Take Control
of Your
Aging

Take Control
of Your
Aging

William B. Malarkey, M.D.

The Wooster Book Company
Wooster • Ohio
1999

612.68
MAL

The Wooster Book Company
205 West Liberty Street
Wooster, Ohio • 44691

Copyright © 1999 by William B. Malarkey

ISBN 1-888683-60-0

Library of Congress Cataloging-in-Publication Data

Malarkey, William B., 1939–
    Take control of your aging / William B. Malarkey.
        p.   cm.
    Includes bibliographical references and index.
    ISBN 1-888683-60-0 (hbk. : alk. paper)
    1. Longevity. 2. Aging. 3. Health. I. Title.
RA766.75.M35   1999
612.6'8—dc21   99-32910
                                                        CIP

∞ This book is printed on acid-free paper.

For additional information or to contact the author:
    www.ControlAging.com

This book is dedicated
to my wife Joan, who for
over 37 years has walked
with me on this journey
of understanding.

Acknowledgments

Many people have provided helpful suggestions, review, and encouragement for this book. The collegiality, encouragement, and knowledge of my research friends, John Cacioppo, Ron Glaser and Jan Kiecolt-Glaser, Phil Marucha, John Sheridan, Carol Whitacre, and Bruce Zwilling challenged me in their areas of expertise. Long conversations with my friends, Drs. Charles and Sandra Alcorn, Dr. Jay Lehr, Richard Arndt, Dr. James Slay, Henrietta Albright, and my sons Kevin and Gregg and daughter Ashley provided helpful insights and encouragement.

Thanks to Dr. Diane Habash and Denise Marcil for their review of the nutrition section. To Richard Arndt, John Cacioppo, Donald Kenny, and Kevin Malarkey for their review of this book.

I appreciate the scholarly editing of Dr. Barbara Rigney.

Thanks to the Relationship Centered Care group at the Fetzer Foundation, particularly the November group for providing some of the early motivation for writing this book.

Weekly encouragement was also provided by the Thursday morning group at Upper Arlington Lutheran Church; Richardt Arndt, Mark Bonifas, Stewart Eilert, Wayne Fitz, Brian Foy, John Gayetsky, and Stan Mack.

The expertise and friendship of my assistant David Phillips throughout the process was deeply appreciated.

My "true north" throughout this effort was my wife Joan, whose legendary reading of fiction and nonfiction helped me with that continual question, "Am I communicating?" She was also tolerant of my mood swings when the question was raised if this work would ever be completed.

Table Of Contents

Take Control of Your *Aging*

Introduction

As I left the clinic for the day, I reflected on the patients I had seen in the last hours. First was the young woman with excessive sweating, dizziness, fatigue, and weight gain; the referring physician thought there might be an endocrine cause for these symptoms. Neither her story, the physical examination, nor the previous lab work supported an endocrine diagnosis. She looked much older than thirty-eight. She showed me a bag of medications which contained numerous drugs for a variety of symptoms, including irritable bowel syndrome and anxiety. Nothing had helped. When asked about possible conditions for stress in her life, she and her husband both began to detail a litany of family, financial, and job stresses. As we talked, they quickly came to the conclusion that there was a link between these life events and her physical symptoms. Wife and husband agreed that many of these symptoms could best be treated by such approaches as exercise, better diets, behavioral therapies, and relaxation techniques. We put a hold on more testing and additional medications and, in fact, we reduced the number of medications she was presently taking.

That same afternoon, I saw a man who had acquired adult onset diabetes mellitus. The referring general practitioner had had great difficulty controlling the swings in the patient's blood sugar levels. Again, I looked for stress or depression as a participating factor. Here was a dynamic and energetic business executive who had recently slowed to 55-hour weeks from the more than 70-hour weeks he had pursued in the past. He looked much older than the age noted on his chart. Little exercise, high job stress, strained relationships at home, excessive ingestion of fast foods with an accompanying weight gain, and coronary artery disease characterized his story. Clearly, his lifestyle was accelerating aging and would most certainly lead to worsening of his disease without aggressive approaches at changing his behavior.

Both of these patients were aging before their time. Both were overweight, had prominent facial lines, noticeable softening of musculature, and facial and verbal expressions that reflected anxiety and anger. I couldn't help but recall the seventy-year-old triathletes I had studied who were twenty years older and yet looked younger than my patients today. But both of my patients still enjoyed life and could smile at their predicament, yet clearly they were searching for healthier bodies. In the first instance, symptoms were not associated with any established disease, and in the second, they were associated with a known diagnosis. In each situation, it was easy for me and for them to see the link between their pre- and/or post-disease behavior and the problems we had just discussed. They were able to see that the stresses in their lives were interacting with their own particular genetic backgrounds, personalities, and emotional states to produce their individual symptom complexes.

My counseling focused on the interrelationship of their present health status, the stressors in their lives, and the ways in which each had failed to deal with this stress. Patients often come to my office seeking a new test, a new diagnosis, and a new medicine that will cure their misery. Frequently, their symptoms are not representative of a specific disease entity, or, even if they have a known disease process, symptoms may not be related to that disease. Frustration for both the patient and physician in not being able to find a disease may lead to the prescribing of an anti-anxiety drug with short-term success before the problem returns. Following this unpleasant encounter, the physician begins to feel, like the patient, that he or she too is aging prematurely!

Looking for important cues in the patient interview about the effects of life event stress and how this interacted with emotional and relational factors to influence health and aging was not always an important focus for me. I am a professor of Internal Medicine and Endocrinology at a major university medical center and had been trained in high-tech medicine at some of our finest academic teaching hospitals. I marveled at how the scientific knowledge explosion of the last 30 years had dramatically enhanced what I was able to provide for my patients compared to what I was taught in the early sixties in medical school. I was challenged and encouraged by the newest imaging technique or laboratory test that sharpened my diagnostic skills and provided me with more precise treatment information. My days were full with teaching, administering a clinical research unit, directing a research laboratory, writing research papers, raising research support, and seeing patients.

Then about ten years ago I became associated with a group of researchers at The Ohio State University who were interested in developing a program to investigate the ways stress influences the human immune, cardiovascular, and endocrine systems and how these systems respond to minor and major stresses. I was trained as a neuroendocrinologist with a long-standing interest in how the brain signals the endocrine system to function, but I realized I knew little about the influence of psychological factors.

Discussions with my psychology and immunology colleagues convinced me that investigating the physiologic changes that occur during common life events and how they affect health would be an exciting topic for research. We initiated a series of studies concerned with a variety of subjects: medical students during examinations, couples dealing with areas of conflict in their marriages, college students encountering math and speech stress, and caregivers of a spouse or relative with Alzheimer's disease. We found that immediately after a stressful episode, people have changes in their endocrine, immune, and cardiovascular systems and that these changes may persist for hours even after the stressor has been removed. In studies with young newlywed couples from whom we obtained blood samples while they were arguing, we noted that stress hormones in the women were elevated for many hours after the argument ended, while elevation was of shorter duration for men. We concluded that the women probably reflected the replay of that conflict throughout the day, whereas the men promptly forgot the discussion and turned on the television set. We noted similar physical reactions in students taking exams; for example, examination stress could delay the immune response to hepatitis vaccination. In caregivers of Alzheimer's patients, stress was associated with more frequent illness, a decreased ability to respond with protective immunity to an influenza shot, and delay in the healing of wounds.

My health and social psychology colleagues also introduced me to a literature that I had never encountered. I read numerous articles detailing the associations between emotions, relationships, and health. Optimism, self-esteem, and feeling connected were positive factors for good health, whereas pessimism, hostility, and loneliness were risk factors for disease. I was also becoming more aware of articles in the medical literature supporting these points of view, including the work of Dr. Redford Williams, who described the negative influences of anger and hostility on the heart. I also read an article detailing research conducted by Dr. Lisa Berkman's group on the role of friendship in helping patients survive a heart attack, indicating that the quality of relationships could actually predict how long one might live after suffering such an event. This study, reported in *The Annals of Internal Medicine*, found that men in their 70s who had no one in whom they could confide about the important issues in their lives had a 70-percent mortality rate within six months, but a relationship with one close friend decreased the mortality to 50 percent, and two or more close confidants decreased the mortality to 23 percent. In this study, all the known risk factors for heart disease were controlled for. I began to realize that a prescription for friendship might be the best medicine I could provide for my patients with heart disease.

If the way we think and relate to others influences the development and progression of disease, could they also be involved in how we age? That seemed a reasonable question based on all of our observations of what happens to our friends going through a divorce or the change in the faces of our Presidents after four or more years in office. Therefore, anti-aging strategies, which are also anti-disease approaches, would have to involve more than cessation of smoking, moderating alcohol intake, taking vitamins, eating well, and exercising daily. These issues were now beginning to influence the way I looked at my own health and were also dramatically influencing the way I was practicing medicine. Focusing on biological issues only without placing them in the context of the person's emotional, spiritual, and relational being was to miss vital information in disease pathogenesis as well as to inhibit successful management of the patient's problem. If a person's anger is out of control, his or her hypertension is more difficult to treat. If people view themselves as worthless, then telling a person to eat less in order to lose weight will be ineffective. If a patient is fearful about a potential side effect of a medicine, he or she will be less likely to adhere to the treatment regimen. If job stress has the individual at work 70 hours a week, that exercise regimen will probably not be initiated, and the increased adrenaline will probably drive the blood sugar in the diabetic to new highs.

The competition of the global marketplace, the introduction of new technology, unrealistic productivity goals, the situation in which both parents in a family are working, the reality of random acts of violence, the experience of road rage, the nightly news, fast foods, and limited discretionary time have all impacted on the harmonious functioning of our bodies. If you question this point of view, take a blood pressure cuff to work and, after your next exasperating meeting, take a reading and also measure your pulse rate.

My research colleagues and I believe that it is the accumulation of these daily hassles and other negative life events which lead to the stress response and eventually to the initiation of symptoms followed by established disease. The signature of the symptom package and disease you may develop is dependent on your genetic background as well as on the particular organism that decides to reside for a while in your body. For example, the chronic stress-induced decrease in immunity makes us susceptible to the common cold. Or, the infection may initiate an antibody response that not only helps eliminate the organism but, in the process, may react against our tissues as well. This reaction to infection may produce numerous diseases, from endocrine deficiencies to neurological disorders and even heart disease. When discussing with patients that stress can lead to serious illness, I have little difficulty convincing them of the merit of this position. My medical colleagues, however, have been more reluctant to accept this argument, although their resistance is beginning to diminish.

It is clear that people want to develop preventive health strategies so they can age healthfully and delay the diseases of aging. Traditional medicine has been slow to respond to this challenge, hence the proliferation of alternative practitioners and non-pharmacological approaches to prevention, from acupuncture to an enormous number of herbal and other supplements. People are increasingly convinced that self-care has to be the cornerstone of any effective aging and health care paradigm. Self-care continues to play a critical role in health, even when a disease becomes established and a physician is consulted. Hopefully, the professional consulted will have an appreciation of the emotional and relational elements that will be critical to our healing. When our chronic condition develops and we know we are in for a long haul with its attendant physical and emotional suffering, we often look to our health team for compassion and support. At this juncture, white coats, scientific arrogance, and the sterile environments of many of our health institutions are negative factors in the treatment process. As Dr. Naomi Remen states in *Kitchen Table Wisdom,* "Expertise cures, but wounded people can best be healed by other wounded people. Only other wounded people can understand what is needed, for the healing of suffering is compassion, not expertise."

Writing this book on health, aging, and disease produced numerous challenges for me, not the least of which was stress; not only is my topic broad, but my schedule is cramped. In the process of writing, I was able to experience what I was writing about, namely that the stress of numerous personal and professional deadlines can be accompanied by a variety of physical symptoms. This was certainly an unwelcome affirmation of these principles!

In this book, I will share my own new insights into how our physical, intellectual, emotional, relational, and spiritual lives influence our aging process and health. My journey toward understanding is rerouted daily, and my goal is not to claim absolute truth but to provide a report of a work in progress. I believe in this comment by Paul Tournier, a famous Swiss psychiatrist, in his book *Learning To Grow Old:* "It is necessary even in a book to give something of ourselves if we are to sound the intimate chord that will resist the passage of time. Many of my readers said to me, you have not told me anything new, but you put into words things that I only vaguely felt." I hope also to provide information, encouragement, and even inspiration that will help my readers to better understand their own journeys toward our mutual goal of a good and long life.

SECTION ONE

Am I Aging Healthfully?

Chapter One

Stress, Relationships, and Disease

I T IS 8:00 A.M. MONDAY MORNING, AND THE TIME HAS ARRIVED for me to begin writing this book on health, aging and disease. Where does one begin so daunting an objective? The phone is ringing, and I breathe a sigh of relief. I can put off the task for at least the length of the phone call. I pick up the phone with glee but with a sense of guilt, as I have been schooled in Stephen Covey's "7 *Habits*," and I know that this upcoming conversation will probably be a type "C" task helping me to avoid my assigned "A" task for this morning. The caller is Maggie, whom I have known for several years, and she wonders if I have a minute to talk to her about a health concern. I happily respond, "Take as much time as you wish, Maggie," secretly thinking what a nice way to delay having to stare at the blank computer screen.

"Bill, Friday I was diagnosed with breast cancer." There is a brief pause as she permits me time to focus and respond to the word CANCER which we all dread one day having to hear from our physician. She then relates that several months ago, during a day that was particularly stressful, she was in a hurry to answer the phone and ran into a high banister in her house, striking her right breast. Pain and swelling continued for weeks, but she hesitated to seek medical advice as she had no health insurance. Finally, after medical consultation, a physical exam, mammogram, and a biopsy, she received a phone call telling her that she had breast cancer.

Maggie was calling to ask me the question we all ask, "How did I get this disease?" There was no breast cancer in her family, and she had never had a serious illness. "Most cases of breast cancer are related to life-style or environment, but exactly which factors affect the risk of breast cancer is difficult to define," states Dr. Anne McTiernan in a 1997 *New England Journal of Medicine* editorial. Dr. McTiernan was commenting on an article that reported a 37-percent reduction in the risk of breast cancer in women who exercised regularly. The risk reduction was greatest in those who continued to exercise regularly over a period of three to five years. The authors speculated that exercise could act by decreasing estrogen levels, lowering body weight, or enhancing the immune system, all of which are considered important in breast cancer risk. Sarah indicated that her weight was higher than she would like, and she had no regular exercise program. Stresses in her life over many years had made it difficult to initiate many self-care preventive programs.

Stress

I asked Maggie if she believed that stress could be involved in causing or promoting disease, and she indicated that it might be involved in her present situation. She was divorced seven years ago, had been forced into the workplace, and, although a resourceful professional, she had encountered difficult work environments over the preceding five years which had become particularly stressful during the past year. She described an employer who repeatedly attacked her personally in the presence of co-workers. She became so distraught after one such incident that she cried for eight hours. Her boss refused appropriate compensation or health benefits. She resigned, and, several weeks later, she was diagnosed with breast cancer. Additional stresses in her life included having been the primary caregiver for her dying mother for several years and enduring as well the verbal and physical abuse of her ex-husband, who now continued his abuse through his treatment of their children. For years, he had reminded her daily of her shortcomings and about how unattractive he perceived her to be. Yet in public, both her former husband and former boss had praised her. Their behavior had provided almost daily material for painful rumination. Could the stress in Maggie's life have played a significant role in causing her breast cancer?

The answer to this question depends on whom you ask. A basic scientist involved in cancer research might respond that Maggie had acquired a mutation of genetic material in one of her breast cells which eventually led to a population of cells undergoing uncontrolled growth. Why had the mutation occurred? Environmental exposure to a carcinogen, a lack of antioxidants in the diet, too much estrogen, and numerous other physiologic factors possibly acted in concert to produce the lesion. Most researchers would find little to disagree with in this analysis. However, a growing number of scientists would insist on including psychosocial factors in the list of possible causal factors for a variety of disorders, including cancer. The purpose of investigating the role of the mind in causing disease is not to induce guilt or to make us feel that we are responsible for all that befalls us, but rather to sharpen our understanding of how our mental imagery affects our health.

Relationships

I have been involved in the practice of medicine for over 35 years, and I continue to be impressed by the importance of social and emotional experiences in defining our physical health. I was still in medical school when I first began to understand these connections. A young child was admitted to a university hospital for failure to grow. It was assumed that his pituitary gland was not functioning properly, and so a series of tests was recommended. In the early 1960s, it took weeks to do hormone tests that today can be done in a matter of hours. Before the test results were completely returned, the youngster began to grow. Yet, the test results demonstrated poor pituitary function. The doctors then repeated the tests and found normal levels. They decided to investigate the home when it became apparent that the child improved immediately upon removal from that environment. Investigators found in the home an indescribable amount of emotional trauma, the stress of which had precipitated growth failure. There is now a recognized syndrome of failure to grow due to emotional deprivation.

Most of my medical training placed little emphasis on such connections, yet circumstances kept reminding me of their importance. I can remember almost twenty years ago listening to an audio tape while driving through the mountains of North Carolina. It was about the importance of a father's love in raising a young woman. The thesis was that women derive self-esteem and feelings of being attractive through the affirmation of a father; if this were not provided by a father or a surrogate father, women would suffer emotional trauma resulting in somatic complaints throughout their adult lives. At the time, I believed that such assumptions were examples of "soft science" that rigorous examination would prove unfounded. However, I remembered the tape, and when I saw a woman who was referred because she had physical complaints but whose tests were normal, I would ask her, "What kind of relationship did you have with your father?" This frequently proved to be a painful question which often revealed that the father had left when she was a child, that he was an alcoholic, or had been emotionally, physically, and/or sexually abusive. Counseling often improved the physical as well as the emotional problems indicated. Increasingly, my experiences with patients confirmed my growing belief in the importance of significant relationships in our lives and in our general health.

Margaret was 40 years old, a single professional woman who had been referred to my office by a gastroenterologist. She had had numerous tests to determine the cause of her significant weight loss. The referring physician wondered if she might have an endocrine problem. She was just over five feet tall and weighed 91 pounds; she had almost no body fat, which had led to a cessation of her menstrual periods. She had great abdominal discomfort whenever she ate, and her evaluation revealed delayed emptying of her stomach after a meal. This highly intelligent woman stated that she was satisfied with her present weight and her diet of 600 calories daily. When told that this was a starvation level, she responded that limiting her food intake had enabled her to heighten the intensity of her meditation in which she spent a great deal of time daily. When questioned about her relationship with her father, she responded simply, "It's terrible." Further conversation revealed that neither she as a person nor her achievements were ever up to his standards, and he had been emotionally abusive in other ways. She admitted that her withdrawal into an extremely meditative life had probably been initiated to avoid criticism by her father or others. She entered counseling and is presently making progress with her eating disorder.

With this and similar cases, I was more and more convinced that relational issues and their associated emotional influence could have important health consequences. Therefore, I was not surprised to see articles in the internal medicine literature over the past five years which report the frequency, more than 60 percent of the cases, with which women patients who complain of abdominal pain for which there is no apparent cause have a history of abuse, often by a family member.

Research

Both my clinical practice and my research agenda were increasingly influenced by these recognitions. I had been involved in endocrinologic research at The Ohio State University College of Medicine for 16 years, evaluating the regulation of pituitary hormones in numerous disorders, including pituitary tumors and breast cancer. In 1988, however, I began working with several colleagues who were interested in stress and its role in human disease. Janice Kiecolt-Glaser, a psychologist; her husband Ronald Glaser, a virologist/immunologist; and John Cacioppo, a social psychologist, were well-recognized international experts in their fields. Our mission was to evaluate short-term and chronic stress in human subjects to investigate ways in which stress influences the cardiovascular, immune, and endocrine systems. Ultimately, we hoped to show how stress could produce human disease. The Glasers had been interested in short-term examination stress and the chronic stress of caring for a spouse or relative with Alzheimer's syndrome. We also decided to add to our research areas the brief psychological stress of doing serial subtractions, the brief social stress of giving an extemporaneous speech, and the intermittent or even long-term stress of marital relationships. Over the past 10 years, we have made intriguing observations and developed concepts related to the definite role of stress in promoting disease processes.

In the examination stress studies performed with medical students, we noted a decrease in immune function during exam week. Also, the amount of stress that an individual experienced on the day of the exam determined the ability of his or her immune system to respond to a hepatitis B vaccination. In studies of chronic stress, we found that problems of caregiving related to the social isolation that occurs with being "on call" 24 hours a day produced marked decrease in immune function. The caregivers had more frequent infections, had diminished responses to influenza vaccinations, and did not heal as rapidly from wounds when compared to individuals of the same age, weight, and sex. The increased stress in their lives seemed the only viable explanation for these health outcomes.

Also of concern was the observation that, in some caregivers, the immune function remained suppressed even years after the death of the person for whom they were caring. An important immune function that was uniformly depressed in the caregivers was natural killer cell activity. These cells are a type of lymphocyte important in immune surveillance and presumably involved in the daily cleaning of malignant or potentially malignant cells from our circulation. Of note in Maggie's story, recounted in the introduction, were the many years of stress, including caregiving, an activity that decreases natural killer cells. Could this stress-induced decrease in her natural killer cell activity have contributed to the development of her breast cancer?

The role of stress in breast cancer is not completely understood, but one study, published in *The Lancet* in 1989 by Dr. David Spiegel, has stimulated a great deal of discussion. His group was able to demonstrate that psychological treatment for women with metastatic breast cancer (stage two) doubled the duration of their survival, even though all the women eventually died of their disease. Psychological therapy was done in groups and occurred once a week for one year. Therapy included discussions of fears, family problems, body image, and sexual concerns among other issues. The survival curve for these women looked so good compared to the standard treatment, that if the intervention had been a drug, every woman with breast cancer would be requesting the prescription.

I am presently collaborating in a study with Dr. Barbara Andersen of The Ohio State University Department of Psychology, who is evaluating a psychological intervention in patients with breast cancer in which hormone and immune function is being examined. After several years of study, preliminary data suggests that dealing with emotional issues related to breast cancer produces a significant increase in natural killer cell immune activity. A change in the patients' emotional health, therefore, produces changes in immune function, which will presumably have long-term effects on these women's outcome with breast cancer. The skeptic still cries for more data, but I believe it will be forthcoming.

In Maggie's case, stress was long-term and severe. Many of us would have trouble identifying with her experience. But, what about daily hassles, like the person who cuts in front of you on the freeway, or the broken shoelace just before a major presentation? We have discovered in our research that the type of stress is less important than our personal interpretation of it in determining our physiologic response. Our math and speech tasks may barely faze some individuals, whereas others shoot their pulse rate and blood pressure through the proverbial ceiling. Often our stress questionnaires are not predictive of who will be the "hot reactors," those subjects whose immune systems could change in a matter of minutes following a math or speech test.

Usually, the pulse and blood pressure falls back to baseline shortly after stress ceases, but occasionally, in more stressed individuals, we would see prolonged activation in the endocrine and immune system; this occurred most frequently following a marital conflict session. Just after we started the marital conflict study in which couples discuss areas of disagreement in their marriage while we sampled continuously for heart rate, blood pressure, hormones, and immune variables, I noted a bizarre and dramatically elevated stress-related adrenaline profile in one of our couples. My research nurse reminded me that this was the couple that had mentioned they had no sexual difficulties in their marriage because they didn't believe in intercourse. These two people had very little insight into themselves or into their relationship, but their physiology was tracking it very closely as reflected by their marked elevation of stress hormones. They were divorced several years later. We also noted that the more hostile couples continued to be so when studied 3 years later, as evidenced by their greater suppression of immune function when compared to the less hostile group of married couples. This finding suggests that harmful personal habits and unresolved hostilities persist and may eventually have undesirable health consequences.

Daily hassles, job stress, and health

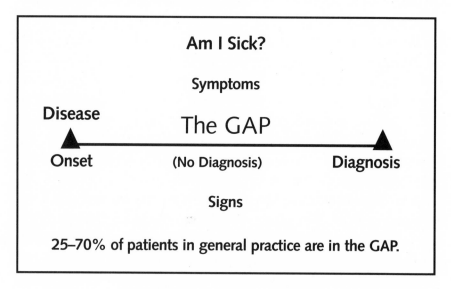

It becomes increasingly obvious that daily hassles produce frequent disturbances in our endocrine, immune, and cardiovascular systems. In those of us more reactive to the stressors, eventually a window of susceptibility occurs for an infectious agent or other abnormal physiologic process to do some damage. The way in which this damage is expressed depends on our genetic makeup. For example, if thyroid disease or colitis runs in your family, your stress may express itself in these diseases. However, before you develop a full-blown disorder that can be diagnosed by your doctor, you may experience minor symptoms such as headaches, low back pain, or fatigue. It is now recognized that almost two-thirds of visits to a family practitioner's office are for complaints related to the hassles of living. The lab tests and x-rays are normal, but you are miserable. There is, in fact, something wrong with you, but not wrong enough for a disease label.

Your symptoms are not yet associated with a specific disease entity, and I refer to this situation as being in the "GAP," as shown in the accompanying diagram. Three hundred years ago, we frequently made diagnoses after death in the autopsy room. With the advent of scientific medicine we have produced sensitive and specific tests that allow us to make diagnoses earlier in the course of a disease. There remains, however, a "GAP" where physical signs and symptoms are occurring but they are not yet adequate, even with laboratory testing, to produce a diagnosis.

A laboratory test can only tell you that your value is within the range of values expressed by a population of individuals. Your "normal" result is an expression of how you compare with the population at this time, not with how you were several weeks ago. For example, let's say your pituitary gland decided to produce 50 percent less stimulation to the thyroid gland, and your thyroid levels fell by one half. Now, instead of a normal level for you of 10, you have a "normal" level of 5. You would not be out of the population range of normal until you fell to 4, but your new level of 5 is too low for you and would probably produce symptoms. At this point, no matter how you tried to change behavior, you would still be tired all the time.

This example demonstrates the problem with normal ranges, but it is misleading as an explanation of the major reasons for unexplained fatigue in our population which has nothing to do with thyroid hormone. A great number of individuals who have unexplained fatigue or other undiagnosed complaints after a thorough evaluation by a skilled physician, often are dealing with the consequences of unresolved stress in their lives, which, with or without the addition of other poor health practices, leads to these complaints. I interpret these symptoms as the body's early warning system that there is a problem that must be addressed. Failure to respond to these signals will eventually lead to an easily diagnosable condition.

Several weeks ago I was discussing these concepts with a friend who is a hospital administrator. He told me of a physician at our institution who had a heart attack and was about to undergo cardiac rehabilitation. At the introductory session he attended was a group of physicians, attorneys, and other professionals who also had experienced a heart attack. The first question asked was, "How many of you are under stress in your job?" Only one individual in the entire group responded that he felt any job stress. These were intelligent and observant individuals who yet had no insight into the stress that their careers were causing. Their intellects were coming to different conclusions than their cardiovascular systems in answer to that question. I have noticed in others and in myself that the long training process of our professions develops a "learning how to play hurt" mind-set. Initially, the long hours of work and study produce signals of fatigue, anxiety, and questions about the appropriateness of our behavior, but the group culture, which says, "Don't be a wimp; everyone else is doing it," wins out. Soon the body tires of sending signals to which no response is elicited, and we no longer see our behavior as stressful. The aging process, however, has been given a jump-start, and it becomes more difficult over the years to deny the telltale signs of stress in the mirror.

Chapter Two

Aging: Accelerated or Healthy?

NTRINSIC TO THE CONCEPTS OF STRESS, HEALTH, AND DISEASE is the aging process. Genetic studies such as those on identical twins have recently shown that our genes may be only responsible for about 30 percent of the variance in our lifespan. Our genetic makeup is most important in its connection to the early onset of diseases like cancer, but twin studies show that, once we reach middle age, there is little connection between genes and life span. Even the distant possibility that infecting our cells with the telomerase gene (an important molecular clock for aging) or other anti-aging genes will probably not be able to correct the damage of poor health behaviors.

Embedded in any definition of aging is the concept of wearing out and not being replaced. Despite a beautifully presented proposal by Dr. Deepak Chopra that we can realize a timeless mind and an ageless body, most individuals over 30 are experiencing some decline in bodily function. The important question we have to ask ourselves, however, is how steep and how rapid is the slope of decline. Over the years, I have noted how fast the aging process occurs in some people, but I have been even more impressed by how gradual it is in others. Certain individuals that I haven't seen for some period of time look younger than when I previously saw them.

We read in the paper that George Bush has jumped out of an airplane above 10,000 feet, and, not to be outdone, a 79-year-old woman duplicates this feat. My friend Jay, at age 62, skydives regularly, plays hockey with 20-year-olds, participates in the Iron Man world championship triathlon, and will be playing lacrosse at his 40-year reunion at Princeton this week.

As I have looked at aging through my research, experience, and reading, I have been less impressed by the gradual decline in body function that occurs in the population over time than by individuals in that population that do not seem to follow that trend. If you look at data on aging, the averages for each decade of life will show a decline, but within each decade you will find individuals who have values of people 40 or 50 years younger. This observation of radical differences in the aging process was the basis for Doctors Rowe and Kahn to describe healthy or "successful"

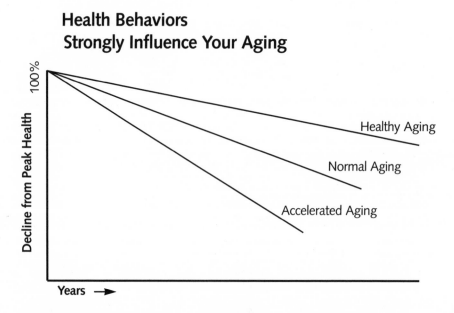

This figure shows three different scenarios of how an individual might age based on how well he or she balances the PIERS principles.

aging in contrast to normal and accelerated aging. If we think of aging as a decline in a certain function, the downward slope for accelerated aging is quite steep, for successful aging is minimal, and for normal aging is somewhere in between. This observation doesn't apply to chronological age, which is dependent on date of birth, but applies to one's "physiologic" and "psychologic" age, which is not fixed but rather is dependent on how one lives.

Physiologic and psychologic age

What is physiologic aging? Here I am referring to your physical appearance and any measure of body function as these compare to the average of people in your age group. For example, if you are a regular participant in some aerobic activity such as swimming, your conditioning as expressed by your capacity to consume oxygen during maximal output will be much higher than a couch potato of your same age. The greatest disparity I have witnessed between chronologic age and physiologic age was at the Iron Man world championship triathlon in Kona, Hawaii, which I attended, not as a performer but as a researcher. My project was to examine endocrine and immune function in superbly conditioned world-class triathletes, one group in their 20s and another group above 50. Yes, above 50, and some contestants were in their 70s. This race consists of a 2.4-mile swim in the ocean, followed by 112 miles of cycling, and finishing with a 26-mile marathon. During my first day of blood sampling, I evaluated three men in their 70s, one of whom was 74, who said, "I'm not sure about the race tomorrow as I'm not fully recovered from a double marathon I ran several weeks ago." This was a different 70-year-old than I was used to seeing in my medical clinic. The rigor of this event is amazing. I rode the cycling course which consists of huge stretches of asphalt through black lava fields where, at race time, temperatures are above 100 degrees, and the winds are so strong that the bike will stop going downhill if you are not turning the crank. As I was watching the race at the transition area where the swim ends and the cycling begins, I was speaking with a gray-haired man about the event. I asked him if a friend or child was participating in the race. He said, no, that his 65-year-old wife was a participant. He pointed her out to me as she burst out of the cycling area, cruising up the hill to initiate her 112-mile ride as a warm-up for her marathon. Her cardio-vascular and muscular physiologic age was of a woman in her 20s. She provided a dramatic example of the positive gap between our chronologic and our physiologic age that we are all capable of creating though our peers may be in assisted-care facilities.

It was also obvious that these triathletes above 50 had different psychologic orientations than their peers. Although most were dealing with nagging injuries, they nevertheless exhibited high energy, excitement about today, and the anticipation of new challenges tomorrow. They were clearly living in the present with enthusiasm, not in the past with regret or in the future with fear. Their psychologic state had many features of what we would expect from someone much younger.

The attainment of what has been traditionally considered a young physiology and psychological outlook is what contributes to successful and healthy aging. Although inheriting a good genetic constitution is desirable and sets a ceiling for the aging process, our behavior is a critical dimension in whether we are on a rapid downhill course toward physical symptoms and disease or the more preferable shallow slope of change that reflects healthy aging. We don't need to participate in triathlon training to improve our physiologic and psychologic age. An assessment, however, of our present state and initiating changes in areas that we will discuss later can change our "slope of decline." As we grow older, putting an emphasis on "growing" rather than older will pay health dividends. With this kind of mental imagery, our view of significant personal and sexual relationships in our life, the kind of retirement we envision, and physical conditioning possibilities may all be reimagined.

Avoiding the popular myths that limit our potential may also be a good health tonic. Fortunately, some of the more famous false assumptions of the past were not blindly followed. For example:

"I think there is a world market for maybe five computers."
—*Thomas Watts, Chairman of IBM, 1943*
"There is no reason anyone would want a computer in their home."
—*Ken Olsen, President, Chairman and Founder of*
Digital Equipment Corp., 1977
"Who the hell wants to hear actors talk?"
—*H.M. Warner, Warner Brothers, 1927*

"Heavier than air flying machines are impossible!"
> —*Lord Kelvin, President, Royal Society, 1895*

"Stocks have reached what looks like a permanently high plateau."
> —*Irving Fisher, Professor of Economics,*
> *Yale University, 1929*

"Everything that can be invented has been invented."
> —*Charles H. Duell, Commissioner,*
> *U.S. Office of Patents, 1899*

Being careful about the "one liners" we hear about aging may help us make a positive correction in our own aging slope.

Who is old?

By the year 2020, there will be approximately six million Americans over the age of 85 and 200,000 people over the age of 100. The centenarian population will increase by about 100,000 every 10 years. At present, many people over the age of 84 have impaired hearing or vision, have suffered falls resulting in hip fractures, have had strokes, cancer, and cardiovascular disease. Almost a third of the oldest old have some degree of dementia. When asked if they want to live to be 100, most people would say yes if they could have a life as vital and ailment-free life as the Delany sisters, who became authors and media celebrities at the age of 100. Often, the images associated with longevity are those of mental or physical impairment and the loss of autonomy. This negative view of aging was the subject of several essays in *Newsweek* several years ago. Eighty-four-year-old Anna Seaver wrote in notes found after her death: "Am I invisible? Have I lost the right to respect and dignity? I don't much like some of the physical things that happen to us. I don't care much for a diaper. I seem to have lost the control acquired so diligently as a child. The difference is that I'm aware and embarrassed, but I can't do anything about it. I've had three children and I know it isn't pleasant to clean another's diaper. My husband used to wear a gas mask when he changed the kids. I wish I had one now."

Eli Rubenstein has a similar view in his essay, "The Not So Golden Years." He states, "On a personal level, getting up in the morning is a mixed blessing. It's reassuring to know that I'm still alive, but the days inexorably tick off on the calendar in my mind. Yesterday another of my close friends was taken to the hospital with a serious illness. Almost every day, I myself feel a new twinge here or an ache there, and I begin to worry about what will be revealed when I take my annual physical next week. It is truly a winter of discontent, with no better forecast in sight." He concludes, "In my opinion, any retiree—happy or even content—with his or her present condition either is lying or forgetting the past or belongs to a very fortunate minority."

Lack of autonomy, loss of respect and dignity, and the inability to perform basic bodily functions characterize Anna's concern, whereas boredom, hopelessness, perception of ill health, depression, and negativism pervade Eli's comments. Almost all of these psychologic characteristics have been found to predict poor health outcomes.

Men who are aging healthily

In contrast, we have the comments and lives of a growing number of seniors who have had better health and more positive views of aging. We rarely read about men who are active in their 100s, but there are men with notable accomplishments in their 80s and 90s. Most of the examples in the popular press have to do with physical accomplishments that would make a man 40 years younger self-satisfied. Joe Weiss was just retired for the second time at age 88 from a foot messenger service in Manhattan. Sixty-nine-year-old body builder Billy Frazier, after months of working out for seven hours a day won the Southern states over-65 trophy. Paul Schipper is a 73-year-old man who has, for 17 seasons, hit the slopes for 2,628 consecutive ski days in a season stretching from September to May. Jasper Hubbert is 85 years old and participates in a hundred-mile bike ride, the "Hotter 'N Hell Hundred," each year into the teeth of Texas August heat.

When it comes to intellectual pursuits, we have had presidents in their 70s but few can top the longevity of Senator Strom Thurmond of South Carolina. He just turned 95 and holds the record as the oldest member to serve in Congress. He will be 100 if he serves out his present term. When asked why he thinks he can stand up to the rigorous life of a senator, he responds, "Do you think the average person has a diet like I do? Do you think the average person has an optimistic attitude toward life like I do?" His daily exercise regimen consists of 50 minutes of weightlifting, stretching, and riding a stationary bicycle. He has a high-fiber, low-fat diet. Hard work, living in the present with hope for the future, regular exercise, and a good diet characterize his successful aging program.

Women who age healthily

Now let's look at some women described in the popular press who are helping redefine what it means to grow old gracefully. In 1997, a 63-year-old woman gave birth to a child conceived by in vitro fertilization. Helen Klein, a 73-year-old woman, last April rafted, mountain biked, canoed, rock climbed, rode horseback, and hiked through Utah on the nonstop 370-mile test of endurance called the Eco-challenge. She has participated in 49 marathons, 100 ultra-marathons (greater than 50 miles), and one Ironman triathlon. She waited until she was 55 and after her mother had died to switch from walking to running. She then worked her way up to 10 miles daily, six days a week. "The reward is excellent health," says the retired nurse. "It's great to know that if my car breaks down and I have to go 50 miles for help, I can." It's not competition that motivates her: "I just don't want to be a quitter. If I'm tired so that I think I can't go on, I tell myself, 'That's just your body.' I work on my mind to say I can go farther. And I do." She understands the value of goal setting and endurance at any age of life.

Eighteen years Helen Klein's senior is Tiny Riley, 91, of Helena, Montana. She runs every other day at dawn on city streets and at a school track. Cross-training consists of occasional hikes up the face of Mount Helena, cross-country skiing, and bowling once a week. She has been married for 72 years to her 96-year-old husband, Roy. "Every day I get up and look at the sky," says the great-grandmother. "It's a pretty place up here in the mountains. I notice everything when I go out and run. You can be ALIVE as long as you live," says Tiny, "but you have to keep moving. If I didn't have so many chores, maybe I could really train and try something longer." Discipline, planning for the future, a daily sense of awe when experiencing the creation, a sense of gratitude, continual activity, and a long-term successful marriage all seem to characterize her vitality.

In December, our local paper ran an article on Cecelia Hurwich entitled, "Still Learning at 77." She gives new meaning to the term, "late bloomer." At 77, after getting a master's degree at 61, a doctorate at 70, and becoming an internationally known speaker on aging gracefully, it is obvious that she knows her topic. She feels that one of the most important things in life is doing what you're passionate about. She also feels that having a variety of friends of all ages and having an optimistic attitude is important. "Being open to new things, having something to look forward to. The hardest thing for me in writing my dissertation was learning to use a computer, but now I know how." Continuing to stretch the mind also figures into longevity, she believes. You have to keep growing and learning, to challenge yourself. "And you have to exercise your body, as well. About three years ago, I realized that I couldn't open mayonnaise jars anymore," she said. "I have arthritis, and I was losing my strength. I've walked a lot, and I ran for 20 years, so I was very strong in my lower body, but women of my generation didn't go to the gym, didn't lift weights. So I went to the gym, and within six months I could notice the difference. I felt better. I could carry my own groceries, my own suitcases. So I'm a big booster of weight and cardiovascular training. You have to make each day count, live in the present. Reminisce—pay respect to the past—don't live in it." She was organizing a symposium next year in Australia. We can see that development of the mind is possible at ages we normally think of as retirement years. She continues to expand her definition of physical exercise; she exudes optimism, travels the world, and lives in the present. She looks much younger then her chronological age, and I doubt that anyone would challenge the fact that she is aging successfully.

The Delany sisters

One of the more extraordinary examples of successful aging that has captivated many Americans is the Delany sisters' story. They were daughters of a former slave who became an Episcopal bishop. Sarah was New York City's first black home-economics teacher; Bessie was the second black woman in the state to be licensed to practice dentistry. Their lives were described in a best-selling book, *The Delany Sisters' First Hundred Years.* Bessie died in 1995 at the age of 104, and in a recent book, *On My Own at 107,* Sarah Delany gives her views on life and her reasons for having lived actively for so long: "Folks ask me why I've lived such a long and happy life, and I always say the Lord deserves the credit. Another factor, I'm sure, is that it runs in the family. My mama lived to be 95 years old with no medical intervention whatsoever. Another reason is the way we live—exercise, eating lots of fruits and vegetables, no smoking, things like that. I still get up early in the morning and say my prayers and do my yoga exercises." Sarah takes life one day at a time and avoids confrontation. "I think you can keep going past the century mark as long as you're healthy and have got a reason to live. I don't see why folks should retire at sixty-five. I retired at 70 myself and, looking back on it, I bet I could have kept teaching for a long, long while yet. Of course, they make you retire … To think I've been collecting a pension from the New York Board of Pension since 1960. I bet they never thought they'd have to pay it this long. They'd have been better off if they'd let me keep teaching."

She continues, "Well if I'm going to make it to the year of 2000, I figure I had better increase my stamina. So I've been climbing the stairs at least once a day, even if I don't need to. And when I'm lonely and I can't sleep, I'll do an extra set of my yoga exercises, even if it's in the middle of the night." She jokes about her age: "I ain't buying green bananas anymore, if you know what I mean." Prayer is also important to Sarah: "I have said my prayers every day for 107 years, and I'm not about to skip a day now. Mama was the busiest woman alive married to a priest and having 10 children, yet she always had time for prayer. Prayer is the comfort that keeps you going in good times and bad. During good times it is a way of saying thanks and acknowledging your blessings. In bad times, it's something to lean on during your hour of trial."

Sarah's words of wisdom about her longevity are consistent with what we know about good health behaviors. Daily exercise, good nutrition, a tranquil personality, a strong sense of gratitude, a good sense of humor, and a spiritual perspective about life which she practices daily are combined with good genes, all of which have enabled her to reach a vital 107. Also once again, we see a successfully aging senior challenging the wisdom of classic retirement.

Chapter Three

PIERS and Health

*T*HE THESIS OF THIS BOOK IS THAT WELLNESS AND healthy aging depend on how we manage the Physical, Intellectual, Emotional, Relational, and Spiritual aspects of our lives. Our success in delaying physiologic and psychologic aging is embodied in these five areas, which I will refer to as PIERS. Successfully aging people have continuously nourished these areas of their lives. They are riding the desirable shallow slope of the aging curve rather than careening down the steep path of accelerating aging leading to disease.

We are frequently reminded that attention to exercise, good nutrition, and prevention activities are requisites for wellness. It may not be as obvious that our emotions, relationships, and spirituality also have powerful influences on our health. For example, the cardiovascular system is strongly affected by our emotional life; stress and hostility produce hypertension and precipitate heart attacks. Our relational life, for example, can affect survival after a heart attack. If you have a heart attack in your 70s,

The PIERS Model

Figure 1

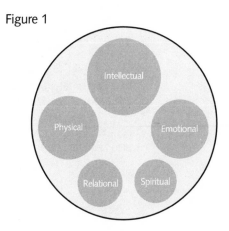

Person A. represents an individual for whom intellectual pursuits such as work, good nutrition, and daily exercise are the major influences. Little energy is available for relational and spiritual involvement.

the number of friends you have to talk to about your problems will have an effect on your 6-month survival. Similarly, the intensity of one's religious commitment has been shown in numerous studies to be directly related to good health.

These five areas of influence vary in the magnitude of their contribution to the health of any individual. If presented with circles containing the words Physical, Intellectual, Emotional, Relational, and Spiritual, how would you arrange them to depict the influence they have in your life? Would one circle be on top of the other four? For example, if concern for good nutrition and exercise dominate your thinking, then the circle containing the word physical would be placed on top of the other four. Conversely, if spiritual and relational concerns were the organizing principle of each day of your life, then those circles would sit on top of the other three. Would any of the circles on your second level be smaller than the other circles? If this is an accurate representation of important health variables, then the way you are presently balancing them may be responsible for present good health. How one arranges these circles of influence is, of course, reflective of core values, philosophy of life, and past experiences. It is an interesting exercise to see how many different representations are possible using these circles of influence. Some of these arrangements are more or less conducive to good health. The major value of this

The PIERS Model

Figure 2

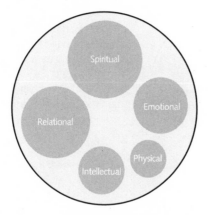

Person B. depicts a person whose major integrating influences are spiritual, relational, and emotional, whereas nutrition, exercise, and intellectual pursuits are of lesser value.

Figure 3

Person C. In these individuals, all areas have equal weight and influence in their lives.

exercise, however, is that it permits us to determine those areas of our lives that we have neglected at peril to our health and then to develop strategies that may help correct these deficiencies.

We all know people who have developed one area of life at the expense of other domains and yet seem to be healthy and aging successfully. This would appear to be at odds with the PIERS concept. If they have neglected the physical area of their lives, however, they may develop a heart attack in their 50s or 60s. Similarly, individuals who have put all their energies into their exciting careers at the neglect of the relational, emotional, or

PIERS Review

Physical:

_____ I eat properly.
_____ I exercise.
_____ I am free of illness.
_____ I abstain from smoking and drinking excessively.
_____ I get refreshing sleep.

Intellectual:

_____ I am analytical.
_____ I read.
_____ I am learning.
_____ I use my mental ability at work.
_____ I reflect on my life.

Emotional:

_____ I am peaceful.
_____ I like myself.
_____ I am optimistic.
_____ I laugh.
_____ I relax.

Relational:

_____ I am a good listener.
_____ I feel supported by friends.
_____ I attend social functions.
_____ I talk with my parents/family members.
_____ I feel close to my co-workers.

Spiritual:

_____ I pray or meditate.
_____ I appreciate nature.
_____ I give to or serve others.
_____ I attend religious services.
_____ I feel my life has meaning.

Rarely (if ever) scores 1 point
Occasionally   scores 2 points
Above average   scores 3 points
Very frequently scores 4 points

This will produce a maximal score of 100 if you obtained four points for every statement.

spiritual domains of their lives develop physical symptoms on retirement or on losing their jobs. It appears that making frequent deposits into each of these areas during periods of stability will serve as a buffer against adverse health consequences when the unpredictable stresses of life strike.

I have devised a review based on the research which will be addressed in these pages that suggests that the elements of the PIERS plan are associated with better health and longer life. It should serve as a useful guide for us to evaluate where we presently reside in our search for a life plan to go with our financial plan.

What score would place you in the successfully aging category? If you recall the interviews provided earlier in this book by individuals in their 80s and 90s, many would have scored very high on this review. The absolute number you achieve is not as important as is the quartile in which you reside. The quartile score will suggest trends that may be affecting your quality of life and whether you are setting into motion habits that are promoting normal, accelerated, or healthy aging. By looking at each of the five sections, the reader can find his or her strengths and weaknesses and which areas need improvement.

Individuals with a score of 75–100 have probably given themselves 3 or 4 points for each of the 25 items. This shows strength and balance in most, if not all, of the categories. Although you are enjoying good health, you probably have found areas which need improvement.

Individuals with a score of 50–75 are probably healthfully engaged in two or three of the categories and in need of improvement in several others. Although you are presently in good health, there are certain actions which you can do to promote healthy aging.

Individuals with a score of 50 or below, depending on present age, may already be struggling with a chronic non-genetically linked illness. The following chapters will provide ways to engage in self-care that could help you prevent accelerated aging and crippling illness.

The concept of PIERS also gives us a view of health as something that we are profoundly influencing on a daily basis by all of our thinking and actions. We are, in essence, conducting the symphony of our lives, and the music that we and others want to hear is not only the percussion of our vocations but also the strings and woodwinds of our emotional, relational, and spiritual selves.

There are so many myths about aging and disease, many of which we will explore in this book. We are all like the insect I see on my window, repeatedly traversing the glass seeking a way out but unaware of the possibilities of freedom, even after I have opened the latch. Finally, a breeze convinces him of new opportunities, and he stretches his wings and flies away. Many of us are trapped in myths and behaviors that are influencing the quality of our lives and that are placing us on a rapid slope of decline. We would like the freedom of escaping from certain behaviors but have been unwilling to take the risk of spreading our wings and taking flight.

A survey was given to eighty-year-olds which asked, if you had your life to live over, how would you do it differently? Three ideas were at the top of most respondent's lists: first, they would have left more than a financial legacy to others; next, they would have reflected on various issues and areas of their lives more frequently; and, finally, they would have taken more risks-gone down the road less traveled. My hope is that, as we explore the PIERS of our lives, we will be willing to take the risks that change requires. Perhaps it will entail getting off the couch, turning off the television, calling a friend, dealing with our hostility, or taking daily walks. Maybe we can place the emphasis on growing, rather than on growing older.

SECTION TWO

Nutrition and Health

CHAPTER FOUR

What Should I Eat?

I HAVE JUST EXAMINED FRED, A 48-YEAR-OLD BUSINESS EXECUTIVE, for a possible thyroid problem but have not found any evidence to support that diagnosis. When discussing his general health, he states that his father developed coronary artery disease in his 60s, and there is a distant family history of diabetes. He is concerned about his recent weight gain and dietary habits. He then asks if chromium supplementation would help him to lose weight. Fred's dilemma is a common one in our society. The weight gain associated with aging, confusion about what constitutes a healthy diet or lack of desire to implement one, and a wish to find a supplement that will prevent him from facing the more appropriate dietary alternatives is something to which we can all relate. I can remember when any meal for me without meat was considered incomplete and often necessitated a visit to the cupboard for a handful of potato chips or cookies. Changing those habits took education, the tincture of time, and continual reflection on the benefits of good nutrition.

There is now abundant data that our dietary habits are killing us. It has been estimated that poor dietary choices over many years may be responsible for 30 to 50 percent of heart disease and cancer. The influence of diet on health is dramatically demonstrated by Japanese who move from Japan to Hawaii where they change from rice and fish to a more Western high-fat diet. From having one-fifth the breast cancer incidence in Japan as in America, the female immigrants have acquired a much higher breast cancer rate in Hawaii. Also, as American-style food and restaurants invade Japan, the Japanese are developing higher rates of breast cancer and coronary artery disease. Dr. Kwame Osei in our Division of Endocrinology, Diabetes and Metabolism at Ohio State has been evaluating diet, weight, and tendency to develop diabetes in immigrants from Ghana. After a few years of ingesting a typical American diet, Ghanians gain weight and frequently develop abnormal blood sugar and insulin levels seen in the pre-diabetic state.

Dietary guidelines

Only 10 percent of Americans eat five servings of fruits and vegetables each day as recommended by the National Cancer Institute and the National Research Council. Excessive salt intake and inadequate fluid intake are also common. In the early '90s, recommendations for what constitutes a healthy diet were revised. Instead of referring to four food groups, including milk, meat, vegetables and fruits, and bread and cereal, the food pyramid became the new standard. It recommended daily intake of *six to eleven* servings of bread, cereal, rice and/or pasta; *three to five* servings of vegetables; *two to four* servings of fruits; *two to three* servings of milk, yogurt, or cheese; *two to three* servings of meat, poultry, fish, beans, eggs, or nuts; and sparing use of fats, oils and sweets. Some of these recommendations are debatable but the fruit and vegetable recommendation is very solid.

These recommendations have not been embraced by the American public. Nearly half of Americans eat no fruit on a given day, 25 percent eat no vegetables, and 11 percent eat neither. The four major food groups as interpreted by many of us are fat, sugar, caffeine, and chocolate.

Why have fruit and vegetable intakes been emphasized so extensively? The answer is that we will live longer and with less illness if we follow these directives. The evidence that fruit and vegetable intake decreases the risk for cancer and heart disease is overwhelming. Over 90 of 100 studies have shown that eating fruits and vegetables protects us from getting cancer of the lung, mouth, larynx, esophagus, stomach, pancreas, cervix, and bladder. The data is less strong for colorectal, breast, ovary, and prostate cancer but still impressive. The quarter of the population with low dietary intake of fruits and vegetables has double the cancer rate when compared to those with the highest intakes. The same trends are found for coronary artery disease. Why do we have such a low vegetable and fruit intake? Cost, availability, preferences for the taste of fatty foods, poor dietary habits, and lack of information about health benefits all may contribute to this low intake.

How many calories?

Other than lots of vegetables and fruit, what else should we eat, how often, and how much? First, how many calories? This has been an important question in the field of aging research in which some investigators feel that the larger your caloric intake over time, the faster you will age. Most of these studies have been performed with rodents and have shown that caloric-restricted animals live 50 percent longer than the "eat what you want" litter mates. When the food intake of mice and rats was decreased by 30 to 60 percent, the average life span and the maximal life span were increased by similar amounts. Also, caloric restriction virtually prevents the development of autoimmune disease in several susceptible strains of mice, and retards the development of spontaneous tumors in these animals. An interesting theory has been developed to help explain these benefits. Damaged cells in our bodies are either repaired or removed by a process called programmed cell death. This process is important because it eliminates oxidatively-damaged cells and old cells which can become premalignant. It appears that caloric restriction may increase programmed cell death, which would result in longevity and anticancer benefits. Another theory is that caloric restriction decreases the oxidative damage to cells which is involved in cancer promotion and aging of cells. One researcher in this area, Dr. Ray Walford, a well-known gerontologist at UCLA, so strongly believes in this concept that he has placed himself on a lifetime caloric-restricted diet. His approach is to gradually restrict calories until weight reaches what one weighed in one's 20s and 30s. There are clearly benefits to be gained from achieving an "ideal" body weight. This approach, however, doesn't factor in exercise or all the other qualities that seem to be common to people who live to be 100.

Most of us are not interested in such a radical approach to nutrition as marked calorie restriction, and our bookstores are not overstocked with books on the virtues and details of periodic fasting, a practice which would probably benefit most of us. We do, however, have an interest in establishing some idea about how many calories we need. Estimates of the number of calories needed per 24 hours to maintain present weight are available, assuming an average metabolic rate and energy expenditure. Even when reasonable estimates are provided, most people aren't willing to invest the time in doing calorie counts. The easiest way to determine if you are eating an appropriate amount is to do a "mirror" test: undress and stand in front of a mirror. There are some sophisticated techniques to determine your percentage of body fat, but your estimate by the mirror test of too much body fat is almost always correct unless you have a tendency toward "anorexia." My friend David challenged me on this concept by squeezing his 30-year-old slight increase in abdominal fat and said, "I don't like this paunch when I stand in front of the mirror, but is this a health risk?" Our risk assessment yardsticks aren't sophisticated enough to answer this question for an individual. We can cite population statistics which say twenty percent above ideal body weight begins to produce health risks, but when we speak about an individual who has a wonderful health profile versus a person loaded with health risks, the answers are probably different.

Whether the excess fat is located in our abdominal area with its attendant increased risk for coronary artery disease and diabetes, or is present in the hips and buttocks which produces less cardiovascular risk, it reflects excessive calorie intake for our activity level. The obvious goal is to match our food intake and energy output via our daily activities if we wish to maintain our present weight, or to make adjustments in these parameters if we wish to gain or lose weight.

How much fat and carbohydrate?

There seems to be little argument about the recommended amount of protein, which is estimated to be about 15 percent of our caloric intake. Most of the debate occurs with fat and carbohydrate, but most experts in nutrition suggest that fat intake should represent less than 30 percent of our caloric intake and carbohydrate intake about 55 percent. There is more debate about the percentages of fat and carbohydrates in the diet for postmenopausal women. A more liberalized amount of fat is recommended by some, but in the form of the more healthy unsaturated fats such as certain vegetable oils, olive oil, and nuts rather than the cardiac villain, saturated fats. Clearly, the saturated fats found in meats and dairy products (less than ten percent of total dietary fat should be saturated) are more prone to produce atherosclerosis, and provide twice as many calories given portions of similar weight of protein and carbohydrates.

The role of dietary fat intake and the risk of coronary heart disease in 80,000 women were evaluated over 14 years, during which time 939 nonfatal heart attacks or deaths occurred. It was found that an increase of five percent of energy intake from saturated fat as compared with equivalent energy intake from carbohydrate was associated with a 17 percent increase in the risk of coronary disease. Researchers also evaluated (trans)unsaturated fat, which includes margarine and the typical fat in a glazed donut. Dr. Tim Byers stated, "Transfats keep our margarine stiff and our pastries firm. They are produced when the healthier polyunsaturated vegetable fats are artificially hardened, a process that increases their firmness and resistance to spoilage." The transunsaturated fats were associated with twice as much coronary disease as polyunsaturated or monounsaturated fats (e.g., olive oil). It is estimated that the replacement of five percent of energy from saturated fat with energy from unsaturated fats would reduce the risk of coronary disease by 42 percent. Also, reducing one's intake of saturated fats may help delay the progression of prostate cancer.

With a lot of the carbohydrates coming from fruits, vegetables, bread, cereals, and rice, these guidelines are fairly clear. We can determine how serious we are in following the guidelines, however, by how we shop at the grocery store. Our American style is to look at the item and, if it looks appealing, grab it off the shelf and pitch it into the cart. Do we examine the label for percentages of fat and if the label says over 30 percent of the calories in the item are from fat do we return it to the shelf? Also we should avoid items that read low or no fat but are loaded with calories. Obviously some of the meats and dairy products will be around 40 to 50 percent fat and high in saturated fats. Sweets and snack foods must be very critically examined for fat and caloric content before they are purchased or there is no hope for success in following the recommendations. This process takes time, but it pays healthy dividends.

There is also evidence that excess fat in the diet may impair mental function as we age. In an article in the *American Journal of Epidemiology,* researchers noted that men between the ages of 69 and 89 who had higher intakes of total fat and polyunsaturated fat were two and one-half times more likely to have impairment of mental function. The good news in this article was that eating fish helped to preserve mental functioning.

Even if these dietary guidelines are available to all Americans, it is apparent they're not being followed. Obesity is rampant in America. Obesity is of value only if you are a Sumo wrestler or interested in competing in the world gut-barging contest. This is popular in London where Mad Maurice defends his crown by bouncing opponents out of a 12-foot by 8-foot mat using gut power alone. However, for most of us, obesity is detrimental to our health and quality of life. It is estimated that one in three of us is overweight (rankings by state and city of America's most obese people are available in bookstores). The weight loss industry earns billions of dollars annually with supervised diets, over-the-counter diet products, and diet medication aides.

Points to Remember:

1   Five servings of fruits and vegetables each day are a major preventive step to decrease the incidence of cancer and heart disease.

2   Our daily caloric intake should be established to allow us to achieve normal body weight or a weight that lowers our health risks.

3   Abdominal fat, in contrast to hip and buttock fat, is associated with an increased cardiovascular risk.

4 Protein intake should approximate 15%, fat less than 30%, and complex carbohydrates 55% of daily caloric intake.

5 Low intake of saturated fats as found in cheeses, meats, and pastries, with more intake of "good" fat, monounsaturated and polyunsaturated, as in olive oil is desirable.

6 Resist placing high-caloric items and food with greater than 30% fat in the shopping cart. If it's not on the shelf at home you will eat less of these items.

BMI* Conversion Chart

Chart 1

kg	45	50	55	59	64	68	73	77	82	86	91	95	100	105	109	114
wt Ht.	100	110	120	130	140	150	160	170	180	190	200	210	220	230	240	250
5'0"	19	22	24	25	27	29	31	33	35	37	39	41	43	45	47	49
5'2"	18	20	22	24	26	27	29	31	33	35	37	38	40	42	44	46
5'3"	18	20	21	23	25	27	29	30	32	34	36	37	39	41	43	45
5'4"	17	19	21	22	24	26	28	29	31	33	34	36	38	40	41	43
5'5"	17	18	20	22	23	25	27	28	30	32	33	35	37	39	40	42
5'6"	16	18	20	21	23	24	26	28	29	31	32	34	36	37	39	41
5'7"	16	17	19	20	22	24	25	27	28	30	31	33	35	36	38	40
5'8"	15	17	19	20	21	23	24	26	27	29	30	32	34	35	37	38
5'9"	15	16	18	19	21	22	24	25	27	28	30	31	33	34	36	37
5'10"	14	16	18	19	20	22	23	24	26	27	29	30	32	33	35	36
5'11"	14	15	17	18	19	20	22	23	25	26	27	29	30	32	33	34
6'0"	13	14	16	17	18	19	21	22	23	24	26	27	28	31	31	32
6'2"	13	14	15	17	18	19	21	22	23	24	26	27	28	30	31	32
6'4"	12	13	15	16	17	18	20	21	22	23	24	26	27	28	29	31

BMI Weight Indicator: above 25 overweight
above 27 obese

*BMI is defined as $\dfrac{\text{body weight (lbs)} \times 705}{\text{height (in)}^2}$

CHAPTER FIVE

I'm Overweight. So What?

OBESITY CAN SHORTEN OUR LIVES! THE GREATER our body mass index (BMI) (see chart 1), the higher the death rates from all causes, and from cardiovascular disease in men and women up to 75 years of age. This index is a composite of weight and height. As we gain weight after we stop growing, each pound increases our BMI as our height obviously remains stable. A BMI of over 25 is where many experts believe health problems begin. This is not a perfect tool, particularly in muscular people as muscle is more dense than fat. As we get older, the health risks from obesity gradually fall, reflecting the higher risk among younger people. We can cite hundreds of research articles which discuss the relationship of weight and longevity. Everyday experience and observation, however, are the best teachers. During your last visit to a retirement community, how many people in their 80s and 90s did you see who were grossly overweight? If your experience is like mine, most of these individuals are thin with a modest amount of abdominal fat. Therefore we have to conclude that their grossly overweight peers have already died. I'm reminded of a person who most of us have seen in the cinema, actor John Candy, who had such prominent obesity and suffered a premature death.

There are many reports which support our observations that excessive weight hastens our deaths. A large study which involved 115,000 nurses was initiated in 1976 when the subjects were 30 to 55 years old. They still periodically report their weight, diet, activity levels, and other lifestyle variables. Through 1992, more than 4,700 had died, and it was estimated that 25 percent of the deaths were because of obesity, which made it only secondary to cigarette smoking as a preventable cause of death. A woman of average height and moderately overweight at 160 to 175 pounds was 60 percent more likely to die than the thinnest woman.

Yet for modest weight gain there are many unanswered questions. Will a healthy person who loses 25 pounds acquire the same health risks as a person who started 25 pounds lighter? If we encourage this individual to lose weight, might the cure be worse than the condition? Yet in those individuals with diabetes, elevated blood fats, and high blood pressure, a 10 to 15 percent weight loss can greatly improve their condition.

Obesity (body mass index greater than 25) increases the risk of heart disease, breast cancer, and hypertension. From a study of 82,000 U.S. female nurses, we are provided some clues as to the role of even modest weight gain in general health. This study demonstrated that a weight gain of 50 to 60 pounds produced a five-fold increase in risk for hypertension, but even a 10-pound weight gain could be significant in producing hypertension. Researchers also found that weight loss decreased the risk for high blood pressure, and they also noted that the protective effect of weight loss was stronger in younger women.

Yet a new survey indicates that fewer overweight individuals are improving their diet to correct the problem. The survey, commissioned by Shape Up America, an antiobesity campaign founded by Dr. C. Everett Koop, the former U.S. Surgeon General, found that 78 percent of overweight people were not using acceptable dietary practices, and many were not even aware of the health risks of obesity.

Is it in my genes?

Why do we have such a national problem with weight control? The obvious answer is that we are eating too much and exercising too little.

Yet, we also have to deal with the fact that many individuals consume an average number of calories and gain weight, while another person with equal activity and ingesting the same number of calories might be losing weight. The control of body weight is complex and poorly understood. There are multiple genetic, physiologic, and behavioral issues involved in establishing our present weight. We now know that there are numerous genetic factors that influence our body weight and fat stores. We don't need to do research on genetic factors but just observe our family and even our friends. What we observe is that we tend to have fat stores that mimic one or both parents. Is that because we eat the same food as other family members, which certainly could play a role, or are genetic factors involved in why family members tend to have similar body fat distributions? Several important studies have documented the importance of genes in weight control. A Danish study has shown that there is a strong correlation between the weight of the biologic parents and the child but not between the child and his adopted parents.

In a study of identical twins, 12 pairs were overfed 1,000 calories per day for over 3 months. The weight gain ranged from ten to 30-plus pounds for the group as a whole, but, amazingly, the weight gain within each twin pair was quite similar. The twins also tended to put the fat in the same areas of their bodies. The authors argued that our genes govern the tendency to store energy as either fat or lean tissue and also direct the various factors that govern resting expenditure of energy. Findings in this latter study were recently complemented by another overfeeding study. These scientists found that the amount of weight gain in the volunteers could be predicted by the amount of these excessive calories that were burned up by nonexercise activities like fidgeting and maintaining posture when not recumbent.

More recently, other powerful genetic factors have been found that influence our fat metabolism. Evidence has been presented that obese children may be resistant to the fat breakdown hormone, adrenaline, and a reduced rate of energy expenditure as a risk factor for weight gain has been found to aggregate in families of obese Pima Indians. We also know that fat cells make a hormone called leptin which increases in our circulation when our fat stores increase. This hormone binds in the hypothalamus of our brain, where our satiety center resides and decreases our desire to eat.

This hormone may even be responsible for the onset of puberty, as a critical body weight is important for the beginning of menstruation. For example, thin gymnasts who would presumably have low leptin levels have a marked delay in the initiation of puberty.

This hormone is now known to be produced at very low levels in at least a few children with massive obesity, caused by the fact that they have lost the signal that tells them to stop eating. Additionally, children with relatively lower leptin levels were more likely to gain weight 12 months later. Also, some extremely overweight individuals have been found to have a defect in the leptin receptor, which inhibits the action of leptin. In the previously mentioned three-year study of Pima Indians, a group prone to obesity, it was found that those with lower leptin levels gained more weight than those with normal levels. Could minimal, yet still significant, decreases in leptin occur in those of us who never seem to feel full during a meal?

Another neuropeptide, orexin (from the Greek word for appetite), has been recently found to increase food intake in rats. Made by the brain, this hormone is increased during fasting to promote eating. Studies on human beings have not yet been published, but this finding suggests that additional peptides that regulate our feeding behavior wait to be discovered.

A mutation in a genetic regulator of fat cell growth and fat accumulation has recently been found in some obese individuals. In addition, there is a gene which resides in the mitochondria, or energy factories of cells, that regulates fat burning. This gene plays a key role in shunting calories toward heat and energy production rather than to fat storage. The deposit of fat tissue, including that located in "love handles" and in the thighs, is also controlled by this gene.

Are my endocrine glands responsible?

As an endocrinologist, I would be remiss not to mention something about hormones and weight control. For example, too little thyroid and too much cortisone, as in hypothyroidism and Cushing's syndrome, respectively, can be associated with an unexplained weight gain. There may be few clues as to the presence of hypothyroidism other than fatigue or weight gain, but if one feels cold all the time or develops extremely dry skin, these are reliable signs of hypothyroidism. Patients with Cushing's are also hypertensive, and, therefore, all obese patients with high blood pressure should be evaluated for this disorder. However, most overweight individuals will have neither of these disorders. The most common cause of obesity with an endocrine basis that I see in my practice is in women with hyperandrogenism. These patients complain of one or more of the following: weight gain, post teenage acne, irregular menstrual periods, and excessive hair growth on their bodies often associated with thinning of scalp hair. The word hyperandrogenism refers to the production of too many male hormones or to increased action of a "normal" level of androgens such as testosterone or DHEA, which come from the adrenal gland and/or the ovary. Blood tests from these patients may indicate a normal level, but still high enough to cause the disorder. Some women with this disorder also have very high insulin levels, a problem which may be involved in causing the disorder or it may occur secondarily to the weight gain. Weight control has been a problem for these patients since they were teenagers. We have medical therapies for this condition which control the acne, hair growth, and irregular periods quite predictably, but weight loss is quite variable. My impression has been that those with disciplined eating and exercise programs in place before therapy lose weight with treatment, whereas others have little success. Thus, endocrine contributions to obesity exist, but these are often associated with behaviors that aggravate the problem.

These genetic and physiologic aspects of fat metabolism are proof that we all have our unique metabolic fat profile. Some have been gifted with the benefit of a high basal metabolic rate and other helpful genetic influences which make weight maintenance much easier. Perhaps this information will make us less judgmental about the supposed slothfulness of those with a weight control problem. In fact, the person with whom we need to be less judgmental may be ourselves.

Behavior and weight gain

Lest we be guilty, however, of the victim mind set pervasive in our society which would allow us to blame our genes for all our weight problems, it is also important to mention that behavioral issues are involved in obesity. When we are under stress, many of us notice an altered eating drive. This is probably associated with alterations in the chemical agents which regulate that center in the brain. Some individuals consume fewer calories, but many of us increase our caloric intake. Eating makes us feel less stressed, and therefore we get positive feedback that perpetuates this cycle. Our eating behaviors may then become more erratic, with increased snacking on fat laden foods of high caloric density (remember fats have twice as many calories per unit of weight as protein and carbohydrate) and calorie-containing beverages. Many of us with a weight problem may consume half of our calories this way. I have seen many individuals who are consuming over 1,000 calories a day in soft drinks and fruit juices. Binge eating and night eating are also frequently increased by stress. Obese night eaters may consume most of their calories after dinner.

Unhealthy eating behaviors and the subsequent weight gain can sometimes lead to or be associated with failure to recognize the amount of food consumed and activity performed on a daily basis, as was first reported in a *New England Journal of Medicine* article in 1992. Researchers evaluated obese individuals who repeatedly failed to lose weight while reporting caloric intakes of less than 1,200 a day. Using very sophisticated techniques for evaluating energy expenditure and caloric intake, the researchers found that these overweight individuals underestimated their food intake by 50 percent and overestimated their physical activity by 50 percent! In other words, their true intake of calories and energy expenditure were not adequately recorded in their diaries or in their consciousness, as was done by the control normal weight subjects. Such a phenomenon has been referred to as the eye-mouth gap or the mind-body gap. Non-obese subjects can also underestimate their food intake, as can athletes and elderly subjects, although obese individuals are more likely to have this problem.

The intensity of the emotional attachment to food in some individuals who overeat is revealed in the following statement I received from a friend.

Dear Food,

Ever since I can remember you've been one of the greatest loves of my life. You were my bridge over troubled waters, my shelter from the storm. Thousands of times my cravings for you were uncontrollable, and I ran to you with open arms. We made love everywhere: in the car, living room, kitchen, bathroom. At somewhere along the way, you turned on me, and I began to grow up.

Growing pains at any age are painful, but I had to face some realities. Your price tag was too high. You helped me bury all my feelings, but you also buried me. You made promises you could not keep.

Whenever we made love at night I couldn't respect myself in the morning. And although I loved you, I never wanted to be seen with you in public. I became a sneak just to be with you, and it grew into a cheap back-alley affair. I'm writing you this letter to let you know it's over. And I'm free ... free at last.

Points to Remember:

1 Obesity increases the risk of heart disease, breast cancer, and hypertension and produces higher death rates in men and women up to 75 years of age.

2 Numerous genetic factors influence our body weight and fat stores.

3 Hormonal abnormalities such as low thyroid function, elevated cortisol levels, or increased androgen (male-like) levels in women can accelerate weight gain.

4 Stress-induced eating, erratic eating schedules, increased intake of snack foods and beverages with a high fat and/or calorie content, binge eating, and late-night eating all can lead to obesity.

Chapter Six

I'm Ready to Lose Some Weight

LL RIGHT, I'M INTERESTED IN DECREASING MY risk of getting heart disease, high blood pressure, breast cancer, prostate cancer, arthritis, decreased lung function, and diabetes. Also I want to fit into some clothes I haven't been able to wear and want to feel and look better! How can I best lose this weight and, more importantly, keep it off? We are all barraged daily in the media by new therapeutic approaches. A new diet, a machine that will take off the excess abdominal fat, a health spa with a guarantee of losing so many pounds in a week, and a new diet suppressant drug. As we try one after another of these approaches and fail either to lose or keep off the weight, the more depressed we feel. In fact, having a major weight problem increases our risk of depression five-fold.

Emotional factors

Perhaps the best way to begin our search in this area is to consult those who have been successful in losing weight and keeping it off. From those individuals, I have learned that dealing with the emotional issues of why they ate excessively was important in their long-term success. I have observed that the more intense the emotional reasons for overeating, the less likely the overweight person's goals will be achieved. If we are eating to treat some symptoms of unresolved conflicts in our lives, then our major area of engagement needs to include treatment directed toward our emotional life. A clue that this is part of the problem is that we continually eat when we are not hungry. Issues of uncontrolled anger, abuse, low self-esteem, as well as marital and job stress usually have to be addressed for a successful long-term weight control program.

This is where self-assessment using the PIERS plan can be helpful as it forces us to ask ourselves certain important questions. Is the weight problem from a poor diet and lack of exercise (a Physical cause), lack of information or understanding of good nutrition (an Intellectual issue), a toxic Emotional life, a bothersome Relationship, or some Spiritual, ethical, or moral conflict? You may discover, as you go over this checklist, that you spend a lot of energy each day ruminating about an unresolved issue in one of these categories. Sometimes, these issues consume so much of our energy each day that there is not enough left to apply to effective weight-loss strategies. Therefore, a vicious cycle is initiated consisting of unresolved conflict, the uncomfortable individualistic symptoms that occur from this stress, eating for comfort not because we're hungry, and decreased self-esteem.

Weight gain then occurs in a stepwise fashion over weeks, months, and even years, punctuated by short-term efforts at weight management schemes. The increase in food intake can involve bingeing, food craving, and night eating, but often it is more subtle with only a small increase over daily needs. For example, let's say you eat a few cookies each day, which puts you 250 calories over your daily energy needs. By the end of the month, you would have ingested 7,500 extra calories for the month, which would translate into more than two pounds of excess body weight (3,500 excess calories = one pound of weight gain). If this practice were to be continued—and you may substitute beer in the illustration for cookies—you would gain 24 pounds over a year's time.

Some insights into the emotional aspects of obesity were provided by researchers who noted that women binged when they felt lonely, sad, angry, or bored, and ate less when they felt happy and in control of their emotions. In contrast, men tended to use food to assert themselves in social situations, and reported that they overate during celebrations and on happy occasions. Overweight men often report feeling inadequate and ineffective because of their obesity.

Often I see individuals who would like to lose some weight, but it is really someone else's goal for them such as spouse or friend. They themselves are not committed to establish weight-loss goals. That becomes quickly apparent when they are asked to begin keeping a food journal. This is a very effective way of monitoring our calorie intake and helping us to modify our eating behavior if distortions are revealed. A failure to keep such a record does not bode well for successful weight loss.

Getting started

We have previously discussed the basics of good nutrition, but there are several other items of importance. The word "diet" implies something temporary, and so I would rather avoid the word altogether, although you will continue to see it occasionally on these pages. Our perspective needs to be long-term. If it took two years to gain the 50 pounds, why not take two years to lose it? Remember the cookie illustration earlier and realize the reverse: if you cut out those four extra cookies each day, you would have lost 24 pounds in a year. Somehow, we have to convince ourselves that these nutritional recommendations which will help us to lose weight and then maintain our new-found level is just good common sense.

Most people who endorse and follow a health-producing nutrition plan are satisfied with the taste of their food. A very tasty menu can still keep fat content below 30 percent of calories consumed. Very highly-motivated individuals, such as those with heart disease, may even restrict their fat level to that found in the Ornish program, in which the diet contains only 10 percent fat.

Eating out at restaurants on a regular basis is also a formula for failure. In a study that surveyed 200 dietitians about the caloric and fat load of five restaurant meals, they underestimated the caloric content by an average of 37 percent and the fat content by 49 percent. For example, a hamburger with onion rings was estimated by the dietitians to contain about 860 calories and 44 grams of fat. Standard analysis of the common restaurant portions revealed 1,550 calories and 101 grams of fat. A tuna salad sandwich thought to contain 374 calories and 18 grams of fat was found to have double these numbers. Even snacks are deceiving, as the old 200-calorie muffin may now contain 900 calories. If dietitians have trouble determining what is in restaurant meals, what hope do we have of accomplishing this task? We should especially avoid the "all you can eat" restaurants. I am reminded by my wife, however, that one can eat sensibly at most restaurants if we use good judgment in ordering and are willing not to eat all that is placed before us. The "Clean Plate Club" may not be conducive to healthy lifestyle changes!

Low-calorie diets

Most nutrition experts frown on very low calorie diets. First, it has been shown that taking in fewer than 800 calories per day does not increase weight loss but does increase the risks for failure of this program. Second, rapid regaining of weight is very common. We are continually bombarded by fad diets like the cabbage soup diet, high-protein diets, or unusual food combination diets such as grapefruit and eggs. These diets are touted to either "rev" up your metabolism, increase fat burning, or just fill you up by eating the same food each day. Temporary weight loss is often experienced with these diets when they lower the number of calories you had previously been eating, decrease your appetite for a period of time, or just cause water loss, but there is no evidence that they accomplish long-term weight control. Instead, they are potentially dangerous, particularly as they cause vitamin and mineral deficiencies if used long term. This usually doesn't happen, however, because people become bored with the regimen or displeased with the amount of weight lost and therefore don't stay with them for long periods. To check out any reported heart diet, consult the American Heart Association's website at www.americanheart.org. General questions about diets can be found on the website of the National Council Against Health Fraud at www.ncahf.org. The American Dietetic Association's website also provides excellent dietary information. Teams of ADA dietitians will answer your e-mail questions and will even refer you to a local dietitian for more in-depth help. Their site can be found at www.eatright.org.

Weight loss medication

What about prescription medications for weight loss? For many years this has been a controversial subject among physicians. The concern is based on the observation that short-term weight loss occurs with appetite-suppressing drugs but is quickly regained after stopping the medication. You may ask, "Isn't that true of almost any chronic medical disorder you treat with medication, that when you stop the treatment the condition reactivates?" The response to this question has to be, "You are correct." The problem is that most of us have continued to see obesity as a behavioral disorder rather than as a disease, which then lumps everybody into the same category, even those whose problems are complicated by genetic factors and endocrine conditions. The irony of the situation is that we treat many such conditions with medications for years, while all along a major contributor to the disorder has been poor behaviors which continue even while medication is given. Examples include diabetes, hypertension, emphysema, and coronary artery disease.

As a consequence, few long-term studies have been performed with weight-loss medications, with the exception of a study by Dr. Weintraub and colleagues that was continued for 5 years using phentermine and fen-fluramine. A long-term combination therapy for weight control is feasible, this study has shown. The medications created greater weight loss than did the placebo, and some effects were sustained for over three years. Weight loss tended to stabilize at six months, though some increase occurred at two or three years while the drugs continued to be taken. In those who stopped the medication, weight returned to baseline. Some patients, however, did not respond to treatment. And, for these individuals, an increase in dose did not improve the weight loss.

Are there valid reasons for restricting these medications to those with major problems? I think we all want our treatments to create fewer problems than we have with the disorder. As is true for any medication, appetite-controlling agents such as phentermine and fenfluramine, the so-called "phen-fen," have side effects. These include diarrhea, dry mouth, sleep disturbance, frequent urination, and depression. There has also been much concern about the side effect of primary pulmonary hypertension, a serious cardiopulmonary condition. The potential for this side effect is increased several-fold for patients taking these medications for less than three months, the absolute risk is in the vicinity of from two cases per million to 12 cases per million per year in the population. With treatment over 12 months, the risk for pulmonary hypertension may increase 30-fold.

Additional risk factors from these agents include alterations in heart valve structure. The surprisingly high incidence of heart valve abnormalities in initial reports led to the removal of phen-fen from use in treating obesity. Both physician and patient face the dilemma that occurs with any medication which has the potential for a serious side effect. Again, such problems emphasize the need for serious attention to nutrition, exercise, and nutritional approaches before appetite-suppressive drugs are prescribed. I would also hope my clinical and research colleagues will give similar intense scrutiny to other agents which are being prescribed for numerous conditions where diet, exercise, and behavioral approaches would prove to be equal or more effective than standard drug regimens.

Recently approved by the FDA, another weight-loss medication works by decreasing fat absorption by inhibiting the enzyme which digests fat in preparation for absorption. It decreases the amount of fat absorbed from the diet by 30 percent, and is not absorbed into the body. One long-term concern for the use of this agent will be its effect on inhibiting absorption of fat-soluble vitamins.

Obviously the use of these types of medication will prove of little long-term value if changes in diet or exercise are not instituted. Researchers continue to develop medications with a minimum of side effects that may help patients sustain long-term decreases in weight despite social and biologic pressures to regain the weight. Weight loss of even 5 to 10 percent of initial body weight has been shown to have positive influences on risk factors for disease, and this is quite a reasonable goal for most individuals.

Other weight-loss strategies

It's possible, however, for most of us to avoid having to use medications. Remember the food pyramid with its emphasis on fruits and vegetables. Also, as that spare tire begins to form around the belly or excess pounds cling to the hips, don't forget the importance of exercise in weight control. We are fighting the following aging scenario—a decrease in muscle mass leading to a decrease in the total number of mitochondria, or energy-burning factories. Seniors can normalize their ability to burn fat by doing 45 minutes of cycling four or five times weekly. Similarly, an exercise regimen with walking, rowing, jogging, using a treadmill, or cycling can reduce abdominal weight gain in people aged 60 to 70.

You say, "I'm only 45 and I'm gaining weight even while I continue the same exercise regimen I did 10 years ago." Our failure to increase our duration or intensity of exercise as we age leads to weight gain because our metabolic rate decreases about two percent each decade after age 25. In addition to aerobic regimens we can increase our metabolic rate by strength training with its associated increase in muscle mass and presumed increase in the number of muscle mitochondria to burn calories.

For those of us with a weight problem or any area of imbalance in our lives where we need help in dealing with the anxiety of our struggle with weight, a 1990 *Newsweek* article by Ken Hecht gives advice that he used on himself:

For me the key to breaking that cycle was to finally decide one night to give in to the anxiety. Not numb it with the food, but instead go, rather than eat, cold turkey. I wanted to just sit there and see if the nightmarish anxiety I so feared would in fact total me. So I sat and felt god-awful and eventually felt feelings of self-loathing and disgust and worthlessness. And finally the panicky desire to eat passed. It lasted less than 30 minutes. It was an awful experience, and one that I highly recommend. Sit with yourself. Don't eat, don't go to a movie, don't turn on the television. Do nothing but sit quietly, be miserable, and feel what you're terrified of. It is the part of yourself you've been using food to run from. It is a part of yourself and you need to know. Doing this just once changed my life. No, I didn't immediately and easily diet the weight off from that point forward. There were many binges. But there were also many times when the anxiety came and I drew upon that one experience and knew I could tough it out. And the next morning there's a wonderful feeling: an absence of self-loathing. You actually feel a little bit good about yourself.

So forget excuses and magic bullets. When you blouse your waist or put on dark colors, don't tell yourself you don't look so bad. You do. You know the anxiety will soon come again and all your mind will want to deal with is food, the binge. So pick a time to sit with that anxiety and meet yourself. Have this one experience that lets you know you can survive what you dread. I've lost and kept off 128 pounds. I did it and so can you.

Points to Remember:

1 The benefits of weight loss include a decreased risk of getting: coronary artery disease, high blood pressure, breast cancer, prostate cancer, arthritis, sexual impotence, and diabetes.

2 Successful weight loss with long-term maintenance at a lower level is greatly benefited by dealing with unresolved emotional conflicts such as uncontrolled anger, abuse, low self-esteem, and marital and job stress.

3 A personal review using the PIERS model may prove helpful in understanding one's problem with overeating.

4 A modest caloric excessive intake of 250 calories a day over daily metabolic expenditure will produce a 24-pound weight gain in one year.

5 An indicator that losing weight is your goal and not that of your spouse or physician, is monitoring your food intake with a daily food journal.

→

6 When establishing goals for weight reduction, have a long-term perspective of taking months to years rather than a short-term program of days to weeks which is almost guaranteed to fail.

7 Refrain from frequent "eating out" and particularly "all you can eat" restaurants, as even dietitians underestimate the caloric load of restaurant food.

8 Avoid very low calorie diets as they are unsafe and produce rapid regaining of weight.

9 Some appetite-suppressing medications are associated with abnormalities of heart valves.

10 A decrease in muscle mass leads to a decrease in the number of calories burned daily, so increase your muscle mass with aerobic exercise and weight training.

Chapter Seven

Should I Use Nutritional Supplements?

NE OF THE MOST CONTROVERSIAL ISSUES IN THE field of nutrition is whether we need to supplement our diets with vitamins, minerals, or other additives which have antioxidant and other properties.

The only guidelines we have are the RDA, or recommended dietary allowances, which were last revised completely in 1989 by the Institute of Medicine at the National Academy of Sciences— the group that develops the RDA. Presently, the considerations that have to be addressed are the role of these substances in maintaining health, the role of these nutrients in preventing chronic disease, and requirements for subgroups such as the young and older segments of our population. New recommendations will have to deal with safer upper limits of nutrient intake for nutrient supplement users and reflect information that has been accumulated about disease prevention. Setting an upper limit for these agents will be useful, as too high an intake of one nutrient can affect the absorption of other nutrients and they can also be toxic.

In recent months there have been reports extolling the need for increased intake of numerous vitamins, including B vitamins, folic acid, and Vitamin C. In this review, we will also be evaluating compounds not essential to life, and which therefore don't have an RDA.

Antioxidants

We read often in the popular press about the need for antioxidants and their role as an antidote to the damage that occurs to our cells daily. The culprits in exerting this damage are the free radicals that are produced as by-products of normal cellular metabolism or by physical events such as energy-carrying particles of light. They include such agents as peroxide. Remember how that felt when mother put it on your cut finger or what it did to your hair color? Free radicals are unstable compounds with an unpaired electron that attaches to a weak bond in cells, forming a stable compound which then generates another free radical. This can lead to a destructive chain reaction that eventually causes tissue damage. It has been estimated that the number of free radical hits per day per cell in humans is about 10,000.

Antioxidants are free radical scavengers that prevent this chain reaction. The genetic material of our cells "dislikes" free radicals which damage DNA and therefore, over time, promote aging of cells and pre-cancerous lesions if DNA is not being properly repaired. Free radicals alter cholesterol so that it becomes toxic to blood vessel walls, leading to coronary artery disease. Impaired immunity, cataracts, brain disorders, cancer, infertility, arthritis, and ulcers all seem to have free radical damage as an important component in their development. Free radicals also damage mitochondria, the cell's energy factory, and cellular protein. In diseases of accelerated aging in humans, such as progeria, these damaged proteins accumulate at a much higher rate than normal.

In order to combat this free radical attack, the body utilizes an internal antioxidant system. The importance of this system in the aging process has been dramatically demonstrated in experiments with fruit flies which were given extra gene copies to produce antioxidants. This group of fruit flies with extra antioxidant protection lived 30 percent longer. Research suggests that the internal antioxidant system needs help and that eating fruits and vegetables decreases the risk for cancer and heart disease. Although the health benefit of these foods could be from something other than their antioxidant content, many people attribute their beneficial effect to this feature. Only 10 percent of people eat the recommended daily amount of fruits and vegetables, and these foods differ in their nutrient content depending on what field they were grown in and how they are cooked. Because of questions like these, millions of Americans are using dietary supplements daily even though many of them have not been endorsed by any major scientific or medical group.

You might be taking enough vitamins and minerals in your diet to prevent the expression of deficiency disorders which, however, are rare and usually seen in the chronically ill or the malnourished, as for example in chronic alcoholism. The need for supplementation, then, is to decrease the aging process, if that is possible, or to delay the onset or progression of the diseases of aging (cancer, heart disease, arthritis, diabetes, and brain disorders). The value and need for supplementation will undoubtedly be intensively investigated over the next decade. One of the problems with existing studies on supplementation with vitamins is that they are cross-sectional, or they examine people at only one point in time. The more valuable studies follow people over long periods of time and control for such conditions as being sure that the health behaviors of the supplement and control groups are equal at baseline. The cross-sectional studies are less expensive and time consuming, but can't tell us whether the supplement users were or were not using other good health practices.

Another problem in assessing benefits of antioxidant supplementation is that it may take a long time to see the benefits, as shown in a study appearing in a 1998 *Annals of Internal Medicine* article. In a study of 88,756 women nurses, it was observed that a significant drop of almost 80 percent in the number of colon cancer cases was not seen until after 15 years of usage of such vitamins as folic acid.

As we see more and more studies on supplementation coming to similar conclusions with sound biological reasons why supplements may be beneficial, we have to conclude, even before definitive statements can be made, that their use is appropriate. I know many scientists who understand these issues quite well and who are personally supplementing with vitamins and minerals. To keep you from guessing about my personal preference, I use supplements.

The increasing accumulation of literature on the benefits of supplementation is impressive. In 1993, for example, a report was published of a study of rural Chinese people for whom stomach and esophageal cancer were ten times higher than anywhere in the world and 100 times higher than in America. After five years of a combination vitamin pill, the incidence of cancer of the esophagus was reduced four percent and stomach cancer 21 percent. Since we know that cancer of the stomach is frequently caused by a chronic infection which would generate a lot of free radicals, it is believable that these antioxidant vitamins prevented the expression of stomach cancer. Several years later, additional results from the same study in China documented that these same supplements lowered the incidence of stroke by 30 percent.

Antioxidant supplementation has also been associated with decreased illness due to infection in elderly individuals and even improvement of mood in another study. Elderly individuals with the highest intake of Vitamin C have the lowest risk of stroke, slower progression of osteoarthritis, and better performance on tests of memory during old age. Vitamin C prevents the clumping of white blood cells, thus helping to prevent coronary disease in cigarette smokers. Vitamin C has also been shown to inhibit the growth of ulcer-causing bacterium *H. pylori* and to interact with alcohol to decrease gallstone formation. People with chronic sinusitis may have decreased antioxidant levels in the mucus membranes of the nose, and Vitamin C may decrease the severity of cold symptoms.

I find these latter findings of interest in that I have been told by several patients that antioxidant regimens improved their sinus allergies, which may also be related to the antihistaminic effect of Vitamin C. Exercise-induced asthma may also dramatically improve with the use of two grams of Vitamin C just before exercise. I have found it easy to accept these observations and studies, as my own seasonal allergies have responded to Vitamin C, allowing me to discontinue antihistamines. It seems almost certain that recommended levels for Vitamin C for health maintenance will be increased in the future from 60 mg. per day to 200-500 mg. per day.

Another supplement gaining enormous popularity is Vitamin E, and leading journals have shown that higher Vitamin E intakes or serum levels are associated with less heart disease, lower incidence of cataracts, less adult onset diabetes, a boosting of immunity in the elderly, the slowing of the progression of Parkinson's and Alzheimer's disease, a lower incidence of cancer including prostate cancer, a lower risk of chronic obstructive pulmonary disease, and a delay in the progression from HIV positive to the development of AIDS. It is difficult to get enough Vitamin E from a low-fat diet, and while we may not want to add Vitamin E to the drinking water, its recommended daily allowance will almost certainly be increased from 30 International Units (IU) per day to somewhere from 100 to 400 IU per day.

Just when we think that one of the supplement recommendations is secure, confusing data arrives. It appears that the gamma-tocopherol form of Vitamin E is best at inhibiting the DNA and cellular damaging effects of inflammation, pollution, and cigarette smoke. While 75 percent of the Vitamin E consumed in food is from the gamma form, most supplements contain less than ten percent gamma and consist mostly of the less beneficial alpha-tocopheral form. With an inadequate diet content of gamma-tocopheral, the alpha in the supplement may deplete the body of the more important gamma form. Some preparations on the market already have the gamma form included, and more should follow.

What about beta-carotene (a Vitamin A precursor) supplementation and the report that it may increase the incidence of lung cancer? One highly-publicized report stated that beta-carotene supplementation increased lung cancer in heavy smokers and drinkers. This finding seemed to be at odds with the 200 or more papers that suggested that beta-carotene plays a role in preventing cancer. Even the authors of the paper felt that this finding may be due to chance. However, it has been recommended that people who drink or smoke heavily should not take beta-carotene, but others may take 10 to 20 mg. daily to improve their cancer risk profile.

In the last several years, much attention has been given to an inadequate amount of folate in our diets. Folate is usually found in fruits and vegetables, and inadequate maternal intake can lead to a 70 percent increase in birth defects such as spina bifida in infants. Up to 50 percent of women of childbearing age may have inadequate folate levels. Low intake in humans is now recognized to be a major risk factor for stroke, thrombophlebitis, and heart attacks. This occurs because low folate levels increase a toxic blood vessel amino acid, called homocysteine, in the circulation. Homocysteine elevation increases the cardiovascular risk in smokers four-fold and in patients with high blood pressure 11 times. Blood levels can be measured and supplementation with folic acid can restore levels into the safe range. Adults should consume at least 400 micrograms of folic acid a day, which is the amount contained in most vitamin pills. In response to this data, the FDA is requiring that grains and cereals be fortified with 140 mcg. of folic acid per 100 grams, which is still probably inadequate, but is a good start.

The latest entry into the antioxidant supplement derby are the dietary flavonoids, which are water-soluble antioxidants found in fruits, vegetables, red wine, and tea. Research conducted in non-human systems suggests that flavonoids could have useful anti-cancer and heart disease properties. In a Finnish study, in which the primary source of flavonoids was onions and apples, those who consumed the largest amounts had the lowest risk for death from any cause. Also, lycopene (a flavonoid) and beta-carotene levels have been found to be lower in newly-diagnosed diabetics than in people with normal glucose levels.

Some manufacturers of nutritional supplements now offer in capsules what is considered the most important antioxidant from these fruits and vegetables. Therefore you can take lycopene, which is an antioxidant from tomatoes, sulforaphane, which is extracted from broccoli, and anthocyanins, which are extracted from grape seeds and skin. Firm support for these supplements, and the many others like it, is lacking, but I am not aware of studies suggesting harm from their ingestion.

Additional minerals and vitamins

There has been some concern that iron supplementation could increase the risk of heart attacks. Several subsequent studies found no support for this contention. Recent evidence suggests that 10 percent of adolescent girls and women of childbearing age are iron-deficient, and in half of these women, levels are low enough to produce iron deficiency anemia. Only one to two percent of males have iron levels low enough to produce anemia. In contrast, one in 200 people are iron over-absorbers, which can cause disease of various body organs. Some researchers argue that a blood iron test should be done before beginning an iron supplement, but because of the rarity of over absorption, this warning is generally disregarded. Iron supplementation should probably not occur unless the person is a vegetarian or has increased need for some other reason such as heavy menstrual bleeding.

The possible need for calcium supplementation to prevent osteoporosis, and to reduce the risk of colon cancer and hypertension has also been considered. Although supplementation may benefit some hypertensives and people with a risk of colon cancer, the data is much stronger for osteoporosis prevention in women, and in men as well. Yes, men, if you are a heavy drinker or have a low testosterone level, you can also get thin bones, particularly of the hip, which can lead to hip fractures. Most women need to supplement their calcium intake as their dietary intakes are inadequate. Being thin and having a low muscle mass will also increase a woman's risk for osteoporosis. A 1,000 to 1,500 mg. supplement of elemental calcium daily is recommended. Remember, it is the calcium content of the supplement that should be at this level, not calcium plus what it is bound to in the tablet, and you may have to read the label carefully. Speak with your pharmacist or your doctor about the preparation you are using.

In order for calcium to be adequately absorbed, you must have Vitamin D in its active form, and Vitamin D deficiency is common. In a study of 290 consecutive patients admitted to the hospital, Vitamin D deficiency was noted in 57 percent, which indicates that Vitamin D deficiency is common in the general population. As you age, you make less active Vitamin D, and it has been estimated that 80 percent of women and men get less than two-thirds of the RDA. Since the body makes Vitamin D when exposed to sun, your needs may vary with the season, but for those over 60, an 800 to 1,000 IU daily supplement is indicated. Those with osteoporosis will get the additional benefit of Vitamin D to decrease the bone loss and fractures of this disorder. In addition, Vitamin D may have anti-tumor effects which could reduce the incidence of breast cancer or combat tumor cell invasion.

In 1998, the Institute of Medicine released new recommendations for daily intake of the B vitamins and choline. These are shown in the Chart. Choline is one of the B-complex vitamins occurring in foods such as eggs, meat, fish, nuts, legumes, and soy, as well as in human breast milk. Choline is an important component of the neurotransmitter acetylcholine, the chemical messenger that many nerve cells use to communicate. Scientists believe choline is an important building block which is essential to the healthy development of various types of cell membranes (including neural membranes) during fetal gestation. In rats, the mothers which were supplemented with choline produced offspring that had a larger memory capacity and were able to hold more items in memory without forgetting them. They also displayed lifelong enhancement of their ability to remain attentive during various tasks and didn't show the same age-related declines in memory that was seen in normal rats. Whether choline has the same effect on the human brain remains to be demonstrated.

For other vitamins that we require, the need for supplementation is less clear. These vitamins seem to be more relevant as we age, and a decreased absorption and lower intake become operative. For example, older single people eat less often because they don't want to cook for themselves, are often depressed, don't want to go to restaurants alone, have decreased taste sensation, and have bad teeth, all of which may make eating difficult. Many published studies have confirmed nutritional deficiencies in the elderly. One report documented that low normal Vitamin B_{12} levels, which are more often found in older individuals, decreases the protective response to a pneumonia vaccination. But again, over-supplementation may be dangerous, as recent studies on Vitamin A indicate: doses above 10,000 but particularly above 20,000 IU daily increased the risk of birth defects.

Supplementation with trace minerals has also stimulated public and medical interest. For example, magnesium supplementation for eight weeks provided a significant decrease in blood pressure. The decrease was greater in those with higher levels of blood pressure. A study performed with 1,312 individuals given 200 micrograms of selenium daily for four to seven years demonstrated approximately a 50 percent reduction in lung, prostate, and colorectal cancer. Selenium is a trace metal present in wheat grown in soil rich in this element from such places as South and North Dakota. This is an example of a plant food in which some of the nutritional benefit is determined by the soil in which it was grown.

Zinc is also a trace element which, if not supplied, can cause loss of appetite, skin changes, and immunologic abnormalities, among other problems. There is some evidence, which is yet to be confirmed, that taking a calcium supplement can decrease zinc absorption in the diet from about one percent to 13 percent. This drop can be offset by adding about 8 mg. of zinc to the diet. Care must be given not to supplement with excessive doses of zinc, such as those 200 mg. tablets found in stores; overuse can decrease copper absorption and lead to a weakened immune system. Yes, zinc lozenges may even be useful in decreasing the severity of the common cold. The recommendation for zinc intake is in the range of 15 mg. per day.

Also a trace element, chromium is being taken as supplementation by thousands of Americans. It is taken in the trivalent form as opposed to the hexavalent form, which is toxic. Chromium has been shown to improve sensitivity to insulin and decrease the blood fat triglyceride, and thus help improve the cardiovascular risk profile of overweight and diabetic individuals. However, it has not yet been shown to decrease body weight, which is the major reason so many people are taking it. The National Academy of Sciences recommends 50 to 200 mcg. per day, and the standard American diet probably contains less than 50 mcg. daily. Therefore, supplementation with chromium seems worthwhile for most of us. I would not agree with those who choose doses five to ten times the amount stated above, as there is no research supporting that position.

There is a tendency for many who supplement to begin "stacking" antioxidants, which means that they are mistakenly acting on the principle that if a little is good, more will be better. This can also happen with "overdoses" of certain foods. Diane Habash, a research dietitian, told me of a nursing student she was teaching whose husband made and drank juice from ten bags of carrots every day. He soon had liver problems and orange hands. Many agents can produce undesirable side effects at high doses or, when combined with other agents, may interfere with absorption of some minerals or vitamins. Hopefully, future research will enable us to make sounder decisions concerning appropriate combinations of vitamins, trace minerals, and flavonoids as antioxidant supplements. As we await this information, we have to remind ourselves continually that our supplement regime is probably a minor player in the health we all wish to have. Supplements are poor substitutes for other neglected areas of our lives, as illustrated by the PIERS plan.

Chart 2

Recommendations for Daily Intake

Vitamin/Mineral	Amount
Vitamin A	1000 IU
B Vitamins and Choline	
Thiamin	1.2 mg.
Riboflavin	1.3 mg.
Niacin	16 mg.
B_6	1.5 mg.
Folate (Folic Acid)	400 mcg.
B_{12}	2.4 mcg.
Pantothenic Acid	5 mg.
Biotin	30 mcg.
Choline	550 mg.
Vitamin C	250 mg.
Vitamin D*	400-1000 IU
Vitamin E	400 IU
Vitamin K	80 mcg.
Calcium**	1000 mg.
Copper	2 mg.
Chromium	100-200 mcg.
Iron	18 mg.***
Selenium	50-100 mcg.
Magnesium	400 mg.
Manganese	1.8 mg.
Molybdenum	75 mcg.
Zinc	15 mg.

*Individuals over 60 should have a daily intake of 1000 IU of Vitamin D.
**Most men don't need calcium supplements.
***Because of the possibility for toxicity, iron should be supplemented only as directed by your healthcare provider.

For the intakes listed above, you will need to take several capsules or tablets per day to get this in the form of supplements. Most programs have not incorporated choline or the higher Vitamin D doses.

Herbs: Should we take them?

We would be remiss to conclude an examination of nutritional supplements without a look at the use of herbs. They have been used for centuries as health maintenance tonics and medicinal agents, yet most of us in American medicine have scarcely any knowledge of their efficacy and prefer to lump them with "snake oil" remedies. This view has been strongly challenged by Dr. Andrew Weil, who writes and speaks on the value of these agents. He argues that centuries of experience of their healing potential provides support for their usefulness, and they should not be disregarded. When we ask for more evidence, he says that much more than we realize is available and challenges us to read *Plantica Medica,* a German journal, and other publications. Indeed, this is true, for when I asked my assistant to do a Medline search on garlic, herbs, and green tea, he handed me three and one-half pounds of abstracts. Unfortunately, large controlled trials are not found, but that has been a problem for all the supplement field. Probably the best studied plant has been garlic, which has been shown even in reviews in U.S. journals to reduce cholesterol. In the herb chart, I have listed some commonly used herbs and their reputed benefits.

As is true for all medicinals and supplements, there are known and unknown risks associated with the use of these preparations. For example, the herbal supplements with Ma Huang contain the stimulant, ephedrine; deaths have been reported with its use. Ginkgo biloba has been associated with eye hemorrhage, the herbal laxative chomper produces an abnormal heart rhythm, and plantain has been contaminated with digitalis. For those who argue negatively about pharmaceuticals, supplements, or herbs, they can find evidence to support their contentions. Obviously, we wish to be as informed as possible, and, hopefully, those that we choose for advice will offer a balanced approach.

Nutrition and Health

We are always in need of more solid research in the nutrition area, but there is enough information available to provide dependable guidelines. We are clear, for example, that our caloric intake should be geared to keep

Chart 3

Commonly Used Herbs

Name	Possible Benefits
Echinacea	Immune system stimulant Enhances wound healing
Garlic	Decreases cholesterol levels* Antiseptic properties Decreases blood pressure Antitumor effects
Ginger	Prevents nausea* Stimulates appetite Treats motion sickness
Ginkgo biloba	Improves memory and social function in Alzheimer's* or stroke Relieves vertigo and ringing in ears Anticoagulant properties *Side effects:* Nausea and diarrhea
Ginseng	Increases stamina *Side effects:* Insomnia
Green Tea	Antioxidant* Treats intestinal disorders, vomiting, and diarrhea *Side effects:* Caffeine-like effects
Saw Palmetto	Treats enlarged prostate symptoms* Treats irritable bladder *Side effects:* Mild headache
St. John's Wort	Treats symptoms of depression* *Side effects:* Nausea, lack of appetite, and increased sensitivity to sunlight

*There is reasonable scientific support for these effects, but studies have not yet proven a definite benefit.

our body fat within reasonable limits, and when those limits are exceeded, we are at risk for numerous diseases. To accomplish this task, our fat intake should be 30 percent or less and our protein intake 15 percent of total calories, with carbohydrates making up the rest of our dietary intake. The majority of these carbohydrates should be from whole grain breads, cereals, pasta, vegetables, and fruits. Although certain individuals will improve their weight control by limiting carbohydrates from bread, pasta, and potatoes, we should all limit foods with added sugars and fats. Our intake of saturated fats, like butter and cheese, should not represent much of our fat intake, and fruits and vegetables should be the cornerstone of our carbohydrate consumption. There is strong data accumulating that many people would benefit from supplementation with minerals and vitamins, but some of the supplements being offered have little or no supporting evidence. Most of us are clearly aware of these nutritional guidelines, but their implementation requires disciplined decisions at grocery stores and restaurants. We are more likely to be successful in these pursuits if other areas of our lives are also in balance. We eat to live, and not the opposite; it is our reasonable desire to provide the right fuel mixture to maintain this wonderful organism we call our body.

Points to Remember:

1 Antioxidants are utilized by the body to counter damage to cells by products of normal cellular metabolism referred to as free radicals.

2 Free radicals damage DNA and over time promote aging of cells and pre-cancerous lesions as well as damage to other body systems.

3 Fruits and vegetables are a rich source of antioxidants which help the body's own antioxidant system.

4 Only 10% of people eat the recommended daily amount of fruits and vegetables.

$\longrightarrow$

5 The argument for vitamin and mineral supplementation is that our diet is either deficient or does not maximize our ability to retard aging and its associated diseases (cancer, heart disease, arthritis, and brain disorders).

6 Herbs have been used for centuries to manage a variety of health problems. The benefits of their use as a daily supplement to prevent the diseases of aging is unclear.

Chapter Eight

PIERS Nutrition Planning for Busy People

B Y NOW YOU MAY FEEL LIKE YOU ARE ON INFOR-
mation overload in regard to nutrition. What
each of us has to do is to reduce this information to something practical that we can use
each day. Taking time to develop an appropriate
daily nutrition plan is of critical importance for our
health. We would never think of putting sand and oil in our gas tank and
then expect to drive successfully across the country. Yet each day we toss
whatever is within reach into our incredibly complex human bodies.

The number of calories that you and I need daily to maintain our ideal
body weight depends on our age, gender, and activity level (Chart 4). The
number of calories recorded in this table is much less than many of us are
eating and we can see that even moderate exercise doesn't increase our
allowances to the levels which we may be consuming. This point is illustrated in Charts 5 and 6 where the typical caloric intakes of the average
American man and woman are recorded. The typical male who eats a

quick breakfast of two donuts, a fast food lunch, dinner, and some snacks will have consumed 3,600 calories. The average American woman eats "on the run" but also while preparing foods for her family and can easily lose track of what she is eating. For instance, she might drink coffee when she first gets up and eat a single bowl of cereal along with a piece of toast. Later, when she arrives at work, she eats some coffeecake someone brought into the office. A couple hours later, she eats some Twizzlers that she keeps in her desk for a little snack. When she goes to lunch, she tries to eat something healthy, so has a toasted bagel, light cream cheese, a cup of soup, a few crackers, and a diet drink. This holds her until late afternoon when she eats a granola bar. She arrives at home and has to make dinner, help the kids with homework, answer the phone, and do laundry. As she makes dinner, she nibbles on pretzels and cheese. For dinner, she

Chart 4

Daily Calorie Requirements to Maintain Current Weight*

Age	Sedentary	Exercise: Brisk Walk 30 min. 3 times a week	Exercise: Brisk Walk 1 hr. every day
Women			
20	2160	2190	2310
30	2130	2165	2280
45	2035	2065	2180
60	1930	1965	2070
75	1925	1955	2065
90**	1925	1955	2065
Men			
20	2955	3000	3170
30	2840	2885	3045
45	2645	2680	2835
60	2455	2490	2630
75	2440	2480	2615
90**	2440	2480	2615

*Based on an "average" woman who is 5'5" tall and weighs 130 lbs. and an "average" man who is 5'11" tall and weighs 172.

**Good nutritional research data do not exist for individuals in this age group.

Chart 5

Typical Male Daily Diet

Food	Calories
Breakfast/Morning:	
2 cups coffee	10
2 tsp. sugar	45
2 donuts	320
Lunch:	
1 large french fries	470
1 double cheeseburger	450
16 oz. cola	190
Dinner:	
6 oz. roasted boneless chicken breast	335
3/4 c. canned corn	100
2 dinner rolls	170
1 cup 2% milk	130
1 cup tossed salad	25
3 tbl. ranch dressing	255
1 fudge walnut brownie	370
Snack:	
2 oz. pretzels	130
1 can beer	145
1 cup ice cream	520
Total	**3665**

eats a chicken breast, a baked potato, some creamed corn, and a tossed salad with fat-free dressing. After dinner, laundry, and kids' baths, she's exhausted. When she finally sits down to relax she treats herself to a fat-free frozen yogurt and a few vanilla wafers. But she realizes she hasn't packed lunches for tomorrow and as she makes them she snacks on a few reduced-fat chips then heads off to bed. She's had very little time for exercise today, but she has eaten over 2,600 calories.

Referring to Chart 5, a 45-year-old sedentary male would have eaten 1,000 calories more than he expended. It is easy to see that he could continue consuming an average of 500 calories more than he needs each day. This would lead to a one pound weight gain each week. A 30-year-old sedentary woman eating a grazing-type 2600 calorie diet would also gain

Chart 6

Typical Female Daily Diet

Food	Calories
Breakfast/Morning:	
2 cups coffee	10
1 oz. frosted corn flakes	110
1 cup skim milk	85
1 piece wheat toast	65
1 tsp. margarine	35
1 tbsp. jelly	35
1 piece coffee cake	170
1 pkg. red licorice bits	135
Lunch:	
1 plain bagel with 2 tbsp. light cream cheese	235
1 cup cream of broccoli soup	235
4 saltine crackers	50
1 can diet cola	0
Afternoon snack:	
1 granola bar	135
Pre-dinner snack:	
1 oz. pretzels	110
1 oz. cheddar cheese	110
Dinner:	
4 oz. roasted boneless chicken breast	225
1 baked potato	145
1/2 cup cream-style corn	100
1 cup green salad	25
2 tbsp. fat-free salad dressing	50
1 dinner roll	105
1 tsp. margarine	35
Snack:	
1 cup frozen yogurt	260
4 vanilla wafers	70
10 reduced-fat potato chips	80
Total	**2615**

approximately one pound per week. One way for these individuals to have eliminated the caloric excess would have been to engage in one of the aerobic activities seen in Chart 7.

Chart 7

Caloric Expenditure During Various Activities*

Activity	Caloric expenditure per hour
Basketball	600–960
Canoeing	180–420
Cycling (5–15 mph)	300–720
Gardening	330
Golf	220–300
Mountain climbing	600
Rowing	300–900
Running (12 min. mile)	600
Skating	300–900
Skiing	480–720
Soccer	540
Swimming	360–750
Tennis	420–660
Volleyball	210–480
Walking	200–420

*Depends on exertion, efficiency, and body size. Add 10 percent for each 15 lb. over 150. Subtract 10 percent for each 15 lb. under 150.

PIERS Healthy Daily Diet

How can a busy person who leaves early for work and is often involved with work-related travel hope to do nutrition planning? It is best initially to focus on how we are going to get our recommended servings of fruits and vegetables. Remember, only one in ten people eat the recommended amount of fruits and vegetables each day.

I suggest fruit in the morning and vegetables at lunch (Chart 8). An easy and tasty way to get your daily fruit intake is to make a simple fruit shake for breakfast. Fresh strawberries, a banana, and a medium apple blended with skim milk, fruit juice and/or ice cubes is an excellent way to

Chart 8

Recommended Nutrition Plan

	1800 cal. diet	2200 cal. diet	2800 cal. diet
Bread: *One serving equals:* 1 slice bread 1/2 c. cooked cereal rice, or pasta 1 oz. ready-to-eat cereal 1/2 bun, bagel, or English muffin 1 small roll, biscuit, or muffin 3–4 small or 2 large crackers	8 servings	9 servings	11 servings
Vegetables: *One serving equals:* 1/2 c. cooked or raw vegetables 1 c. leafy raw vegetables 1/2 c. cooked legumes 3/4 c. vegetable juice	3 servings	4 servings	5 servings

Fruit:
One serving equals:
Typical portion (1 med. apple,
   banana, or orange, 1/2 grapefruit,
   1 melon wedge)
3/4 c. juice
1/2 c. berries
1/2 c. diced, cooked, or canned fruit
1/4 c. dried fruit
	3 servings	3 servings	4 servings

Milk: *One serving equals:* 1 c. milk or yogurt 2 oz. processed cheese food 1½ oz. cheese	2–3 servings	2–3 servings	2–3 servings
Meat: *One serving equals:* 2–3 oz. lean cooked meat, poultry, or fish. Count 1 egg, 1/2 c. cooked legumes, 4 oz. tofu, or 2 tbsp. nuts, seeds or peanut butter as 1 oz. meat (about 1/3 serving).	2–3 servings	2–3 servings	3–4 servings

Note: This table is based on recommendations from the food guide pyramid which
limits foods high in fat and in sugar.

Sample PIERS Healthy Daily Diet

Breakfast	**Lunch**	**Snack**	**Dinner**
Breakfast shake:	Salad	Vanilla wafers	Boneless chicken breast
Skim milk	Green beans	Pretzels	Long grain brown rice
Banana	Corn	Diet cola	Broccoli
Grapes	Roll	Frozen yogurt	Roll with spread
Apple	Oatmeal raisin		
Toast with jelly	cookies		

get your fruit for the day. This can be supplemented with toast or cereal. In summer there are a lot of fresh fruits to choose from, but even in the winter there is some fresh fruit at the market and one can also use frozen fruit in the shakes. When eating breakfast at a hotel there is usually a fruit plate on the menu. Depending on how many calories you need for breakfast you can alter the size of your portions.

At lunch I suggest building your meal around vegetables. Salads that you purchase or take with you to work are a great beginning. At many restaurants you have access to vegetable medleys where you can pick two or three steamed vegetables. Bread, rice, a small order of pasta, meat, or fish are an excellent addition. Chart 9 lists some suggested foods that are healthy snack alternatives. By now you have completed or nearly completed the important fruit and vegetable requirements. In addition, you will have ingested a lot of antioxidants and other vitamins and minerals (Chart 10).

At dinner, the traditional meat along with bread, pasta, or rice (which contribute the B-vitamins not found in fruits and vegetables), along with a vegetable or salad will complete a successful day of supporting the work of our bodies. Remember that your total caloric intake will be adjusted as you monitor your weight after beginning a nutrition program like the 2,200 calorie sample diet (Chart 11).

The second area that we need to keep in mind for our nutritional plan is the proportion of fat, protein, and carbohydrate in the diet. Remember, less than 30 percent fat, 15 percent protein, and the rest carbohydrate (Chart 12). The good news about this issue is that if the fruit and vegetable

Chart 9

Healthy Foods During the Workday

Below are some healthy alternatives that you might want to take to work. Some of the items would work well as lunches. Others could be kept in your desk for those times when the hunger pangs strike.

Snack items:

2 rice cakes	70 cal.
1 tbl. peanut butter	95 cal.
1 oz. bag of pretzels	132 cal.
1 plain bagel	195 cal.
1 oz. cheddar cheese	110 cal.
1 oz. fat-free crackers	100 cal.
1 fat-free granola bar	140 cal.
3/4 cup Frosted Mini-Wheats	125 cal.
1/4 cup raisins	130 cal.
1 tbsp. sunflower seeds, dry roasted, hulled	50 cal.

Fruits and vegetables:

1 medium apple	80 cal.
1 medium banana	105 cal.
1 medium orange	60 cal.
1 celery stalk	5 cal.
5 baby carrots	20 cal.

Lunch alternatives:

2 oz. light tuna in water	65 cal.
3 slices lean ham	110 cal.
3 slices lean turkey	60 cal.
1 whole wheat pita pocket	170 cal.
2 slices whole-wheat bread	130 cal.
1 tbsp. fat-free mayonnaise	10 cal.

Salad:

1 cup tossed salad	25 cal.
1 cup tossed salad with tuna (as above)	90 cal.
1 cup tossed salad with ham (as above)	195 cal.
1 cup tossed salad with turkey (as above)	85 cal.
2 tbsp. ranch dressing or 1 tbsp. fat-free mayonnaise	10 cal.

Foods High in Antioxidants

Food	Serving Size	% of RDA
Vitamin A		
Beef liver	3 oz. fried	100+%
Carrots	1/2 c. shredded raw	100+%
Corn flakes, fortified	1 oz.	38%
Mango	1 med. raw	80%
Pumpkin	1/2 c. canned	100+%
Spinach	1 c. raw	38%
Squash, butternut	1/2 c. baked	83%
Sweet potatoes	1/2 c. cooked	100+%
Turnip greens	1/2 c. cooked	60%
Vitamin C		
Broccoli	1/2 c. cooked	97%
Brussels sprouts	1/2 c. cooked	83%
Grapefruit juice	3/4 c. fresh	100+%
Kiwi	1 med. raw	100+%
Mango	1 med. raw	97%
Orange	1 med. raw	100+%
Red bell pepper	1 c. raw chopped	100+%
Snow peas	1/2 c. stir fry	67%
Spinach	1 c. raw	30%
Strawberries	1/2 c. fresh	70%
Tomato juice	3/4 c.	60%
Vitamin E		
Canola oil	1 tbsp.	35%
Cashews	1 oz.	25%
Corn oil	1 tbsp.	100+%
Soybean oil	1 tbsp.	100+%
Spinach	1 c. raw	20%
Sunflower seeds	1 oz. dry	80%
Sweet potatoes	1/2 c. cooked	45%
Tofu (soybean curd)	1/2 c.	40%
Wheat germ oil	1 tbsp.	100+%

Chart 11

Healthy Daily Diet: 2200 Calories

Food	Calories
Breakfast:	
Breakfast Shake:	
1 cup skim milk	85
1 medium banana	105
15 grapes	50
1 medium apple	80
2 pieces whole-wheat toast	135
4 tbsp. jelly	75
2 tsp. soybean oil-based margarine	70
Lunch:	
2 cups tossed salad	50
1 cup canned green beans	40
1 cup canned corn	150
1 whole wheat dinner roll	100
2 oatmeal raisin cookies	130
Snack:	
5 vanilla wafers	85
2 oz. pretzels	270
Diet cola	0
Dinner:	
4 oz. roasted boneless chicken breast	225
1 cup long grain brown rice	215
1/2 cup frozen broccoli	35
1 dinner roll	105
2 tsp. soybean oil-based margarine	70
1 med. scoop nonfat frozen yogurt	125
Total	**2200**

recommendations are being followed, the guidelines for fiber, potassium, and sodium intake will also be easily met. Additionally, it will only take a small amount of low-fat or skim milk, fish, or meat to meet the essential amino acids (building blocks of protein) requirement not found in vegetable proteins.

With this program we will have done an excellent job in obtaining our vitamin and mineral requirements. It's possible that individuals following this regimen may need little if any vitamin supplementation. For those not following a similar nutrition program, supplementation is probably important. We need to keep in mind, however, that there are many helpful compounds in fruits and vegetables that are not included in most supplement programs and probably also other fruit and vegetable compounds that we have not yet discovered. In Chart 2, I included the recommended daily intakes for the B and other vitamin and mineral groups. If it were possible to know exactly the micronutrient content of our food we could subtract it from this recommendation and take the remainder in the form of supplements. Since this is not feasible for most people, supplementing with the doses in this chart will not produce toxic side effects. Megadoses of supplements, however, have no research base of support and may be dangerous.

Because of the difficulty of finding a supplement which would provide all the vitamins and minerals on Chart 2, I have put together a reduced list of those items for which inadequate intakes would have clear-cut health-related consequences.

The "PIERS Short Program" is easier to put together than the long program in Chart 2, but still somewhat difficult. As you roam the aisles of your pharmacy, grocery, or health food store, you will become frustrated trying to match these recommendations even for the ULTRAShort program. For example, multivitamin tablets will often contain about 30 IU of Vitamin E and 60 mg. of Vitamin C. These are the presently recommended levels set by the RDA, but almost certainly will be increased in the future. Therefore, one may have to buy individual bottles of Vitamin C and E to get the 250 mg. of Vitamin C and 400 IU of Vitamin E. The folate and Vitamin D levels in these "one-a-days" are usually the desired 400 mcg. of folic acid and 400 IU of Vitamin D. It is harder to match the short program without buying several bottles and it may be difficult to stay

Chart 12

Recommended Intake

Food Component	Amount
Fat	30% of calories
Saturated fat	10% of calories
Protein	15% of calories
Carbohydrate (total)	55% of calories
Fiber	11.5 g. per 1000 calories
Sodium	2400 mg.
Potassium	3500 mg.

Chart 13

PIERS Short Program

Vitamin/Mineral*	Amount
Folate (Folic Acid)	400 mcg.
Vitamin C	250 mg.
Vitamin D**	400 IU
Vitamin E	400 IU
Copper	2 mg.
Chromium	100 mcg.
Selenium	50-100 mcg.
Zinc	15 mg.

*Women need 1000 mg. calcium.
**Over age 60, 1000 IU Vitamin D daily.

Chart 14

PIERS ULTRAShort Program

Vitamin/Mineral	Amount
Folate (Folic Acid)	400 mcg.
Vitamin C	250 mg.
Vitamin D*	400 IU
Vitamin E	400 IU

*Over age 60, 1000 IU Vitamin D daily.

within the intake levels you want to achieve. If the program you choose has additional agents other than these items, you most likely will not have a problem, but you should probably have the label reviewed by your health nutrition consultant.

There are several manufacturers that produce multivitamins that approximate these recommendations. Nutrition stores have a variety of preparations, giving you options to compare labels. Several network marketing companies produce preparations that also come close to my recommendations. Their products aren't on retail shelves but you may wish to investigate them.

You may wonder how one can make recommendations for individual supplementation without knowing how much a person ingests from food, the person's age, the individual's ability to absorb nutrients, metabolism and excretion rates, gender, weight, and exercise routine, to name just a few important variables. These are the same problems doctors have when they prescribe a diet or medication. It is an imprecise science which depends on ranges of acceptable intakes—always attempting to produce levels well below those which might produce toxic effects.

At this point we have the information we need for successful planning of our daily fuel intake. At issue is whose value is good nutrition? If it is our spouse's, friends', or physician's goal for us we will probably not be successful. Perhaps those of us who need to restructure our eating habits can test our resolve by keeping a daily record of what we are eating and drinking. This effort would be a reflection of how much we have endorsed healthy daily nutrition.

Points to Remember:

1 Taking time to develop an appropriate daily nutrition plan is of critical importance for our health.

2 The number of calories we need each day to maintain our daily weight depends on our age, gender, and activity level.

3 Fast food, grazing throughout the day, eating out, and a sedentary lifestyle often produce excessive caloric intakes.

→

4 Only one in ten people ingests the optimal amount of fruits and vegetables each day.

5 Building a diet which emphasizes fruit in the morning and vegetables at lunch increases the likelihood of getting the right amount of fat, fiber, protein, carbohydrate, vitamins, minerals, and calories.

6 For us to have a healthy nutrition program it must be our own value and not that of our spouse, friends, or physician.

7 Those of us who need to restructure our eating habits can test our resolve by our willingness to keep a record of our daily food and beverage intake.

SECTION THREE

Your Health and Exercise

Chapter Nine

I Don't Have Time

S TAY FIT," "NO PAIN NO GAIN," "USE IT OR LOSE IT," and "I've got to earn my calories" are frequently heard phrases at the local health clubs where people of all ages are pumping iron, running on treadmills, and using a variety of aerobic and strength machines to produce what they perceive to be the benefits of exercise. Beginning in the late 1960s, Kenneth Cooper and others challenged Americans to get off their couches and enjoy the health benefits of aerobic exercise. A medical student at the time, I had heard little about the importance of exercise, but Cooper's words were like a challenge.

Over the last 30 years, the virtues of exercise have been extolled in published reports. Numerous individuals began to exercise regularly and seriously. However, about ten years ago the curve of increase began to flatten. It's my understanding that presently less than 40 percent of Americans have a regular exercise program.

Health benefits from exercise

The benefits of a regular exercise program are impressive. Improved health and longevity, as well as improved functional capabilities, are the results of a disciplined exercise program. An important study on the value of exercise in extending life span was performed by Finnish investigators with a group of 434 pairs of twins. One sibling died during the study period, but the surviving twins who engaged in vigorous conditioning (30 minutes at least six times per month) reduced their risk of death by an average of 43 percent compared with sedentary twins. Occasional exercisers were able to reduce their mortality by 19 percent compared with non-exercisers. These differences remained after controlling for other risk factors. The researchers concluded that regular exercise is a preventative factor for premature mortality, independent of genetic influences.

In another study performed in non-smoking retired men 61 to 81 years of age, those who walked two miles or more a day had one half the mortality rate as those who walked less than one mile each day. The group who walked greater than two miles a day had one third as much coronary disease and one half as much cancer.

Improvements in endurance and in sleep patterns are quickly noted by the new exerciser. Soon after beginning an exercise program, you note a change in body composition which reflects a decrease in body fat and an increase in muscle mass. Body weight may not be changing rapidly, but inches around the waist decrease. Your metabolic rate goes up with an increase in muscle mass, burning calories more rapidly. It has been reported that aging may result in a yearly half-pound loss of muscle mass, which may be responsible for an annual one-half percent reduction in metabolic rate. It has been estimated that every pound of muscle you gain, increases by 50 the number of calories you burn each day. That is one reason why strength training adds to the benefits of aerobic exercise when weight loss is desired. In the elderly, strength training has also been successful in reducing the number of falls.

The cardiovascular benefits of exercise are well known, with an increase in the maximal amount of oxygen that an individual can consume during aerobic testing reflecting improved cardiac conditioning. If you are 60 years old, frequent aerobic exercise can give you the oxygen carrying capacity of a sedentary 30-year-old, which means that the 30-year-old would be watching your back in a jogging or cycling competition.

Exercise also produces a dramatic decrease in a number of cardiovascular risk factors as it lowers blood pressure, cholesterol levels, body fat, the incidence of diabetes, and stress levels. Its effects in lowering blood pressure are even more impressive in hypertensive men. It was reported that a single bout of 30 minutes of bicycling at less than 50 percent of the maximum speed could reduce blood pressure by 6 to 10 points in men with hypertension. This reduction in blood pressure lasted for almost 13 hours. Exercise decreases blood pressure in part by decreasing the influence of the sympathetic nervous system which causes blood vessels to constrict. Thus, exercise decreases the tension in the blood vessel walls as well as in the rest of the body, producing its well-known calming effect. Exercise also increases blood volume; vigorous exercisers may increase their volume by over a liter. The amount of blood the heart pumps during exercise increases and produces the same output with a slower heart rate. In well-conditioned athletes, the heart chambers enlarge and the volume of blood ejected with each beat at rest can be so large that resting heart rates fall to fifty beats per minute and occasionally lower.

Exercising also reduces blood fats such as the cholesterol-rich triglycerides. There is an enzyme in our tissues that digests triglycerides and therefore lowers our cholesterol levels. This enzyme is increased in people who exercise. The decrease in body weight with exercise also decreases the risk of diabetes, which is a very strong risk factor for heart disease.

A variety of other disease risk factors are also minimized by exercise. The incidence of all cancers, including breast cancer, are decreased by exercise. A 1997 *New England Journal Of Medicine* article revealed a 37 percent decrease in breast cancer in those who exercised regularly. The reduction in risk was greatest in lean women, especially if they continued to exercise regularly over three to five years.

Sedentary men have an increased risk of developing symptomatic gallstone disease. For example, men who watched television more than 40 hours a week had a higher risk for symptomatic gallstones than men who watched less than six hours a week. The authors of this study suggested that 34 percent of cases of symptomatic gallstone disease in men could be prevented by increasing exercise to 30 minutes of endurance-type training five times a week.

Exercise results in less depression and anxiety as well as in fewer illnesses. Looking younger and having a better sex life are additional benefits we receive from a regular exercise program.

I received a phone call the other day from a patient of many years who had been treated with surgery for a pituitary tumor and subsequently lost most of her hormone production. We had been able to replace these successfully, and she was doing well except for a problem with weight control. Susan was a vegetarian, and, as a teacher of advanced yoga practices, she meditated daily. She told me with some disappointment that her long-time dream of entering a three-year meditative retreat in a Buddhist Ashram had ended for several reasons. First, her father died, and, shortly thereafter, her mother developed Alzheimer's disease. Susan was aware of her tendency toward severe depression, and she decided that a better alternative would be to begin a rigorous exercise program. She ran daily and did some weight training, and, within six months had lost 35 pounds and lots of inches around the middle. She continued to grieve, but her energy level never lessened; in fact, her whole attitude toward life was cheerful. She now looks better, and her sex drive has markedly improved. In her excitement with this newfound friend called exercise, she is thinking, in her 40s, about getting a master's degree in exercise physiology. We may not share Susan's interest in getting a degree in exercise physiology, but improved appearance, increased energy, improved mental outlook, weight loss, and an enhanced sex life all seem to be on most of our wish lists.

Chronic fatigue

A large number of Americans complain of fatigue, and some have developed what is referred to as the chronic fatigue syndrome. A 1997 article in the *British Medical Journal* suggests that when individuals with the chronic fatigue syndrome begin a regular aerobic exercise regimen, they feel better overall with less fatigue and their functional capabilities increase. This study included 66 men and women with the chronic fatigue syndrome who were assigned to a 12-week program of graded aerobic exercise or to 12 weeks of stretching and relaxation. The program, in which walking was the main exercise, was increased by one or two minutes a day up to a maximum of 30 minutes daily. Researchers found that 16 of 29 individuals rated themselves as better after exercise treatment, whereas only eight of 30 in the relaxation group could say the same. Individuals who then switched from the relaxation to the exercise group also improved, and these improvements were still present one year later. Whereas few of us have chronic fatigue syndrome, we do however often come home from work drained of all energy. Many people find that exercise at this time restores energy. Others note that regular morning exercise helps prevent their "wasted" feeling in the afternoon.

Benefits of exercise

I have previously discussed examples of incredible exercise achievements in elderly individuals. Yesterday I was discussing exercise with a 52-year-old fellow bicyclist who complained that his physician brother, recently discharged from the hospital after bypass surgery, had not been advised about the importance of cardiac rehabilitation on coronary artery disease. Ed was also concerned about the myth that older people can't be athletes or even very physically active. He indicated that exercise in the form of cycling was high on his list of priorities. His concern about the lack of exercise for older Americans is valid. At least 40 percent of people over 65 are sedentary, and 70 to 80 percent of older women report levels of physical activity less than recommended in public health guidelines. Since fewer than 10 percent of women over the age of 75 smoke, one could conclude that physical inactivity is the leading health problem in this group. Several reports in a 1997 issue of the *Journal Of the American Medical Association* describe benefits of exercise for people over 60 that have not been previously emphasized. One of these studies showed that disabled persons with osteoarthritis of the knee had improvements in measures of disability, physical performance, and pain from participating in either aerobic or a resistance exercise program.

Even more intriguing is the finding that quadricep (the knee extensor muscle) weakness may be a risk factor for the "initiation" and progression of damage to knee cartilage and other tissues in the bone containing osteoarthritis. The authors of this report suggest that this muscle weakness may increase the likelihood of knee pain, disability, and progression of joint damage in persons with osteoarthritis of the knee.

Another study in this same journal showed that exercise reduced the time required to fall asleep by 15 minutes and increased sleep duration each night by 45 minutes. Sleep disorders and osteoarthritis occur frequently in older adults, leading to the ingestion of millions of sedatives and nonsteroidal anti-inflammatory drugs annually with their attendant side effects. These are just a few examples of the value of exercise in the non-drug treatment of disease.

Another group not exercising regularly includes working women. A recent survey by the Women's Sports Foundation found that only a quarter of the working women sampled engaged in regular physical activity, though they acknowledged that exercise was important in feeling good about themselves, and most felt that it would make them happier and more self-confident. One misconception was that long hours at the gym were required to develop fitness. The Foundation has now published a list of recommendations for women to help them squeeze a workout into the workday:

- Make your morning commute work for you. Get off the bus a few stops earlier, and take the stairs instead of the elevator.
- Take a meeting for a walk. Conduct meetings with colleagues as you go for a walk inside or outside the building.
- Make a fist. Use a squeeze ball to flex and tone hands and arms. It's also a great stress buster.
- Visit friends. Need a coffee? Go to another floor in your office building. Use any excuse to use those leg muscles.
- Do lunch—at the gym. Save the eating for your desk while you check your mail.

Your own personal work environment may suggest numerous other fitness-developing strategies.

Why don't people exercise?

With all these potential benefits of regular exercise, why don't a majority of the population participate? There is probably a small minority who are not familiar with these benefits, so that it is lack of education which keeps them from exercising. There are numerous other reasons given for not exercising when I raise this question to patients: I don't like gyms. Health clubs are not nearby or are too expensive. I'm too heavy and embarrassed to be seen working out. My joints are bad. I weigh too much. I'm afraid that I will develop big muscles like the women body-builders. I'm not sure what exercises to do or how hard to train. It was too strenuous. I hurt for days. Plus many others.

The following humorous account of a novice's bad experience with a personal trainer, distributed on the Internet several years ago, describes the hazards of a too-aggressive exercise regimen. The writer enjoyed both his trainer and his workouts on days one and two. By day 3, this new exercise enthusiast had broken all the rules in starting an exercise program. But, not one to throw in the towel this easily, he perseveres:

Day 3
The only way I can brush my teeth is by laying the toothbrush on the counter and moving my mouth back and forth over it. I am certain that I have developed a hernia in both pectorals. Driving was okay as long as I didn't try to steer. But I made it back to the health club. My trainer was a little impatient with me and said my screaming was bothering the other club members. The treadmill hurt my chest, so I did the stair monster. Why would anyone invent a machine to simulate an activity rendered obsolete by the invention of elevators. My trainer told me regular exercise would make me live longer. I can't imagine anything worse.

Day 4
My trainer was waiting for me with her vampire teeth in a full snarl. I can't help it if I was half an hour late. It took me that long just to tie my shoes. She wanted me to lift dumbbells. Not a chance. The word "dumb" must be there for a reason. I hid in the men's room until she sent Lars looking for me. As punishment she made me try the rowing machine. It sank.

Day 5
I hate my trainer more than any human being has ever hated any other human being in the history of the world. If there was any part of my body not in extreme pain, I would hit her with it. She thought it would be a

good idea to work on my triceps. Well, I have news for you. I don't have triceps. And if you don't want dents in the floor, don't hand me any barbells. I refuse to accept responsibility for the damage. The treadmill flung me back into a science teacher, which hurt like crazy.

Day 6
My trainer left a message on my answering machine wondering where I am. I lacked the strength to use the TV remote, so I watched eleven straight hours of the weather channel.

Day 7
Well, that's the week. Thank God that's over. Maybe next time I'll start a project that's a little more fun. Like free teeth drilling at the dentist.

As you may have already figured out, I forgot the most frequently cited reason for not exercising which is, "I don't have enough time." I hear this repeatedly from patients, friends, and even family members. My son, Gregg, and I had this discussion last night when he was giving me his reason for not participating in an aerobic exercise program. We laughed about the spare tire he was growing around his middle as he approaches his 30s. I then asked him if exercise was a priority in his life. He stated, "Dad, you know I love to play golf, and there just isn't enough time to do aerobic exercise." He then admitted that he didn't enjoy jogging and some of the gym-related programs and that was the primary reason that he didn't have a regular exercise regimen. Exercise was my value and not his. Until we develop personal ownership of this value nothing will happen.

I'm reminded of a story I heard at a Franklin-Covey seminar where they discussed Ben Franklin's development of 12 values, one of which he planned to improve each month. A friend, after reviewing his list, felt that Ben would benefit from adding humility to the list. When asked by the same friend months later whether he had made improvements in his value program, Ben stated he had been successful with all of them but humility. It would seem that the reason for his poor performance in the humility area was that it had been someone else's value.

Points to Remember:

1 Why don't people exercise? Numerous reasons are provided including the most common, "I don't have time."

2 The problem is that exercise is often someone else's value. Once you make the commitment for yourself, with a program that you enjoy, you will make it your value.

3 Increased longevity, improved appearance, increased energy, weight loss, decreased arthritic pain, improved sleep, less depression, and an enhanced sex life are a few of the health benefits awaiting the regular exerciser.

4 A study of 434 pairs of twins revealed that 30 minutes of exercise at least 6 times per month reduced their risk of death by an average of 43% compared with the sedentary twin. Occasional exercisers were able to reduce their mortality by 19% compared to non-exercisers.

5 Aging may result in a yearly half-pound loss of muscle mass, which will lead to a reduction in caloric burning. It has been estimated that every pound of muscle you gain by strength training, increases by 50 the number of calories you burn each day.

6 Exercise reduces blood pressure, cholesterol levels, body fat, the incidence of diabetes, and stress levels, all of which are cardiovascular risk factors.

7 Exercise reduces the incidence of all cancers, including breast cancer. It also decreases the risk of developing symptomatic gall stones, depression, and chronic fatigue.

8 Recommendations for women on how to squeeze a workout into the workday are presented.

CHAPTER TEN

Your Personal Exercise Prescription

HETHER A PRESCRIPTION FOR A DRUG OR an exercise, compliance with the proposed regimen must occur for the office appointment to be anything but an intellectual exchange. It is estimated that only 30 percent of recommendations by a physician for medications are followed as prescribed. I assume that exercise prescriptions are followed even less frequently. When we try to help an individual who needs an exercise program, it is important to know the reasons that a program is not presently in place. If it is embarrassment at being with fit people, then an outdoor program or one done in the home needs to be established. If the person has joints that have been injured or aching with arthritis, then water aerobics and water-resistance training can be employed. My daughter-in-law is a personal trainer who is a proponent of water training. She asked me for months to do some water training and to forget the myth that it was only for rehabilitation or for women. It is now clear to me that one can get heart rates near the level found in jogging, and water resistance compares favorably with some of the machines and free weights in the gym. I did only water exercise for one month, giving up cycling and weight training, and, after returning to these programs one month later, was able to resume my former activities without losing a step.

"I'm afraid I will develop big muscles like women body builders if I get into a regular aerobic and weight training program," is a complaint sometimes expressed by women. I have yet to see this occur, however, if the weight training focuses on modest weight levels with a lot of repetitions.

A valid complaint for not initiating a regular exercise program is lack of information on how to start, how frequently to exercise, how intense a workout should be, and what exercise to select. The most important decision, other than starting to exercise in the first place, is the selection of activities. You must select something you think you will enjoy! Remember, you are committing to a program on which you will be spending time for at least three days a week. Visualize yourself participating in this routine when you may be mentally fatigued, or the weather may be hot, cold, or rainy, or you may have to get out of bed early to do it. Given those conditions, what would work best for you? Set reasonable goals which may be augmented if you find them too easy later. Keeping a journal of your activities, such as a record of minutes spent in training, may make it easier for you to see your accomplishments. Also, finding friends to participate in that walk or run will increase enjoyment and facilitate compliance with your regimen. Personal trainers are also helpful in getting you started, but avoid those who hold to the "no pain, no gain" philosophy. Remember the story about the trainer who became a nightmare for the novice exerciser. Although credentials are not the only way to evaluate a good personal trainer, national certification suggests that he or she has received training.

Once you have selected an aerobic and possibly an anaerobic activity such as weight training, set a scheduled time each day or every other day. For individuals who are basically sedentary, I suggest as little as five minutes a day for the first week. The initial primary goal is to build habits, not run a marathon. The objective is for you to look forward to the day when you can exercise 15 or 20 minutes a day. One of the most predictable ways to discourage a beginner is to recommend an overly-ambitious program.

On the second week, individuals may be ready to commit to ten minutes a day, and then increase the time by five minutes a day weekly so that by six weeks, 30 minutes of exercise daily or every other day has become routine. This is plenty of time to build a habit which is being daily reinforced by positive feedback, including the physiologic "high" that comes from stimulating endorphin release and other hormonal signals that have mood-elevating properties. Increased productivity and less fatigue, anxiety, and depression all encourage one to return to the chosen physical activity tomorrow. This approach will generate little if any chronic muscle fatigue or soreness.

Some individuals who are over 40 and have never been active or have an associated medical problem may need to see their physician for a baseline cardiovascular evaluation. Occasionally, individuals don't like to exercise because they get inappropriately fatigued with very little exercise, and this may represent underlying heart, lung, or some other disease process. Following this admonition, plus a gradual increase in your aerobic regimen, is to be recommended over the "weekend warrior" syndrome, that situation in which a person—usually an out-of-shape male—tries a sport or other activity which he hasn't done for years and then suffers a severe soft tissue injury or a heart attack which is sometimes fatal.

A very useful tool for monitoring the intensity of your workouts is to use a heart rate monitor. Although they are a little pricey, costs are decreasing to the point that you can purchase a quality monitor for approximately $60. A wristwatch depicts the beats per minute, and the heart rate is detected by a chest strap which fits comfortably and transmits a signal to the watch. A good training range is in the vicinity of 70 to 75 percent of your maximal heart rate. Your maximal heart rate is calculated by subtracting your age from 220. So, if you are 50 years old, the maximal rate will be 170 beats per minute, and the comfortable conditioning rate would be in the 120s to 130s. These numbers increase for your age if your cardiovascular system is well-conditioned. You will know you are exceeding this training range when your breathing rate is high enough to make it difficult to carry on a conversation. Increasing the heart rate outside this range in brief spurts is referred to as interval training. These intervals can be increased in duration after you are experiencing a training effect and can be useful in advancing cardiovascular conditioning. Therefore, pulse monitoring can be useful in preventing overtraining, but its greatest utility is in preventing undertraining. You can tell by your breathing rate when you are on the high side of your desired heart rate, but a lot of factors can make you feel fatigued while your heart rate is still below the training level.

What about stretching before or after your aerobic or anaerobic activity? For years, most experts have advocated stretching as a way to prevent injuries. However, a 1997 *Wall Street Journal* article challenged its value, arguing that marathon runners who stretched had no more protection from injury than non-stretchers and suggesting that stretchers might even be at increased risk. Another study found non-stretchers suffered less pain after a 20-minute Stairmaster session than did those who stretched prior to exercise. Apparently there are no studies documenting its value, and many athletes have stopped stretching. We may, however, get research support for its benefits in coming years.

I have found that using yoga poses, which are stretching-like activities, result in much less post-exercise discomfort and improved flexibility. I usually do 10 to 20 minutes of stretching following my exercise regimen. Also helpful in preventing soft tissue injury which might occur in primary exercise activity is the performance of cross-training. If jogging is your primary activity, then intermittent cycling or swimming will allow you to develop the muscle groups that may be under-developed by your primary activity and thus more prone to injury.

What about nutrition for the aerobic exerciser? A good nutrition plan, usually carbohydrate-based with a decrease in the fat content of the typical American diet, is of great value when you initiate your exercise program. One of the most important concerns is that you replace fluids after exercise, and, if it is a prolonged exercise event, fluid should be replaced during exercise. In hot weather during running or cycling, at least a quart of fluid an hour will be required. A sports drink with electrolytes is of great value. Dehydration can occur quickly and is often associated with low body potassium levels, low blood pressure, and, less commonly, irregular heart beats, shock, and even death. An unusual feeling of fatigue after excessive exercise in warm weather may reflect a need for fluids and supplemental potassium which can be found in most sport drinks. Both my wife and I have experienced on two different occasions the symptoms of severe dehydration following extended exercise, and I assure you that you want to avoid them.

Many people suffer from exercise-induced asthma and therefore greatly restrict their activity. A 1997 article in the *Archives of Pediatric and Adolescent Medicine* reported that taking two grams of Vitamin C before exercise prevented exercise-induced asthma in nine of 20 individuals exercising on a treadmill. It was thought that the increase in free radicals, which initiate inflammation in the lung during exercise, were decreased by the antioxidant Vitamin C. Many athletes without asthma take a variety of vitamins and minerals before or after exercise to reduce inflammation and increase their rate of recovery. Studies are not available to direct us as to what the combination of these supplements should be or exactly how beneficial their effects are. The advantages of vitamin and mineral supplementation in general have been discussed in the previous chapter.

Musculoskeletal injuries will occur in almost everyone at some time in their exercise career. The best initial response to such an injury is to apply ice immediately and then intermittently during the day following the insult. This will cut down on local inflammation and swelling and increase the recovery rate. Injuries are more common in those individuals who overtrain, which is hard to define but "you know it when you see it." Overtrained individuals have little body fat, exercise performance falls, and fatigue is frequently present. In a study with college wrestlers in which I was involved, we found that when body fat fell below 5 percent, the testosterone levels fell into the low female range. The testosterone levels returned to normal when body weight returned to its pre-weight-loss level.

How intense should my exercise be?

There is really no longer any debate that exercise can improve cardiovascular risk factors and longevity. There is controversy, however, as to what constitutes the appropriate exercise intensity and duration to achieve all of these benefits. Initially, it was felt that at least three bouts of intensive aerobic exercise three times a week were needed to achieve these benefits. Several later articles, however, suggested that even moderate exercise could improve risk factors and survival. Moderate exercise consisted of activities such as housework, gardening, playing with children, and walking. A panel of exercise researchers convened by the Centers for Disease Control and Prevention and the American College of Sports Medicine in 1993 concluded that moderate exercise is sufficient to improve health, a recommendation that has since been challenged by some researchers. More recent research indicates that there is a progressive improvement in cardiovascular risk factors as exercise intensity increases, and that significant cardiac protection requires vigorous exercise.

There are also differing opinions about whether sustained exercise is required for cardio-protection or if intermittent exercise of similar intensity is adequate. In 1997, about the same time that this debate was presented in the journal *Science,* a paper appeared in the *Journal of The American Medical Association* which showed that regular moderate exercise can reduce the risk of premature death by 30 percent in post-menopausal women. The study which was performed with over 40,000 women found that one exercise session a week was effective in reducing the risk of death from a variety of causes. Exercise seemed to be the most closely associated with decreasing the death rates from heart disease and respiratory problems. Women studied were between the ages of 55 and 69 when the study began in 1986, and they were followed for seven years. Two thousand two hundred and sixty women died during the course of the study, many due to heart disease and respiratory illness. Most women in the study participated in regular moderate exercise such as bowling, golf, light sports, gardening, or long walks. Those reporting vigorous exercise such as jogging, tennis, swimming, aerobics, or other strenuous activities had the greatest risk reduction, but even modest exercise reduced the death rate. This was the first study to show a risk reduction even with light exercise, and it should encourage older women to engage in some form of physical activity. Since it is estimated by the Center for Disease Control that inactivity accounts for more than a third of the 500,000 annual heart disease-related deaths, it is obviously important for us to exercise and also to encourage others to do likewise.

Points to Remember:

1 Why don't you have an exercise program? Sore joints, embarrassed being with fit people, a woman afraid you will develop big muscles, or other issues?

2 The most important decision is the selection of a particular exercise activity. It must be enjoyable!

3 Visualize yourself participating in this exercise routine when you are mentally fatigued, or the weather may be hot, cold, or rainy, or you have to get out of bed early to do it.

4 Set reasonable goals.

5 Keep a journal of your activities which will make it easier for you to see your accomplishments.

6 Find friends to participate in your exercise activity which will increase your enjoyment and facilitate compliance with your regimen.

7 Set a scheduled time for exercise every day or every other day. Build the habit before developing your conditioning.

8 Over time, increased productivity, less fatigue, anxiety, and depression will encourage you to return to the chosen physical activity tomorrow.

9 A gradual increase in exercise is preferred over the "weekend warrior" syndrome.

10 Monitoring your heart rate is useful when starting an aerobic program or when you increase your conditioning level.

11 Stretching and good nutrition are beneficial.

12 Avoid overtraining. Men whose body fat falls below 5% have a marked decrease in testosterone levels, and women lose their menstrual cycles when their body fat gets too low.

13 Even modest exercises can reduce the risk of death from a variety of causes.

14 Inactivity accounts for more than a third of the 500,000 annual heart related deaths. It is important for us to exercise and also to encourage others to do likewise.

Chapter Eleven

Motivation and Exercise

WHEN I HAVE URGED FRIENDS TO INITIATE an exercise program, some have responded, "Whenever I get the urge to exercise, I wait until the impulse passes." Your motivation to exercise regularly will probably include some of the benefits already discussed, and your list will also have some features that are unique to you. For those who have become regular exercisers, however, there are some commonly expressed motivational characteristics as discussed in a 1997 article published in the *Journal of Clinical and Consulting Psychology.*

- For some people, having a friend or workout buddy is helpful.
- For others, workouts are a good time to relax and sort out some thoughts.
- Always have a plan B. If you were planning to walk outside and it's raining, head for the exercise bike.

• View exercise as a welcome break, not an imposition.
• Reward yourself for your perseverance.
• Expect some obstacles.
• Don't over-exert.
• Keep yourself entertained. Add music to your exercise routines.
• Exercise in the morning. It's easier to find excuses as the day moves on and other activities come up.
• Learn how to win those internal dialogues about exercise between the inner sloth and the inner athlete.

I have had a regular exercise program for many years, starting with basketball, tennis, and jogging, and, when the knees began talking back in the form of osteoarthritis, bicycling became my passion. My motivation to exercise has been driven by some of the previously described health benefits, but also by its contribution in helping me to integrate the physical, intellectual, emotional, relational, and spiritual aspects of my life.

To illustrate this point, accompany me, my wife Joan, my friend Jay and his wife Janet on a bicycle tour into central Ohio farmland. Joan and I prefer our tandem bicycle, which permits us to arrive at our destination at almost the same time.

It is early Saturday morning in June, and the sun has been up only a short time. We are in rolling hill country, and the tandem powerfully soars down a country lane at 25 miles an hour. The cool breeze feels good as we prepare for the ascent up the next hill, which on this day occurs almost effortlessly. At the top of the climb, Joan points to a home sitting in a meadow surrounded by wildflowers of almost every imaginable color. The colors and shadows created by the emerging sun behind us have produced an almost idyllic vista. At the speed we are traveling, the view quickly changes only to be replaced with one of equal beauty—acres of corn and soybeans as far as the eye can see and a quaint Amish farmhouse with an enormous flower and vegetable garden. We wave to the Amish children working in their dresses and trousers, while yesterday's wardrobe is blowing straight out like a sail on the clothesline, warning us that our elation about what good shape we are in has to be tempered by the fact that we are benefiting from a strong tail wind.

We still have 12 miles to ride before the breakfast break at the Amish restaurant in Plain City, which has been our Saturday morning destination for so many years. Janet comments that she thinks she can smell the home fries and baked goods for which the Dutch Kitchen is so famous. We soon become complacent about the scenery, and our talk begins to focus on current events—the upcoming Presidential race and the commercialization of college athletics. As if these topics aren't challenging enough, discussion turns to prisoner rehabilitation, morality in the work force, and arguments for the existence of God. The wind direction has now changed, and talk has become a little less animated as our pulse rates climb and we acquire a more aerodynamic riding position.

The Kitchen is now in sight, and sweat pours off our foreheads as we race for the goodies we have long been imagining. Forty bicycles already rest against the restaurant wall, so hopefully the early birds didn't get all the worms. As we move inside, we see many familiar people whose names we often don't know but who have also been making this Saturday morning journey for many years. We pick a table with several old friends and soon get updated on the latest about schools, weddings, disappointments, and successes in their lives while gulping down oatmeal, coffee, and the famous rolls. We hope to keep our caloric intake below the energy expenditure of the ride. Stomachs a little too full and the wind having turned up several notches encourage us to take the shorter route back home after another Saturday morning of exercise for the body and mind, relationships reestablished, and enjoyment of nature's beauty. It's been a good day!

This cycling experience provided all the elements of productive aerobic exercise with two hours of constant motion and pulse rates in our target area. It is not the healthy increase in heart rate, however, that motivates us to take a 40- or 50-mile bike ride every Saturday morning. It is the other four areas of the PIERS plan, the deposits made in the intellectual, emotional, relational and spiritual areas of our lives that provide motivation to return each Saturday morning. I have noted similar points of view in talking with other people who have successful exercise programs. Remember Tina Riley, the 91-year-old great-grandmother, who each day when she goes jogging reflects on the beauty of the Montana mountains? For most people, a narrow focus on the basics of aerobic or weight training in an attempt to lose weight or improve cardiac conditioning will not produce the perseverance required to stay with a balanced exercise program. Therefore, bring people, scenery, discussion, and emotion into your exercise equation as you try to find what will work best for you.

The value of exercise is not just a personal issue but also has enormous public health implications. In discussing "The Public Health Burden of a Sedentary Lifestyle," Dr. McGinnis notes that, "The national pattern of physical inactivity, in combination with the dietary patterns to which activity patterns are fundamentally related in producing health outcomes, ranks with tobacco as among the leading preventable contributors to death for Americans—well ahead of the contribution from infectious diseases." Among Americans there has been very little change in their sedentary life style for the past 20 years. He states, "Clearly, we need to make exercise and fitness a social norm, which means that adult role models for children must be strengthened and worksite programs must be expanded. In addition, environmental changes are critically important, including the expansion of urban space and increase in availability of facilities for physical activity in the inner city area." Additionally, the medical care savings that could accrue from an enhanced level of fitness in our population is staggering. These savings could be applied to medical research, preventive care for the young, and other areas to enhance our quality of life.

Perhaps further development of our social consciousness may provide us with an additional incentive to develop a regular exercise program: one of the greatest gifts we can give to society is our health!

Points to Remember:

1 For most people a narrow focus on the basics of aerobic or weight training in an attempt to lose weight or improve cardiac conditioning will not produce the perseverance required to stay with a balanced exercise program.

2 Relationships are often important in initiating and sustaining an effective exercise program.

→

3 Many elements of the PIERS model can be incorporated into an exercise program which adds physical and emotional deposits to our health bank account.

4 Bring people, scenery, discussion, and emotion into your exercise equation as you try to find what will work best for you.

5 The public health financial burden of taking care of people with illness that could have been prevented or delayed by regular exercise is enormous.

6 One of the greatest gifts we can give to society is our health.

SECTION FOUR

Stress, Emotions, and Health

CHAPTER TWELVE

Left Brain, Right Brain

It's July 3rd, and we have just canceled a trip to Maine and have several days to experience vacation at home. My wife calls to me in my upstairs office where I am trying to sneak in a few hours on the word processor on this manuscript. How would you like to take a car trip to Yellow Springs and have lunch? Yellow Springs is a small college town and the home of Antioch College; its appeal to us is provided by its quaint shops featuring art, glass blowing, and coffee. The people we meet on the streets have the dress and hairstyles of a '60s and '90s hybrid. Our last visit, which was associated with a 70-mile bike ride, was to be replaced by a 70-mile ride in a convertible. I pulled out my Ohio bicycle maps and detailed a series of one-lane paved roads through southwest Ohio farm country. One-lane bridges, beautiful wildflowers, golden fields, and green cornfields which were well above "knee high by the fourth" all contributed to a peaceful, relaxing drive. After lunch and a double-decker ice-cream cone from the huge Youngs Dairy, we headed back to Columbus.

We decided to return via Interstate 70 in the interest of saving some time. Within minutes of entering the holiday traffic flow on this four-lane interstate, we could feel our relaxed muscles beginning to tense. I was no longer focusing on flowers and one-lane bridges, but on 18-wheeler caravans snaking through orange construction barrels and frustrated drivers with kids yelling in the back seat. Soon I noticed a small headache beginning as my temple musculature began questioning my sanity about the route change. The contrast between these two routes was mind boggling, and my headache gave resounding testimony to this truth. I stole a glance at Joan, who was obviously having the same physiologic reaction, and almost simultaneously we asked each other whether the time was worth the price we paid.

The fast lane

We are being constantly challenged to take the fast lane! To be a pace setter, to be productive, competitive, and rewarded in the global economy. We have to attack, be macho, be number one, and that requires toughness in driving in the fast lane even if a few folks get run over! The fast laners say, "There are only two kinds of people: winners and losers." Certain coaches remind us that losing is worse than dying, for when we lose we have to get up the next morning. How else can we accumulate competitive skills, earn the wealth, get the title we deserve, and be seen in the right car and country club without placing our lives in the fast lane?

Yet occasionally, because of a comment made to us or an illness we are fighting, we become aware of our rapid shallow breathing and racing pulse. A thought may arise, stimulated by some forgotten words of a prophet or poet of contemporary society, that challenges our frantic lifestyles. Their words temporarily penetrate our armor of indifference. Why are you going so fast? What are you going to do when you get there? Will there ever be enough? Will peace ever replace desire? These are questions for romantics, poets, and philosophers, not for a '90s person, we respond. Yet our lives are being lived as if we had carefully considered the psychologic and physiologic price for achieving these goals and had decided that the fast lane was the only option. A sin of omission with great personal and communal costs, the critic responds! When we are too weak to argue further, we may listen to his verdict. Why do you think you and your friends are fatigued, need to get away, are burned out, and feel like you are constantly under stress?

The critic says, taking aim at the jugular vein, that it is your body speaking to you in physiologic language that you refused to listen to when it whispered in your ear, "Slow down," and it is now creating noise that you can no longer refuse to hear! Come on, you respond to the critic, I have lived like this for 40 years, so why should I now have to look at my behavior. Cellular memory, he responds—you have been disturbing your biorhythms for years, and the beauty of your body is that it has constantly set into motion physiologic processes to bring you back to a comfortable baseline. You have now exceeded the elasticity of these adaptive processes, he continues. Your doctor may not be able to label your symptoms with a specific disorder, but, if you continue these behaviors, you will get a diagnosis that makes you more uncomfortable than your present signs and symptoms. The critic now has our complete attention as we contemplate the diseases of aging which other people get—not us!

Our critic is just getting warmed up. Why don't you look at sunsets anymore? What happened to your sense of wonder about the little successes and joys of today? Your optimism has been replaced by cynicism, anger, and a dislike and distrust of most people. These attitudes multiply daily as you watch the nightly news. Your thinking is occupied by past mistakes and emotional wounds and senseless fears and frustrations concerning the future. Your sense of gratitude is non-existent, and kindness, patience, forgiveness, hope, and optimism are no longer part of your vocabulary. You have no time for the present moment, which is squeezed out by your living in past and future time. With this parting shot the critic departs.

Conflict

This dialogue and later reflection on that which applies to us may itself produce stress, depending on how closely it mimics our struggle. The contest is between our left and right brain attributes as they contend for recognition of their input. Left brain dominant people are analytical, ask for scientifically-acquired information, and decide on a course of action after considering all the options. Left brain dominant people tend to be more competitive and more interested in productivity; they stress accumulation of knowledge and believe in bottom-line decisions. They tend to be goal-oriented people of action. They are doers. They are better at speaking than listening. More often they have a "scarcity mentality" that sees giving or helping others as depleting their own limited resources.

In contrast, a right brain dominant individual would tend to value relationships, intuition, awareness, compassion, service, creativity, and spirituality as equally or more important than the characteristics which flow from left brain thinking. They would also be more interested in meditation than action, emphasize being rather than doing.

Granted this is an artificial model, but it does bring into focus the issues which contribute to conflict for many of us. Left brain qualities are more valued in the work place. Successful relationships in every sphere of our lives, however, are aided by right brain attributes.

Let's look at a left brain-right brain dialog that might occur when a son approaches a busy professional father and requests that his father drive the little league baseball team across town for the big game. The father has just carefully explained to his son that he is in the middle of a big project and needs this Saturday to complete it for a Monday morning meeting. The father carefully explains that a promotion and possible salary increase which will help pay for the son's future college education may depend on the father doing well during this meeting. His son leaves the room saddened but accepting, and the father's left brain says he was brilliant, logical, persuasive, in control of a potentially very emotional situation. The father attempts to smile as he turns on the TV set, but the smile doesn't develop because the right brain, which has not been consulted, voices its displeasure by immobilizing the smiling muscles of the face and subconsciously begins the following response to the left brain. *I've had it, left brain; these aren't my priorities and you know it! We've been down this road before, and I have given in to keep peace, but I no longer can stay quiet as your priorities are inconsistent with my happiness. You have given too much importance to your job, your title, and the accumulation of money and things, while neglecting your marriage, your son, and your friends. As you have climbed the ladder of success, I have become an emotional cripple. My pleas for tenderness, service, intimacy, civility, and shared vision have all been met with your perception that I'm too soft, emotional, and have no idea what it takes to survive in the real world. Divorce is not an option. However, because you have been unwilling to consider any kind of middle road response to requests like that your son just made, I'm going to give us the biggest case of heartburn that we have ever felt—go to it, stomach!*

We have all been involved in such a dialogue with ourselves, but often it is subconscious. All of us, no matter how well-balanced our right and left brain, experience such a dialogue as we face the hassles, worries, hardships, feelings of guilt, and unpleasant decisions of life. Our emotional and physical response to these stressors is influenced by our genetic, physiologic, and psychological endowment, as well as our previous life experiences. Throughout each day, we are processing and coping with numerous experiences, and our bodies register a physiologic response—like heartburn. The greater the gap between our expectations and actual life experiences, the greater the attack on our bodies' physiologic harmony.

Points to Remember:

1   Our lives are being lived as if we had carefully considered the psychologic and physiologic price for achieving our goals and decided that the fast lane was the only option.

2   We don't look at sunsets anymore. What happened to our sense of wonder about the little successes and joys of today?

3   Optimism has been replaced by cynicism, anger, and a dislike and distrust of most people.

4   We have no time for the present moment, which is squeezed out by our "living" in past and future time.

5 Our analytical, competitive, goal-oriented, bottom-line-centered left brain often dominates the civil, intuitive, aware, creative and spiritually oriented right brain functions.

6 We can easily become human doings rather than human beings.

7 Left brain attributes are more valued at school and in the workplace whereas right brain functions are more valued in the establishment of successful relationships.

8 The greater the gap between our expectations and actual life experiences, the greater the attack on our bodies' physiologic harmony.

Chapter Thirteen

Everyday Hassles and Health

REMEMBER THE RESEARCH I DESCRIBED EARLIER which demonstrated that even minimal hassles such as serial subtractions or an extemporaneous speech can produce markedly higher pulse and blood pressures in many people. Any acute stress, like a problem at work or in the home, produces temporary changes in our heart, immune, and endocrine function. When faced with chronic stress, however, we may develop a persistent maladaptive response in which physical symptoms and even established disease may occur. For example, our research on the chronic stress of caring for a spouse with Alzheimer's disease showed signs as severe as increased risk for infection, an inability to respond to an influenza shot, and delayed wound healing.

How stress can produce disease

Researchers are learning more about the ways in which chronic stress could lead to disease by altering immune function. We now know, for example, that many diseases in addition to colds, flu, pneumonia, and other classic infectious illnesses have an infectious origin. These diseases range from serious neurological disorders to cancer, arthritis, and ulcers. It is now well-established that stomach ulcers are associated with a gastric infection with the bacteria *H. pylori,* and it is probably in some individuals responsible for the later development of gastric cancer. We know that stress increases the risk of developing an ulcer and perhaps increases the likelihood of an infection with *H. pylori.*

A surprising study found that multiple myeloma, the second most common cancer of the blood, may be triggered by the same virus that produces cancer in AIDS patients. I'll never forget the comment made to me by a friend who developed multiple myeloma while under incredible stress at work and at home that the diagnosis of cancer was almost a relief to him, such that now he had an excuse for cutting back on some of his commitments. Could the stress in his life have made him more susceptible to a bone marrow infection with this myeloma-producing viral strain?

It has also been reported that an infectious organism, *Chlamydia pneumonia*, was found in a fatty plaque from a coronary artery in a patient with atherosclerosis, and this finding was followed by an observation that patients with recurrent heart attacks are more likely to have been infected with this organism. Individuals infected with *Chlamydia pneumonia*, a common microbe which causes pneumonia, bronchitis, and sinus infection, were four times more likely to have recurrent heart attacks over the next 18 months if they did not receive an appropriate antibiotic.

In another report, researchers found an association between a previous infection with *Chlamydia pneumonia* and chronic severe hypertension as well as narrowing of the aortic valve of the heart. It has also been found that stroke patients were three times more likely than controls to report a history of infection in the week prior to their hospital admission. Those with chronic bronchitis or poor dental status (linked to gum disease) had a two-fold greater risk for stroke. There is also some evidence that a virus can cause vessels that were previously opened by angioplasty to close up again, forcing another intervention.

Research has shown that stress increases the risk of heart attacks and also decreases functioning of the immune system. Therefore, an obvious question is whether stress in some heart attack-prone individuals lowers their resistance to infection and whether this could produce a subsequent infection of the coronary arteries and a defect in the vessel that leads to a cholesterol-laden plaque. We also now know that in a person with a diseased coronary artery, mental stress produces further constriction of the vessel and decreased blood flow, whereas in a normal vessel stress produces dilatation and increased blood flow.

Therefore, one way in which stress could lead to disease is by altering our immune defenses to infection which, when it occurs, could set into motion disease processes to which we have a genetic susceptibility. Hence, stress could produce a window of opportunity for infection and subsequent disease that may not have been expressed until much later in life if at all. This argument is less appealing to the staunch genetic determinist, but my review of the health literature, personal research, and observations with patients make it a very credible hypothesis.

Additionally, stress and the emotional response that precedes or follows it produces many effects on the heart unrelated to infection. This fact was brought home to me recently when my wife told me that the sister of a colleague of hers had suffered a heart attack several days ago. When her husband was told the news, he immediately developed chest pain and fell into the arms of the cardiologist delivering the news. He was admitted with a heart attack to the same hospital where his wife was being treated for her myocardial infarction.

Studies following earthquakes in Los Angeles and Kobe, Japan, have shown dramatic immediate cardiovascular effects from stress. There was a large increase in fatal heart attacks recorded by the L.A. county morgue following the Northridge quake. Long-term studies on the cardiovascular systems of survivors of the Kobe, Japan, earthquake indicated that blood pressure increased in much of the population after the earthquake and often took four to six months to return to normal. Elderly people, in particular, became more susceptible to formation of blood clots, and their endothelial cells, the delicate cells that protect the blood vessel walls, were unable to do their normal metabolic work.

A group of Duke researchers has been interested in the influence of stress on the heart and has been able to make observations outside the laboratory by having patients with coronary artery disease wear heart monitors at home and at work. Patients were also asked to keep diaries of their activities, moods, and symptoms three times an hour during waking hours for two days. It was noted that decreased blood flow to the heart, as determined by a heart monitoring system, was more than twice as likely to occur within an hour of experiencing emotional stress. High levels of negative emotions, such as tension, frustration, and sadness, were often the culprits in affecting the heart blood flow. Even though the studied individuals had already established heart disease, their reactions raise questions about the role of emotional stress in producing cardiac effects in people without heart disease.

Dr. Stephen Oppenheimer, a Johns Hopkins investigator, has written on why stress may have such a profound effect on the heart. He has identified an area in the top part of the brain, the insular cortex, which when stimulated influences heart rate. If this area in a rat is stimulated for hours, the heart muscle suffers damage similar to that found in humans who died with cardiac fibrillation. He has emphasized that the brain's insular cortex is where the autonomic nervous system, which controls functions such as breathing and heart rate, connects with the limbic system, which processes anger, fear, pleasure, sexual arousal, sadness, and other emotions. He argues that this area of the brain may be involved in processing the conflict associated with such events as the death of a loved one and also in the subsequent sudden death which may follow this news. He believes that this area of the brain may be involved in the deaths that follow a "voodoo" curse. He has been able to test this theory in patients who required brain surgery for seizures, and when that area of the brain was exposed and stimulated, heart rate and blood pressure were affected.

Stress and the endocrine system

At this juncture, we may wonder what causes a stress response: the feelings of being uptight, altered breathing, and increased heart rate. The basis for these effects and many others are related to numerous hormones that are turned on by events, thoughts, and our reactions to them. Dr. Hans Selye, the father of stress research, outlined the basis for the hormonal response that is responsible for these effects as illustrated in the following episode.

It is 9:00 A.M., Friday morning, and you have an important meeting across town with a friend you haven't seen in 10 years. It's close to departure time and your baby begins crying with the belly pain that always seems to occur when she senses you are leaving. The phone rings, and a voice reminds you that the mortgage payment hasn't been received yet. You thank the voice for this important reminder, which was also given yesterday, and proceed to take care of your baby. What you weren't aware of as you were on the phone was that your pituitary gland had just received a message from CRH which resides in the hypothalamus of your brain that ACTH is needed to stimulate the adrenal glands to secrete cortisol, a hormone that works on probably every cell of the body, and the need increases during times of stress. Meanwhile, for some reason the usual soothing words aren't working with the baby, and where is the baby sitter? With that thought, the brain flashes a message down the spinal cord to the center of the adrenal gland to increase the output of epinephrine, also called adrenaline, which is increasing your heart rate and blood sugar production to prepare your body for the lurking emergency of not getting out of the house on time.

Epcot at Disney World in Orlando has an exhibit called the Cranium Commander which visually puts together the analytical left brain and the feeling right brain as they dialogue with the Cranium Commander during a rough day that begins with a youngster getting up late and missing breakfast. This is followed by stressful encounters with other students, teachers, and finally the principal. The Cranium Commander is being continually engaged throughout the day in a stressful conversation with the heart, the breathing center in the brain, the stomach, the adrenal gland, and the contrasting right and left brain, which are all reacting to these encounters from their own personal perspective. A recent visit to this exhibit encouraged me to reflect on several problems I had experienced recently and on the right and left brain dialogue and subsequent response of my heart, adrenal, stomach, and breathing patterns that occurred. These issues were still being processed when I entered the large traffic jam at the exit of Epcot. Perhaps my organ-to-organ communication was more tranquil that evening as I considered alternatives to impatience, frustration, and the accompanying adrenaline rush.

We all have had these experiences, and for some they are all too frequent. These latter individuals are referred to as "hot reactors." Their physiologic response to stress is amplified and they may become aware of many uncomfortable sensations such as heartburn, chest pain, dizziness, sweating, and palpitations. They may also be more prone to damage of the hippocampus in the brain, which is a structure vital for learning and memory. Research has shown that people with persistent increases in the stress hormone cortisol can develop shrinkage of the brain hippocampus. A recent study has shown that when the stress hormone cortisol increases in older women over a two-and-one-half year period they are more likely to develop lapses in memory performance—a function of the hippocampus. These lapses in memory are probably not irreversible, however, as women with declines in cortisol production noted improvements. This increase in stress-related cortisol secretion over time could also lead to an increased risk for osteoporosis and diabetes.

Work, stress, and health

The workplace is often a site for major stress. Work-related stress has become pandemic as corporations try to stretch profit margins by increases in worker productivity. An advertisement which appeared in several national publications depicts this stress quite well: four people in business attire are running in different directions in the corporate office; fire is coming out the seat of their pants. The caption reads, "Apparently, your e-mail has been read."

Sweeping corporate layoffs increase the incidents of illness among remaining staff. Researchers have found that "downsizing" significantly increases the general rate of absenteeism, much accompanied by physician-certified, long-term absences. And women seemed more prone to higher rates of health-related absenteeism than men.

Today in the clinic, one of my patients was a woman with hypoglycemia. She had classic symptoms which were relieved by eating. There was some concern that she might have a serious underlying disorder in which a tumor makes too much insulin. Her work history was remarkable for extreme stress. A valued worker at a local bank, she had won numerous sales awards, but her most recent manager ruled by intimidation, demanding that each employee sign a sheet stating sales goals for the week. If those goals were not met, the employees were subjected to an encounter with the manager. Each morning my patient sat in the parking lot at her place of employment, unable to get out of her car as she anxiously anticipated another stressful day. The previous week she had lost a crown from one of her teeth, exposing a nerve root, but when she left 15 minutes early to see a dentist, she was chastised. Fear of her boss contributed to her hypoglycemic symptoms, which disappeared when she took a two-week vacation. Relief from her hypoglycemic symptoms did not require detailed testing and medication—just a job change.

This kind of workplace experience is not rare, and there is a large body of literature describing important health consequences from continual job stress. A series of articles in 1996 and 1997 in four major medical journals documented the role of job stress on cardiovascular disease and mortality. The first study of 12,000 Finnish workers noted that workers who had high psychological demands and low control over the work process had almost a two-fold increase in cardiovascular mortality. Workers who had low control combined with absence of coworker support had over a two-and-one-half-fold increase in cardiovascular deaths.

In a similar study of 10,000 British government workers, aged 35–55 followed for over five years, those with high job demands and low job control were twice as likely to develop a coronary event such as anginal chest pain or a heart attack. Other heart risk factors could not account for these findings. The questionnaires that were used in these studies asked subjects to describe what influence they had over the content of their work, deadlines, and coworkers assigned to help with a particular task. They were asked whether someone else made all the work decisions for them. When people were engaged in boring and repetitive tasks which didn't use their skills, their heart disease risk went up.

In another Finnish study of 1,000 workers, hardening of the arteries in the neck (carotid atherosclerosis) was evaluated over four years by using noninvasive sound wave scanning. Stressed and lower-paid workers had twice as much fatty plaque build-up in the carotid arteries as their more affluent, less-stressed coworkers, thus putting them at more risk for vascular diseases. These findings were supported by a study of men aged 42 to 62 who showed higher blood pressure as they anticipated an exercise test. If these blood pressure reactive men also reported high job demands, they had greater carotid artery thickness than those who perceived job demands as low. These high-job-demands individuals with higher stress-related blood pressure increases had almost 50 percent more thickening of their carotid arteries during the follow-up period. As I am anticipating another busy day, my fingers are sliding up to my carotid artery and I am, of course, unsuccessfully trying to judge my artery thickness as the pulsations hit my finger.

Several recent articles have dealt with studies of the negative influences of the workplace on working mothers. In one report, working women with one child were found to have higher levels of the adrenal stress hormone cortisol than their childless coworkers. Mothers employed outside the home, researchers have maintained, usually retain the majority of child-raising responsibilities, resulting in what has been referred to as a "second shift" for working mothers.

Pregnant women in high-stress jobs may also be at increased risk for preterm delivery. In a study of 1,000 pregnant North Carolina workers during a six-month period, over 400 of them delivered infants before term. Full-time high-stress jobs increased the premature delivery rate by 40 percent. A high-stress job was classified as highly active work with little or no worker control over the pace of labor. The typical participant would be a lineworker who worked as a high-speed packager at a textile factory.

A study of pregnancy in attorneys noted that working a great number of hours during the first trimester of pregnancy was associated with a greater risk of miscarriage compared with lawyers who worked fewer hours. This study of 584 attorneys compared those who worked more than 45 hours per week with those women who worked less than 35 hours per week. The more hours a woman worked, the more likely she was to report feeling stressed. Those women who were partners or associates in a law firm were more likely to report stress, as were those involved in criminal law and litigation. Factors inducing stress were political intrigue, backbiting, lack of opportunity for promotion, advancement not determined by the quality of work, and lack of respect from superiors. Working more than 45 hours a week was associated with a three-fold increase in the miscarriage rate when controlling for other factors as age, smoking, and alcohol intake. Women who drank seven or more alcoholic drinks a week in the first trimester were five times more likely to have a miscarriage.

Workplace stress, often referred to as "burn out," was the subject of a column in *The Wall Street Journal* on work and the family. One stressed professional described the sequence that led to her burnout: "I appreciated your column on burnout. Like you, I have been starting work early, working nights and over the weekend. I extend my maniacal pace to cutting the lawn, cleaning, painting, and other jobs around the house, making the weekend a time of exhaustion, not relaxation. My exercise and diet regimen has slipped, speeding the spiral toward burnout. My breaking point came during an overseas business trip. I operate a one-person firm. That meant cramming an incredible amount of work into the days before my departure, returning calls from Paris, doing my work there, battling jet lag, deciphering French, worrying about clients, then catching up on a week's work upon my return. In short, I reached burnout."

A recent article on the health risks of foreign travel noted the obvious increase in risk for infectious diseases, but also the fact that foreign travel produces psychological problems. A study of 10,884 workers at the World Bank in Washington D.C. noted that health insurance claims of foreign travelers were 80 percent higher for male travelers and 18 percent higher for female travelers. Men who took one trip a year had twice the number of claims for psychiatric treatment as nontraveling colleagues; those who took two or more trips a year had three times the number of claims. The numbers were only slightly lower for women. Separation from family, language and cultural differences, work demands abroad and on return, as well as sleep disorders due to time zone changes may all have contributed to the psychological disorders. Foreign travel seems to be just one more stressor with associated health risks.

We have previously shown how low control over one's job can promote job stress, but being in total control can also be a stressor. A series of articles has appeared over the past several years on successful CEOs who were overstressed by success. A 1991 article in *Newsweek* was prompted by the suicide of Rick Chollet, who built Brookstone into a nationally-successful company. Commenting on this tragedy, his wife stated, "He constantly feared letting people down, and he swung from feeling totally powerful to totally helpless." A psychiatrist who focuses on treating professionals commented that one-half of the successful workforce is depressed. Some suffer because they are perfectionists about their work, and others because they place very high expectations on themselves to be ideal role models.

The suicide of Admiral Jeremy Border, then chief of naval operations, was provoked by his fear that his inappropriate wearing of a medal would dishonor the service that had been his life. Perfectionism seems also to have been one of the root causes for the suicide of John Curtis, who at the time of his death in 1997 was CEO of Luby's, America's biggest cafeteria chain. Perfectionism and the sometimes associated "encore anxiety" is common in people who fear they cannot repeat their previous successes.

Some executives believe their lofty position was achieved by luck. Gerald Kraines, a psychiatrist who treated Rick Chollet for depression, estimates that 20 to 30 percent of CEOs he encounters through his work as a consultant on organizational stress fear that their inadequacy will be found out. He states that they compensate by driving themselves continually, and they can never savor their success because they have to keep working harder. Because they don't want to show weakness, they keep everything to themselves, thus increasing their anxiety and depression.

Therefore, whether we are in a low- or high-control environment, work stress may occur. Prolonged fatigue, loss of libido, decreased ability to concentrate, insomnia, anxiety, eating disturbances, and a great many other symptoms may prompt us to evaluate what is happening to us at work.

The influence of our job on our stress level is probably conditioned by our personality, say the authors of a study on working women. In a study of 152 women at a large corporation in North Carolina, questionnaires revealed that women who had the greatest job strain had higher levels of hostility, anger, and lower social support. Anger, hostility, pessimism, hopelessness, fears, anxieties, and low self-esteem can produce stress and subsequent acceleration of the diseases of aging at any level of employment.

A friend and psychologist research colleague, Dr. John Cacioppo, said that he considered those qualities discussed above to be most detrimental to health. A great deal of research supports this opinion. It is curious, however, that it is much easier for researchers to document the negative health consequences of certain personality variables than to show a health-enhancing effect of positive attributes.

Points to Remember:

1 When faced with chronic stress, we may develop a persistent maladaptive response in which physical symptoms and even established disease may occur.

2 One way in which stress could lead to disease is by altering our immune defenses to infection which, when it occurs, could set into motion disease processes to which we have a genetic susceptibility.

3 The number of diseases which we now know may have an infectious origin has increased during the last several years, including heart attacks, high blood pressure, and ulcers.

4 Events, thoughts, and our reaction to them produce stress symptoms such as feelings of being uptight, altered breathing patterns, and increased heart rate.

5 The stress response is driven by brain hormones (CRH and ACTH) and the adrenal hormones epinephrine (adrenaline) and cortisol. They increase our blood sugar and heart rate to prepare us for the perceived stress.

6 Long-term excessive stress-induced production of cortisol may damage our brain center (hippocampus) responsible for learning and memory.

7 Workplace stress produced by absence of coworker support and low control over the work process is associated with an increase in cardiovascular mortality.

8 Pregnant women in high-stress jobs may also be at increased risk for preterm delivery.

9 Attorneys who worked more than 45 hours per week were 3 times more likely to have miscarriages than those who worked less than 35 hours per week.

10 Two or more foreign trips for business each year increases the number of referrals for psychiatric treatment threefold.

11 Much of the successful workforce is depressed from concerns of letting people down, not wanting to show weakness and thus keeping everything to themselves, as well as "encore anxiety," or fear that they cannot repeat their previous successes.

12 Symptoms of workplace stress include prolonged fatigue, loss of libido, decreased ability to concentrate, insomnia, anxiety, and eating disturbances, plus many others.

13 The influence of our job on our stress level is conditioned by our personality and emotional support. Higher levels of hostility, anger, and low self-esteem are associated with higher levels of job stress.

Chapter Fourteen

Anger

IT IS MONDAY MORNING, AND YOU ARE IN YOUR CAR ON YOUR way to work to begin a long day of one meeting after another without a break. It is a grey morning with mist gathering on your windshield making visibility quite poor. Traffic is heavy, and your headache from a bad night's sleep and no breakfast are not adding to the pleasure of your driving experience. Without warning, a black sedan suddenly swerves into your lane, and the driver then hits his brakes as traffic has slowed in front of him. You instinctively hit the horn and your brakes while checking your rear view mirror to see if the car behind you is going to stop before ramming your recently repaired rear bumper. Relieved that he has safely stopped, you glance forward to the jerk who started this mess and see him deliver the universal sign of displeasure with his middle finger. You can't believe your eyes; he started this mess and now he's flipping you an insult. You retaliate by hitting your horn and blinking your lights, and he responds by slamming on his brakes once more, causing you to do the same. You can feel your pulse racing now, and you wonder what your blood pressure reading is at that moment. You sense the need to gain composure, if for no other reason than that you are suspicious of the sanity of the person who started all of this. You are glad when your exit approaches, and you pull into your parking lot feeling as if you had just completed a long day's work.

Anger and its effects

Many of us can identify with this scenario, which has been referred to as "road rage." The head of the National Traffic Association estimates that of the 41,000 traffic deaths each year, about two-thirds are the result of behavior associated with aggressive driving. The uncomfortable feelings that arise from this kind of encounter, the anger that comes from a sense of danger, not just the physical threat but the threat to self-esteem, all act to trigger the limbic part of the brain to initiate an adrenaline surge from the center of the adrenal gland, the "fight or flight" reaction. Meanwhile the brain is also activating the top part of the adrenal gland to release cortisol. Both of these hormonal responses are producing a heightened attentiveness and probably lowering the threshold for invoking the anger response. Similarly, unkind words from the boss that day will produce an emotional state that needs less prompting by your spouse that evening to produce anger.

Fortunately, most of the anger which we feel daily or see expressed by others is more subtle and expressed nonverbally in body language. It has been recognized for centuries that anger is destructive to our quality of life and longevity. The biblical literature of thousands of years ago makes frequent references to anger and its consequences:

- Refrain from anger and turn from wrath; do not fret—it leads only to evil.—Psalm 37:8
- A hot-tempered man must pay the penalty; if you rescue him, you will have to do it again.—Proverbs 19:19

But anger need not always be a destructive quality if it is a response to an injustice, either personal or civil. An often-quoted biblical example of positive anger is Jesus' response to the money changers when he drove them out of the temple.

In their book *A Woman's Guide to Empowerment—Use Your Anger,* Sandra Thomas and Cheryl Jefferson describe some of the benefits that we derive from the anger response, including:

- Gets other people's attention as it is a clear form of communication
- Protects you against those that would dominate or take advantage of you
- Serves as a warning signal that the stress in our lives may be excessive
- Is a warning that your rights are being violated or your values are being compromised
- Alerts us to relationship problems when others are doing too little
- Serves as an encouragement to explore new approaches

They also suggest that, "Before you become a poster girl for positive anger, acknowledge your own private anger" in order to prevent progression to the more dangerous stages of hostility and aggression.

Major contributors to our understanding of hostility and cardiovascular disease are Dr. Redford Williams and his colleagues at Duke University, who have clarified the critical dimension of Type A behavior characterized by hurriedness, competitiveness, and hostility, with hostility being the factor most clearly associated with poor heart health. A similar finding resulted from a study on doctors and lawyers who had taken the MMPI psychological exam 25 years earlier while students at the University of North Carolina. Dr. John Barefoot found that doctors with high hostility scores were four to five times more likely to develop coronary artery disease than their less-hostile associates. Even more impressive was the finding that 14 percent of the physicians and 20 percent of the lawyers with high levels of hostility were dead by age 50, whereas only two percent of physicians and four percent of lawyers with low hostility had died by age 50. In a further study of the lawyers, it was reported that many experienced a cynical mistrust of people and frequent anger, the expression of aggressive behavior being a specific aspect of the hostility that predicted the higher death rates.

Anger is also harmful once coronary heart disease is already present. Psychiatrist Dr. Gail Ironson noted that even recalling an incident which had made one angry often led to a decrease in the heart's pumping ability.

Hostility exerts effects on the heart over a long period of time, and the physiologic factors responsible for these effects are unknown. Many researchers feel, however, that increased adrenaline levels following an angry outburst is partly responsible, as it can produce an increase in heart rate and blood pressure and influence processes that are likely to speed up the growth of plaques in the coronary arteries. Dr. Kate Stoney has performed studies at our center that show that a brief bout of mental stress can immediately increase the atherogenic makeup of our blood fats such as triglycerides and cholesterol. Another possible link between hostility and poor cardiac health is suggested by a study finding that hostile people are more likely to smoke, consume alcohol, and gain weight.

Drs. Jan Kiecolt-Glaser, Ron Glaser, and I examined the influence of hostility during marital conflict while we continuously sampled adrenaline, other hormones, and immune factors during and after arguments. Remember that these were happily married couples discussing everyday issues. We found that the more hostile couples had higher adrenaline and other hormonal disturbances that are associated with heart disease and decreased immune function. Many of the women continued to have higher adrenaline for many hours after the conflict, suggesting that they were possibly still angry and ruminating about the disagreements.

This constant replay of events that creates anger and hostile feelings can be deadly. In August of 1996, Joe Cruzan, the father of Nancy Cruzan who had an automobile accident that had left her in a permanent vegetative state for many years, hanged himself at age 62. Friends commenting on the tragedy said his efforts to have the life-sustaining support removed resulted in public and private animosity. In a somewhat similar case, the father of an Army helicopter pilot shot down over Iraq by friendly fire from U.S. jets suffered a fatal heart attack at age 55. He had battled the military and politicians in an attempt to get facts that he felt were being concealed from the public. His wife said that he never reconciled his resentment, and his health began to deteriorate just before his heart attack.

Dealing with anger

How do we identify and effectively deal with our anger? Dr. Elaine De Beauport challenges us to be aware of the subtle faces of anger. She states that, "People with a preference for the left brain express or hide anger in disagreements, rapid conclusions, rationalizations, justifications, and disapproval backed up with a long list of reasons. A person with a preference for the right brain becomes disoriented and chaotic, uses absolutes, incomplete thoughts, generalizations, and evasions." She further states that an important skill is to learn how to defend ourselves against other people's anger rather than enhancing it by our own hostile reaction.

There are numerous books in the last few years that provide suggestions for how to deal with our anger. Most of the suggestions appear useful, but after reading these articles I have within minutes been unable to remember their major points that would be useful to quickly review before becoming angry. Perhaps prevention, then, is the best policy for safeguarding ourselves against the negative results of uncontrolled anger and hostility. I believe the PIERS plan can be quite useful for preventing anger. The balance provided by appropriate attention to our physical, intellectual, emotional, relational, and spiritual needs would incorporate most of the suggestions on how best to cope with anger. First, our physical state will influence our anger threshold. If we are sleep-deprived, not exercising, consuming a poor diet, have an acute or chronic illness, or are on medication, we may be at increased risk to respond with anger to any unpleasant life event.

An intelligent approach to anger control involves more of our brain than the center that deals with logic, analysis, and other predominantly left brain functions. Several recent books, including a long-time best seller by Daniel Goleman, reviews the ways in which the brain deals with anger. IQ tests measure only one of many competencies that our brains possess, a fact which is proven in daily experiences as well as by experimental studies. For example, we all know people who earned average grades in school but who are quite successful as defined by a variety of different criteria. Goleman details several studies which support these observations. When 95 Harvard students from classes in the 1940s were followed into middle age, the men with the highest test scores were often less successful than lower-scoring individuals in terms of productivity, salary, or status in their professions. The "good grade achievers" also fared less well in relationships with family and friends and in "life satisfaction," which I would equate with happiness.

A similar study followed 450 boys into middle age, most of whom were sons of immigrants. Seven percent of men with IQ's under 80 were unemployed, but so were seven percent of men with IQ's over 100. There was a general link between IQ and socioeconomic status at age 47, but childhood abilities, such as being able to deal with frustrations, control emotions, and get along with others had the greatest effect.

A study of 81 valedictorians and salutatorians from a 1981 class in Illinois high schools found that these students earned excellent grades in college. However, by their late 20s, they had achieved only modest success. Ten years after graduating from high school, only 25 percent were at the highest level of achievement for young people of comparable age in their profession, and many were doing less well. Therefore, our emotional intelligence or our "character" seems to be critical in the workplace and in our relationships and in how we handle anger.

Emotionally healthy individuals seem to be happier and therefore better able to deal with anger. Viktor Frankl in his book *Man's Search for Meaning*, writes, "Happiness cannot be pursued; it must ensue. One must give a reason to be happy. Once the reason is found, however, one becomes happy automatically. As we see, a human being is not one in pursuit of happiness but rather in search of a reason to become happy, last but not least, through actualizing the potential meaning inherent and dormant in a given situation. Once a person's search for meaning is successful, it not only renders him happy but also gives him the capability to cope with suffering. And what happens if one's groping for a meaning has been in vain? This may result in a fatal condition."

Remember the two fathers we described earlier who each had lost a child, and one hanged himself and another had a fatal heart attack? Anger and hostility were involved in their unhappiness, and they were unable to find meaning in their lives after these tragedies. Sometimes we can more easily understand a concept by looking at an extreme case. Certainly Dr. Frankl had a reason for anger, having been imprisoned in Auschwitz, and his father, mother, brother, and his wife died in gas ovens or in concentration camps. With every possession lost, suffering from starvation and torture and daily expecting to be killed, what remains, he states, "Is the last of human freedoms—the ability to choose one's attitude in a given set of circumstances."

We can choose not to be angry or hostile in a given situation, just as Frankl chose not to focus on anger and hostility but on the meaning of life. It helped him survive, and likewise our choice to avoid hostility may prolong our own lives. I am reminded of a diagram frequently referred to by Dr. Stephen Covey, who describes the habits of highly effective people. He depicts the word "stimulus" separated by a gap from the word "response." In this gap he has inserted the words "freedom to choose." He reminds us that animals don't have this freedom because their response immediately follows the stimulus. In the diagram below the words "freedom to choose," he has inserted self-awareness, imagination, conscience, and independent will, all of which we have at our disposal before we engage in inappropriate and self-destructive responses to those people or events in our lives that stimulate our anger and hostility.

We do have the freedom to choose our response to anger-producing situations, but our success will be conditioned by our general state of well-being, as dictated by our physical, emotional, relational, and spiritual health. We may be able to buffer much of the grief that anger produces, or that we produce in others, if we have paid attention to the PIERS principles. If we are prone to receive or give hostile or angry comments on a daily basis, perhaps each morning before we are confronted by the provoking stimulus, we could do a personal PIERS review. Are there parts of my health maintenance program that I have been neglecting (for example, good nutrition, exercise, relaxation time, sleep)? Have I been developing my emotional intelligence, and are there any features in my emotional life such as worry and fears that need attention? Am I convinced that being civil in my daily relationships is an attribute which is of value to me? Are there spiritual issues in my life which are producing conflict? With this daily brief review, we would be in much better shape to handle our anger and many of life's frustrations.

Anger and forgiveness

This approach should be useful for anger prevention. But what about the anger produced by emotional wounds inflicted in the past by events or broken relationships from which our memory produces images as if they happened yesterday? The answer is that forgiveness heals! When I discuss this concept with others, I often refer to a personal story told by Gregg Anderson in his book *The 22 (Non-Negotiable) Laws of Wellness.* He had a problem with anger, which was intensified at his place of employment where he was in a hostile tug-of-war with another corporate officer over almost every issue. It all came to a head when at a major meeting he reviewed the figures produced by his adversary, and in disgust salted with profanity he belittled the report. During this volatile interchange, he accidentally spilled his coffee into the CEO's lap. He was asked to leave the meeting, and, not long afterwards developed what was said to be terminal lung cancer.

Within 30 days of this diagnosis, his adversary at the company developed prostate cancer. Gregg Anderson was told by physicians that both men had been carrying the cancers for years, and that it was coincidental that both illnesses were discovered at the same time. Gregg felt, however, that their "toxic battles" contributed to the onset of both their cancers. Gregg had a lung removed, and four months later a second surgery confirmed that the cancer had spread from the lung into the lymph system; he was told that he had about 30 days to live.

He was a problem solver, however, and placed phone calls all over the country to cancer survivors whose names had been provided by different organizations. The common thought that emerged from the survivors was the word forgiveness. His first reaction was that this advice didn't apply to him, but on reflection he recognized his anger and hostility and that he had never forgiven those who had wronged him. He then became actively involved in forgiving those with whom he held grudges.

As each individual came to mind, he wrote his or her name on a piece of paper, then visualized the face and recalled the specific incidents which had offended him, making a conscious effort to release the memory. Then, as a final part of the process, he imagined something good happening to that person he was forgiving. He noted that to express forgiveness was easier than to release the hurt. He often had to repeat the release a number of times before he was able to make, "The emotional and spiritual shift that was required. Many times I would say 'God, you take this. I can't handle it anymore.'"

Through this process, he discovered old angers, with his father and others, and he came to better understand their influences on his behavior and his own contribution to the problem. The final act of forgiveness was the comptroller with whom he had battled. He describes a tear-filled encounter and his feeble words of asking for forgiveness, followed by an overwhelming response from his old adversary that he was the one who needed forgiveness. When he left the house he felt his posture change, the tension disappear, and the pain was gone. "'I'm free'. I shouted it. I'm free!'" Following his week of sincere forgiveness, he began to gain weight and to heal physically.

Eleven years later, he is writing this story and is free of lung cancer. "Do I believe there was a link between this deeply spiritual work and my physical improvement? Absolutely. I believe that practicing the Law of Forgiveness changes us biochemically. And in the process, the body is released toward its optimum wellness potential. I know my doctor and scientist friends get very uncomfortable when I state these beliefs. But it seems we can all agree that life quality soars when we sincerely practice The Law of Forgiveness. And this just may be an important determinant in releasing the body's self-healing potential."

Gregg Anderson spoke of the spiritual work involved with forgiveness, a theme which has been recognized for centuries as recorded in the Bible. "Then Peter came to Jesus and asked, 'Lord how many times shall I forgive my brother when he sins against me, up to seven times?' Jesus answered, 'I tell you not seven times but seventy times seven'" (Matthew 18:21). Jesus reminds us of the continual state of mind that is necessary if we are to derive the benefits of a forgiving approach to relationships. For many of us, this probably translates to better health.

The native American shaman, Bear Heart, also has a challenging perspective on forgiveness. "If someone is unkind or throws verbal daggers at you, that person has a problem—why make it your problem too? If you can't forgive, then there's a challenge for you to work on until you can pray for that person and mean it. Until you do that, you carry a nagging, aching feeling all the time. You can't even rest at night. You lie and toss and turn, and all kinds of dreams come up—your inner consciousness is trying to get through to your brain, but it can't because it's all clogged up with anger. It's one thing to talk about love and forgiving, but another to truly forgive. Break apart the word forgiving—'for giving.' Giving what? Giving love. This is why love and forgiveness are intertwined."

As we extol the virtues of dealing with our anger and hostility and forgiveness, we need to again remind ourselves of the danger of unexpressed anger. Several breast cancer studies have concluded that not only those with frequent temper outbursts had an increased incidence of breast cancer, but also those who had only expressed anger once or twice in their entire lives. Either extreme appears to be detrimental to our health.

Gregg Anderson summarizes the anger-hostility issue clearly when he says, "Nothing clutters a life or the life of a nation, more than the 3 R's: resentment, remorse, and recrimination. These three emotional responses to life are based in anger, guilt, and hostility. When held in the mind and in the heart, they occupy a fearsome amount of space, coloring our perception of reality to an alarmingly large degree. They block our potential. They drain our life of any chance for joy and peace." Should we also add that they threaten our good health?

Lest you think that the writer of these words has personally solved the issue of anger, I had no sooner typed the previous sentence when the phone rang. It interrupted my present reflective state, as my assistant reminded me of a problem with patient scheduling, a problem I thought we had solved. My voice immediately increased in volume; I sat more upright, and expressed my displeasure about the new turn of events. I went over a new strategy and then hung up the phone. Still ruminating about this event, I smiled to think how appropriate it was to my previous paragraph.

Points to Remember:

1 Anger, as expressed in aggressive driving behavior, may be responsible for two-thirds of the 41,000 U.S. traffic deaths each year.

2 Anger may be helpful in some situations, but when it progresses to hostility and aggression, it becomes destructive to good health.

3 Doctors with high hostility scores are four to five times more likely to develop coronary artery disease.

4 In a long-term study, 14 percent of physicians and 20 percent of lawyers with high levels of hostility were dead by age 50, as compared to only 2 percent of physicians and 4 percent of lawyers with low hostility who had died by age 50.

5 In the study of lawyers, many experienced a cynical mistrust of people and frequent anger, the expression of aggressive behavior being a specific aspect of hostility that predicted the higher death rates.

6 Recalling an incident which made one angry often leads to a decrease in the heart's pumping ability.

7 Marital conflict can lead to an increase in stress hormone levels that may persist in some women for hours after the episode.

8 We can choose not to be angry or hostile in a given situation, and over time avoiding hostility may prolong our life.

9 The PIERS plan can be quite helpful in preventing anger. The balance we get from appropriate attention to our physical, intellectual, emotional, relational, and spiritual needs incorporates most of the suggestions on how best to cope with anger.

10 We may be able to buffer much of the grief that anger produces, or that we produce in others, if we pay attention to the PIERS principles.

11 How do we approach anger produced by emotional wounds inflicted in the past by events or broken relationships from which our memory produces images as if they happened yesterday? The answer is that forgiveness heals!

12 Nothing clutters a life or the life of a nation more than resentment, remorse, and recrimination that derive from anger, guilt, and hostility. They diminish our potential and drain our life of joy and peace. They threaten our good health!

Chapter Fifteen

Optimism and Health

OPTIMISTIC PEOPLE HAVE BETTER HEALTH. SEVERAL years ago, our local paper reviewed the role of optimism in health outcomes for patients with established heart disease. In one study, 14 percent of those whose heart disease had been established by catherization said they doubted they would recover enough to resume normal activities. After one year, 12 percent of these pessimists had died, compared with five percent of those optimistic about getting better. In another study, heart attack patients who scored high on a test for depression were eight times more likely than optimists to die during the following 18 months. Yet good news which would boost optimism seems to be a losing proposition. Several magazines and newspapers concentrating on good news had lost readership as well as money and were ceasing publication. One economist asked to comment on this trend said, "Good news makes people feel uncomfortable—they feel like the other shoe is going to drop."

Worry

This pessimistic view of life is associated with worry and anxiety, both of which can lead to an increased risk of early death. Christopher Peterson of the University of Michigan analyzed data from a 70-year-old study of personality traits, the Termean Life-Cycle study, and found that people who tend to blame themselves when things go wrong and who believe that one unfortunate event can ruin the rest of their life also expected bad things to happen to them and felt incapable of changing their situations. Males were more likely than females to be classified as pessimistic and were more likely to die from accidents and violence, including suicide.

Researchers have devised a "worry scale" to evaluate the effects of worry in patients who suffered heart attacks. The scale evaluated anxiety about health and possible death, social conditions, finances, and aging. Men reporting the highest level of worry had twice the risk of having a nonfatal heart attack and a 50 percent increase in risk of developing coronary disease. An increase in the financial worry scale produced a 20 percent greater risk for all cardiac events, and an increase in the health worry scale increased the angina risk by 39 percent.

Anxiety and fear are emotions that originate in the amygdala, a walnut-shaped area deep in the brain. It may be that over-stimulation of this area leads to heart disease. If worry and anxiety become chronic, they can lead to a sense of hopelessness which has been associated with increased risk for cancer and heart disease. Researchers then decided to follow individuals over four years to see whether pessimists had more rapid narrowing of their arteries. It was noted that middle-aged men who feel hopeless or think of themselves as failures may develop atherosclerosis, narrowing of the arteries, 20 percent faster than more optimistic subjects. The authors felt that this was of the same magnitude of increased risk as smoking one pack of cigarettes a day.

Hopefulness

Dr. Lydia Temoshok, a psychologist, has written about a patient she was counseling on how to cope emotionally with advanced cancer. Each counseling session led to improvement in her patient, who left hopeful that she might after all lick this disease. At the beginning of each counseling session, however, Dr. Temoshok heard the same depressing news that the patient's oncologist communicated—namely that the patient's condition was hopeless. When the patient expressed optimism that not only would she survive but recover fully, her physician interpreted this as denial. As a health professional, I have never understood why an honest description of a person's status had to be delivered in such a fatalistic fashion. It is one thing to state that you can't provide additional effective therapy and quite another to issue a pronouncement of no hope. Recall the "30 days" death sentence given to Gregg Anderson when he had lung cancer. This example proves that physicians can be seriously wrong when it comes to prognosis in what would seem to be terminal illness!

The importance of optimism and hope for humanity has been recognized for centuries, as revealed in the following passages:

We all hope for the best but an optimist actually expects to get it.
To the optimist, a fireplace is a center of warmth and beauty. To the
     pessimist, it is a source of smoke and ashes.
Hope deferred makes the heart sick.
You cannot live on hope alone, nor can you live without it.
If it were not for hope the heart would break.
Hope is the anchor of the soul, the stimulus to action, and the
     incentive to achievement.

DeBeauport and Diaz have beautifully described hopefulness as it can be created in our minds by using our visual-spatial intelligence. "Spatial-visual thinking can enable you to bring your entire past into the present. You call it memory, but is it really past if you can recover it in vivid detail and enrich your present? Won't you also relive all the horrible memories of the past? Yes, until or unless you learn to select only what you wish to see. Hope is the capacity to visualize a better future. Then with that visualization, that new image, our own mental processes can guide you into making tomorrow more tangibly better than today. The mind has incredible capacities. There is no reason to limit your mental processing to exactly what exists in this moment, at this time and place. Today may actually be horrible. Hope is vision: it is the capacity to imagine and see a better tomorrow. Hope is a new vision of the future, different from what you are living in at the present."

Positive thinking

Wandering through a bookstore the other day, I came across a copy of Norman Vincent Peale's *Power of Positive Thinking*. It was the large print edition, and I could almost read it without my glasses. As I flipped the pages, I was amazed that the concepts he discussed seemed so contemporary. In one memorable passage he tells of a trapeze artist who was instructing a terrified student: "Throw your heart over the bar, and your body will follow." Later Peale states, "A man who is self-reliant, positive, optimistic, and undertakes his work with the assurance of success magnetizes his condition. He draws to himself the creative powers of the universe."

Walter Swan was the best teacher I have had in recent years on the value of optimism and hope. I first learned about Walter in a *Wall Street Journal* article about his one-book bookstore. Walter's bookstore in Bisbee, Arizona, stocked only one book and that was written by Walter. That summer I attended a meeting in Tucson, and my wife and I started a sightseeing trip to a variety of Arizona towns, including Bisbee, where we visited a copper mine. While awaiting our descent deep into the mine, we saw posters advertising Walter's bookstore. I then recalled the *Journal* article and hoped that he would still be there at 5 o'clock on a Saturday afternoon. We found an elderly gentlemen who introduced himself as Walter Swan. For the next two hours, Walter told us his story as if he had never told it before, right up to his recent problems with metastatic prostate cancer. Walter was born in Arizona and also raised his family there. Education and money were as scarce as the water supply, but there was plenty of love and sharing in his family. Without radio or television, Walter entertained his family in the evenings by telling humorous stories with a strong moral and ethical flavor. They were often recorded by his wife on paper and stored in a drawer.

One day they got the idea they should write a book to pass along their wisdom about life and raising a family. So Walter, in his 60s, began improving his writing and spelling skills and his wife learned to type. Unable to find a publisher or a bookstore that would give them a reasonable return, they ended up publishing it themselves and selling it in their one-book bookstore at 38 Main Street in Bisbee. The book's sales took off after the *Journal* article, and it had gone into a second printing when I bought my copies.

Given the almost insurmountable odds of something like this happening, I asked him his secret for success. He handed me The One Book bookstore bookmark on which was written his philosophy of life:

- **Always be kind**
- **Have a good attitude**
- **Never give up**

His optimism derived from being centered on who he was and on his obligation to others.

I am reminded of a frequently-told story about the importance of optimism. A visitor to a stone quarry one hot summer afternoon asked several of the workers about their work and why they were doing it. The first man responded, quite perturbed, "We are cutting stone." A second worker responded less hastily, "I'm earning money to put food on the table." Finally, a third man who particularly seemed to be enjoying his work responded, "Oh, I'm building a cathedral." The same task was associated with markedly different attitudes and degrees of optimism in these working men.

We have seen how pessimism can produce abnormal cardiovascular events, and it also can influence our performance in many areas, athletic contests being excellent examples. I witnessed one example of the power of the mind in directing physical performance at an Ohio State versus Michigan football game a couple of years ago. The Ohio State team was undefeated in their previous ten games and was hopeful of a national championship, with only Michigan standing in the way. There had been a lot written about the Michigan jinx over Ohio State, and I wondered how much the players had taken this rhetoric to heart. At the beginning of the third quarter, Ohio State was dominating the game. But in a single play Michigan scored on an 80-yard touchdown pass when an Ohio State pass defender slipped, and the Michigan receiver ran untouched into the end zone. Ohio State was still ahead, but as the defense walked off the field with their eyes focused on the ground, everyone felt that this was the beginning of the end. The players saw victory slipping through their fingers and this pessimistic visualization probably was a major reason for their subsequent poor performance and loss of the game.

Pessimism can be associated with or lead to depression. DeBeauport and Diaz remind us that, "At last count, fifteen million Americans have been declared clinically depressed. Are they focusing on the harsh or bitter details of the day, projecting them as conclusions onto tomorrow and the rest of their lives? Are they victims of a visualization capacity in their brain that has never been guided, never been taught to be intelligent and life-affirming? Imagine how different it could be for those who are depressed if they had been taught that they govern their minds, that while they are free to focus on the bitter aspects, they are equally free consciously to visualize a better tomorrow to guide their actions. They can change their environment rather than being deeply affected and controlled by it."

My initial reaction to these words was that the authors had forgotten about the genetic predisposition to depression. This comment seems to place the responsibility for depression on the individual's negative thinking. When we in the medical profession see depression, we automatically reach for the prescription pad to write for medication. Self-evaluation is usually not high on our list of treatment options. Perhaps it's time for all of us to ask the question, "Are there things in my life that need changing to produce better attitudes which may help treat these depressed feelings or keep them from happening again?" As DeBeauport challenges us, "Sit down at your enchanted loom and weave a design that can inform you of how to act on behalf of your own life and the lives of those around you. We can all participate in helping create a better future. To visualize the future is a capacity of your mind. Use it consciously."

While reflecting on depression and visualizing the future I was reminded of a conversation I had today with Barb Hillmon, who works in our Clinical Research unit at Ohio State. Her husband, John, was involved in an automobile accident three years ago which left him quadriplegic. The anger, sense of hopelessness, and pessimism that accompanies such a tragedy soon overcame John. With help of family and friends, these feelings were replaced with an enhanced faith and optimism about life. Several months ago he enrolled in college and received his first grade—a B in algebra.

Mother Teresa

Mother Teresa's life was filled with virtue, and one attitude that she demonstrated quite dramatically was her optimism for life even when working in the most difficult of circumstances. There is a sign on the wall of one of her children's homes in Calcutta that reads:

ANYWAY
People are unreasonable, illogical, and self-centered,
> *Love them anyway.*
If you do good, people will accuse you of selfish, ulterior motives,
> *Do good anyway.*
If you are successful, you win false friends and true enemies,
> *Succeed anyway.*
The good you do will be forgotten tomorrow,
> *Do good anyway.*
Honesty and frankness make you vulnerable,
> *Be honest and frank anyway.*
What you spend years building may be destroyed overnight,
> *Build anyway.*
People really need help but may attack you if you help them,
> *Help people anyway.*
Give the world the best you have and you'll get kicked in the teeth,
> *Give the world the best you have anyway.*

What wisdom for living! What strong medicine for toxic moods and emotions. Stress at work or home, anger and hostility, pessimism, and hopelessness would have great difficulty taking hold of our minds if we seriously committed ourselves to these principles outlined by Mother Teresa.

Points to Remember:

1   Optimistic people have better health.

2   Men reporting the highest level of financial or health worry are at greater risk of developing coronary artery disease.

3   If worry or anxiety become chronic, they can lead to a sense of hopelessness which has been associated with increased risk for heart disease and cancer.

4   Prognosis can be seriously wrong when it involves people who seem to be terminally ill.

5   Are there things in my life that need changing to produce more optimism which may help treat those depressed feelings or keep them from happening again?

6   Stress at work, anger and hostility, pessimism, and hopelessness would have great difficulty taking hold of our minds if we seriously committed ourselves to the optimistic principles expressed by Mother Teresa in her poem "Anyway."

Relationships and Health

CHAPTER SIXTEEN

Can My Relationships Influence My Longevity?

I N ONE OF THE OLDEST PASSAGES OF RECORDED HISTORY IN
the second chapter of Genesis, it is stated that "The Lord
God said, 'It is not good for the man to be alone. I will make
a helper suitable for him.'" Loneliness has been dealt with by
God, but this relationship is headed for trouble following the act
of eating of the forbidden fruit from the tree of the knowledge of good
and evil. This act represents a break in the relationship with God, and
changes the relationship between Adam and Eve. It also has a dramatic
consequence as they are forbidden to eat from the tree of life and thus lose
the ability to live forever.

Few of us would deny the havoc that occurs in our lives and those of
our friends when our trust in someone is destroyed. A broken covenant
with another resembles that first set of broken relationships that occurred
in the Garden; it tears at our emotions and physical being. If we were
threatened with the loss of all we possess,

   1) Our house and toys

   2) Our money and all our financial security

   3) Our prestige and accomplishments

   4) Our family and friends

but could keep one of the four, most people would consider this an easy choice and select to keep family and friends. Yet many of us are living as if the first three were the most important! Survey after survey confirms that we desire a happy family life over career and income. Yet family and friends are put on the back burner until the first three items are satisfied, and who knows how much of our lives that will consume. Unhappiness is often the outcome of these choices.

It has been said that a happy person spends his time consistently with his core values. A result of this disconnection between what we value and how we live produces dramatic consequences for us and our communities. The health consequences may not be as dire as those recorded in Genesis, but are nevertheless dramatic.

Emotional support and disease prevention

A 1990 *Newsweek* article was entitled, "For Longer Life, Take a Wife— A New Study Examines Marriage and Mortality." The article detailed research that middle-aged men without wives were twice as likely to die during a ten-year period as married men of similar age. Unmarried men ate less healthy foods, and other emotional and social factors also played a role in the higher mortality. A great deal of literature supports the notion that our relationships have a bearing on how long we live.

One of the first studies to show a relationship between social integration and death from all causes was the Alameda County study published in 1979. Investigators found that isolation from family, friends, and church increased mortality rates two- to three-fold during a nine-year follow-up period. Those who lacked social ties were at increased risk of dying from cancer, cardiovascular, respiratory, and gastrointestinal diseases, and other causes. By 1995, seven more community-based studies revealed an association between social integration and mortality rates from all causes.

In 1997, three articles appeared almost simultaneously supporting this concept. A study performed by University of Iowa researchers followed 2,575 rural people ages 65 to 102 from the early 1980s until 1993. Women and men who lost their social network (spouse, close friends, relatives, or participation in a religious or social group) were twice as likely to die during that period. Those who lost their social support during the study did not die sooner when health problems were taken into account. However, the group at two-fold risk of dying were those who, at entry into the study, were relatively isolated and had lost their social network. In addition, those with low levels of social support who managed to increase their social ties during the three-year period had a death rate similar to those with continued high social support. It appears that continued social isolation is the factor that is important for increasing mortality rates. Similar findings were noted by Dutch investigators who evaluated 2,800 citizens 55 to 85 years of age for two-and-one-half years. They found that people who perceived themselves as surrounded by a loving, supportive circle of friends decreased their risk of dying by 50 percent. The authors felt that friends may provide an emotional buffer to the loss of a spouse.

A third article was written by researchers at the University of Maryland who found that women who were engaged in activities and more integrated into their communities had a longer survival. They followed over 800 elderly white women for five years and found that a large circle of friends (more than three) almost doubled the survival rate in the over 75-year-old age group compared with women without close friends. Women who did not participate in any group organizations had twice the mortality risk of those who were involved in two or more organizations. The author, Dr. "Jay" Magaziner, advised that as people age they should try to stay in places in which they have social connections rather than relocating across the country. His data supported this opinion as women who lived in their communities for over ten years lived twice as long as those who had been part of the community for less than a decade.

Nowhere is the importance of relationships to health more evident than following the death of a spouse. Within six months of the death of a spouse, there is a 60 percent likelihood of a serious medical problem occurring in the bereaved mate. It appears that elderly people who lose their lifelong partner are exposed to a set of physiologic events that often lead to the expression of new disease or the worsening of one already present. All the particulars of this physiologic response are not known, but there is documentation of immune suppression in bereaved individuals. I am looking at a photograph in our local paper at this moment of two daughters and the wife of a Guatemalan man who died in a stampede of soccer fans in which 84 people were killed. The grief on their faces is indescribable, and one finds it easy to understand that a strong physiologic effect is occurring in these young women. Rumination over this lost relationship during the years that follow will almost certainly induce some form of physiologic response.

Individuals who continued to live in the vicinity of Three Mile Island following the nuclear accident at the power plant and continued to ruminate or have intrusive thoughts about the fear surrounding that event were found to have elevated levels of the stress hormone adrenaline for years.

Dr. Joel Dimsdale has defined the essence of emotional or social support as leading a person to believe "1), That he is cared for and loved, 2) That he is esteemed and valued, and 3) That he belongs to a network of communication and mutual obligation." These principles are illustrated in his article with a painting by Winslow Homer entitled, "Lifeline," which depicts a storm at sea with a man carrying a person in distress while attached to a lifeline between ships as waves crash beneath them.

Emotional support and early development

Yet loneliness which occurs in the absence of social support is evident in much of our society. The family has traditionally been the hub of emotional support, but according to an article published in *USA Today*, a new census report detailing the change in family structure between 1980 and 1992 reports that there are presently almost 24,000,000 people living alone, which represents an eight-percent increase since 1980. The number of single mothers and fathers has almost doubled, there has been a ten-percent increase in unmarried mothers, and the divorce rate is plateauing at a high level. Perhaps the growing importance of chat rooms on the internet reflects the loneliness suggested by these demographics. If these figures are accurate, we are increasing the number of children in this country who are at risk for receiving less than optimal support from a very early age.

In the 13th century, the Holy Roman Emperor Frederick II conducted child development research. He removed babies from their mothers and had them attended by individuals who responded to their basic needs but had very little physical contact with them. He wanted to learn what language they would speak if they never heard adults talk. What he learned was that without emotional nurturing all the children died. Whether or not this 13th century account is true, it has been duplicated in modern times by the mistreatment of East European orphans. A recent study evaluated 56 orphans raised in some form of isolation in state-run institutions for months to years. These children were erroneously diagnosed as having severe neurological abnormalities, but on close examination not a single child had severe neurological problems. Half the children, it was found, did have delayed development of social and emotional skills and 59 percent had poor language skills. Additionally, the children's growth lagged one month behind for every five months spent in the orphanage. These findings are similar to those which reported growth failure due to growth hormone deficiency in young children raised in emotionally deprived homes.

Several other studies are in agreement with these findings that early emotional and physical relationships are critical for normal physical development. For example, University of Miami researchers found that premature babies given daily massage gain 47 percent more weight and are discharged from the hospital six days earlier—all at a savings of $10,000 in medical costs. Pennsylvania State University researchers found that the amount of language that is directed at children in child-care centers is an important predictor of the child's acquisition of cognitive and language skills.

There are also some animal studies that give us some clues as to how relationships affect the body. When rat pups are taken from their mothers, they show lower levels of growth hormone. Also, when the rat stress hormone corticosterone, which can suppress growth hormone secretion, was measured in stressed pups separated from their mothers, levels were higher than normal. Early findings in the Eastern European orphans indicate that they also have an elevation of the human stress hormone cortisol. Thus it appears that poor or absent relationships between a child and its mother creates developmental abnormalities, some of which may persist into adult life.

This need to belong doesn't stop at infancy, but nurturing relationships appear to be essential for physical and psychological well-being across the life span. I recently participated in a study of loneliness directed by Dr. John Cacioppo. We tested 2,632 undergraduates at The Ohio State University to determine their feelings of loneliness. Lonely individuals reported higher levels of perceived stress, more frequent and severe hassles, and poorer self-esteem. They also had higher levels of fatigue, hostility, confusion, and dejection than was found in the socially-embedded individuals. We suggested that the unfulfilled need to belong is associated with a complex yearning for intimacy. Yet feelings of insecurity, mistrust, and anger cause lonely individuals to fear negative evaluations from others and therefore they withdraw. It is not surprising that daily encounters provide less encouragement and more frequent hassles for lonely individuals and that their levels of the stress hormone cortisol were elevated. Over a lifetime, the stress of daily challenges in lonely individuals could produce more illness.

Emotional support and cancer

In adults, loss of emotional support has been associated with numerous disease states and progression of others. There are two landmark papers that demonstrate that psychological support can significantly influence cancer outcomes. Dr. Fawzy and colleagues at UCLA have demonstrated that only nine hours of psychological intervention can have a positive influence on immune function in malignant melanoma patients and decrease the number of recurrences and increase longevity. In sessions with patients, therapists stressed health education, enhancement of disease-related problem-solving skills, and psychological support. After five years of follow-up, 62 percent in the standard care group had recurrences of the disease, while only 26 percent in the psychological intervention group had recurrences. Forty-two percent of the standard care group died, whereas only ten percent of the group receiving counseling did so.

Dr. Spiegel and colleagues examined the role of psychological intervention in patients with metastatic breast cancer. The treatment lasted for one year, while both control and treatment groups received their routine oncology care. The intervention groups met weekly for 90 minutes, led by a psychiatrist or a social worker and a therapist who had breast cancer in remission. The groups were encouraged to discuss how to cope with cancer, but the patients were not led to believe that participation would affect the course of the disease. Group therapy patients were encouraged to come regularly and express their feelings about the illness and its effect on their lives. Physical problems, including side effects of chemotherapy or radiotherapy, were discussed, and a strategy was taught for pain control.

Social isolation was countered by developing strong relations among members of the groups. Members encouraged one another to be more assertive with doctors. Patients focused on how to extract meaning from tragedy by using their experience to help other patients and their families. One major function of the leaders was to keep the groups directed toward handling grief. Patients' participation in this intervention was associated with, on average, an extra 18 months of life. If this result had been achieved with chemotherapy, the stock of the company would have soared in value. The authors felt that emotional support could probably account for most of the difference in mortality rates by preventing some of the social alienation that often separates cancer patients from their well-meaning but anxious family and friends.

Emotional support and cardiovascular health

Social relations and the attendant emotional support are also powerful influences in cardiovascular health. Although poor relationships may be involved in the onset and progression of heart disease, most of the published literature deals with the role of relationships in recovery from heart attacks. In her article, Dr. Lisa Berkman summarizes five studies that have shown that social isolation decreases the likelihood of survival after a heart attack. In a study of 2,320 male survivors of an acute heart attack, patients who were socially isolated were twice as likely to die over a three-year period. When social isolation was combined with a general measure of life stress, those in the highest risk category were four to five times more likely to die. In a Swedish study of 150 cardiac patients, those with a large number of risk factors who were socially isolated were three times as likely to die over a ten-year period. In another study of 1,368 patients with significant coronary artery disease, men and women who were unmarried were three times as likely to die within five years.

Berkman then describes her impressive study which I first read in the *Annals of Internal Medicine* in 1992. In this study of both men and women admitted to a hospital with a myocardial infarction, 38 percent of those who reported no source of emotional support died while in the hospital compared to 12 percent of those with two or more sources of support. Emotional support was determined by asking the patients if they could count on anyone to talk with them about their problems or help them to make a difficult decision. During the first six months of the study, 59 percent of those with no source of emotional support had died compared with 41 percent of those with one source and only 23 percent of those with two or more friends. These figures remain about the same at one year following the heart attack.

A study done at Yale on elderly patients hospitalized for heart failure noted that if patients had no one to provide emotional support, they were three times more likely to die or do poorly. The risk was eight times higher for elderly women without emotional support than for elderly men.

These studies are consistent in saying that, when known biologic risk factors are controlled for, heart health is closely linked to significant relationships. How does friendship exert its physiologic effects? Research continues in this area, including work by several of my colleagues at The Ohio State University. Most investigators feel that a more favorable neuroendocrine and immune environment in those with enhanced emotional support almost certainly plays a major role. Animal studies have shown that stable or supportive social environments protect against atherosclerosis. In addition, acute stress produces neuroendocrine events that result in blood vessel injury and also increase the risk of the often fatal heart irregularity, ventricular fibrillation.

Part of this necessary emotional support network might be found in religious faith and in church membership, both of which have been shown to be positively correlated with good health. Dr. Oxman and his colleagues have found that religious strength and comfort, as well as social participation, are related to the survival of elderly individuals after cardiac surgery. The evaluation of 232 patients, of whom 21 died within six months of surgery, revealed that only four percent of those who participated in social or community groups died compared to 13 percent of those with no participation. Similarly, only six percent of those with some or a great deal of religious strength and comfort died compared with 16 percent of those with no religious support. Other studies have also shown a relationship between church attendance and/or self-assessed religiosity and longevity.

Emotional support, suicide, and other societal costs

Loneliness or the absence of emotional support is often the feature that leads to depression and suicide. Our local paper reported the Kevorkian-assisted suicide of a local woman who suffered from a severe neurological disorder and had been divorced for decades and living alone in her apartment for more than 15 years. Similarly, a newspaper article reported the suicide of a prominent Pittsburgh community leader, describing her as single and childless, recently fired from her company, and having lost her beloved mentor, as well as her mother and younger brother in recent months. In a eulogy, she was described as dying from heartbreak, and, we might surmise, the loss of all the significant relationships in her life.

Henri Nouwen in his book *The Wounded Healer* beautifully articulates the significance of relationships. "No man can stay alive when nobody is waiting for him. Everyone who returns from a long and difficult trip is looking for someone waiting for him at the station or airport. Everyone wants to tell his story and share his moments of pain and exhilaration with someone who stayed home, waiting for him to come back." He continues, "A man can keep his sanity and stay alive as long as there is at least one person waiting for him. The mind of man can rule his body even when there is no health left. A dying mother can stay alive to see her son before she gives up the struggle, a soldier can prevent his mental and physical disintegration when he knows his wife and children are waiting for him. But when nobody is waiting there is no chance to survive in the struggle for life. Thousands of people commit suicide because there is nobody waiting for them tomorrow. There is no reason to live if there is nobody to live for."

While I was typing Henri Nouwen's comments, I was also listening to a local radio station which was interviewing my son about his literacy program for prison inmates. Within minutes after the conclusion of the interview, Kevin called to see what I thought about his performance. I told him I missed the show and asked how it went. I could hear and almost see the disappointment on his face. I received a big "all right" when I told him that I actually had listened to the show and gave him rave reviews. I had pretended to miss one hour of an important event in my son's life and the effect was immediately noticeable. Many of the inmates that Kevin works with have never known a father, most rarely ever get a visitor, and many have never received a gift or even a Christmas or birthday card. Their need for relationships is so great that gangs form to provide this necessary human bond. Also, many of these inmates are in poor health. In light of the influence of relationships on health, the absence of positive relationships in their lives must be contributing to their various diseases.

Clearly, absence of emotional support and broken relationships are powerful forces in creating personal and communal bad health. Cardiovascular disease, cancer, life expectancy, suicide rates, childhood development, and crime all seem to be strongly influenced by how we relate to one another.

Points to Remember:

1   Emotional support as obtained through our relationships impacts our health to the same extent as high blood pressure and elevated cholesterol.

2   People who perceived themselves as surrounded by a loving, supportive circle of friends decreased their risk of dying by 50%.

3   Within 6 months of the death of a spouse, there is a 60% likelihood of a serious medical problem occurring in the bereaved mate.

4   A person who believes that he is cared for and loved will enhance both his emotional and physical health.

5 Early emotional and physical relationships are critical for normal physical development. For example, the growth of Eastern European orphans lagged one month behind for every five months spent in the orphanage; premature babies given daily massage gain 47% more weight and are discharged from the hospital six days earlier.

6 Psychological intervention can have a positive influence on immune function in malignant melanoma patients, decrease the number of recurrences, and increase longevity.

7 Psychological intervention in patients with breast cancer was associated with, on average, an extra 18 months of life.

8 In a study of 2,320 male survivors of an acute heart attack, patients who were socially isolated were twice as likely to die over a three-year period. Of 1,368 patients with significant coronary artery disease, men and women who were unmarried were three times as likely to die within three years.

9 Two or more close friends, when compared to having no close friends, can decrease the mortality rate from 59% to 23% in older individuals suffering from a heart attack.

10 Patients hospitalized for heart failure with no one to provide emotional support were three times as likely to die or do poorly. The risk was eight times higher for elderly women without emotional support than for elderly men.

11 Loneliness or the absence of emotional support is often the feature that leads to depression and suicide.

12 Cardiovascular disease, cancer, life expectancy, suicide rates, childhood development, and crime all seem to be strongly influenced by how we relate to one another.

Chapter Seventeen

Our Key Relationships Are in Trouble: Health Implications

RADITIONALLY, THE FAMILY UNIT HAS BEEN THE bedrock of how we learn to relate. This institution has come under enormous stress during the last 30 years as the social development of our children is being increasingly turned over to schools, day care centers, and the television set as baby sitter. An interview by David Blankenhorn entitled, "The American Family Is In Big Trouble," succinctly outlined the problem and made suggestions about what parents and grandparents can do to alleviate the erosion of the family and the loneliness of children.

THE PROBLEM:
- America has the highest divorce rate in the world, with the possible exception of Sweden, with 50 percent of today's children spending a major portion of their childhood in a single-parent home.

- Changing values: Our society stresses individual goals over institutional loyalties.
- Less time spent with family.
- Quality of life for children: One of five children is born into poverty. Fewer children who start school are mentally or emotionally equipped to learn.

WHAT PARENTS CAN DO:
- Make family life a high priority.
- Encourage contact between the generations: Research shows that it's through not knowing that we develop our attitudes about what it means to grow old.
- Restore family rituals: They help bond a family together.
- Bring back the family meal and make it an opportunity for discussion of family and other issues. Food has powerful psychological and social significance.
- Take marriage seriously.
- Be wary of irresponsible media: Movies and especially television tend to portray the family as a subject of ridicule.

Absent fathers

The divorce rate in our country reflects relationships that aren't working, often because one or both partners have never lived in a healthy family themselves. Important qualities have never been acquired, such as shared values and the development of common interests based on good communication. A third of all marriages end within the first four years, which leaves many homes without fathers.

In a Father's Day editorial, the *Wall Street Journal* included comments from a variety of individuals about the importance of fathers. Hadley Arkes, a professor at Amherst College, is quoted as saying, "It is only in our day that we have required sociologists to prove to us what any child can gauge at once: that his father is committed to him in the same way that he is committed to his wife and family, that he can be counted on not to quit this relation when it no longer suits his convenience." He then states that his father made it clear to him, "through countless acts, that grown-ups were competent; that they could be counted on to bear the responsibilities of grown-ups, and that children would not have to bear the burden of keeping the family together and act as therapists."

In the same editorial, Deal Hudson, publisher of *Crisis* magazine, says, "Both parents lose credibility when fathers are absent. Children's cynicism toward parenthood is increased by the inability of parents to raise children together. What follows in the teenage years is lack of faith in the sincerity and integrity of the entire adult world, a skepticism that shapes adolescent views of teachers, clergy, and politicians." I would add that it also creates skepticism toward marriage in general. Both my wife and I are concerned by my daughter's and her friends' distrustful views of marriage. Even though my daughter admits that her parents' marriage should count for something, she states that the boys she knows often have a negative view of marriage and family life.

Although women bear some responsibility for the crisis in family life, the majority opinion from what I have experienced and read is that absent or abusive fathers are at the core of these broken relationships. My wife, whose agency deals with trying to give offenders and ex-offenders life skills to help them succeed in society, assures me that the absent or abusive father is the largest contributing reason for crime in this country.

This point is painfully brought home in a 1993 *Newsweek* essay by Travis Simpkins, who at 20 years old was awaiting trial for armed robbery in an Atlanta jail. His parents were divorced when he was two and his father left for a different state. Even though his visits were infrequent, his father was his hero. He states, "When he called, always a few weeks after Christmas or a birthday, and told me that package I never received must have been lost in the mail, I believed him wholeheartedly. My Dad loved me as only a father can love a son. I don't question that. But he was also a self-centered s.o.b. who let me down when I needed him most. A part of me will always be that kid at the window waiting with his nose pressed against the glass, knowing that if Dad said he was coming, he was coming: but waking up curled beneath the window, alone. I don't want to sit and cry about the scars his actions may have left. I'd like to believe the only real damage done was to our relationship. But I have a very hard time letting people in. Trust is not an easy word for me to say, and it's almost impossible for me to feel it. I learned a hard lesson a long time ago. It's not one I'll risk learning again."

In a hard-hitting essay entitled, "Dear Dads, Save Your Sons," Christopher Bacorn, a Texas psychologist who deals with juvenile offenders, states, "What's become of the fathers of these boys? Where are they? Well, I can tell you where they're not. They are not at PTA meetings or piano recitals. They're not teaching Sunday school. You won't find them in pediatrician's offices, holding a sick child. You won't see them in juvenile court, standing next to Junior as he awaits sentencing for burglary or assault. So if they are not in these places, where are the fathers? They are in diners and taverns, drinking, conversing, playing pool with other men. They are on golf courses, tennis courts, in bowling alleys, fishing on lakes and rivers. They are working on their jobs, many from early morning to late at night. Some are home watching television, out mowing the grass, or tuning up the car. In short, they are everywhere except in the company of their children. Fathers who are on the job, these are the real men of America, the ones holding society together. Every one of them is worth a dozen investment bankers, a boardroom full of corporate executives, and all of the lawmakers west of the Mississippi."

The potential rewards to society of fathers being fathers is enormous. Emotional rewards from relationships with children can be gratifying, and we need to share our perspective with others. I was privileged to have a letter shared with me by my friend Jay, which was written by his step-son on Father's Day, 1997:

To the Greatest Father Ever, on Father's Day:

I will never be able to explain to you in words how grateful I am to have you as my father. Without you I would not be half the person I am today and I would not have the foundation to develop into what and who I will become later in life. You have changed my way of thinking which enables me to live a brighter day every day. I learn from you every day, you teach me how to be happy just by watching you and how to get the most out of life. You have transformed our once small family into a large and happy celebration each and every day. You have changed my mom from a hard-working woman into a happy, confident, secure, hard-working woman. She has a great life now, she is happy every day, and it is all because of you. She has been given a much higher quality of life and it's because of your love, your constant energy and enthusiasm, and your zest for life. I couldn't have asked for anything more in life than to see my mother the way she is today; only you could have made her this happy.

I never understood what a hero or a role model was until now. A role model isn't someone who can play a sport well or can play a role in a movie well. I now know that a role model is someone on whom you want to model all aspects of your life. To know that following his lead will make you a better person. I am fortunate and I am sure I am among a select few that are lucky enough to have a role model. A role model I can be with every day.

I want to thank you for everything that you have done for my mom, my sister, and me. You have made us all better people just for being around you. You have made all of us grow together into a close, loving family. I feel like we celebrate our tight-knit family every time we sit down at the dinner table together or when I greet you two after a long day biking, or when we walk around the yard with the dogs admiring mom's gardens. I cherish all of the time that we live together or play chess together or just watch Leno together. I just enjoy being with you. You are not only my hero, role model, and father, you are also my best friend. Thank you, Jay, for just being you and rubbing off on all of us at the same time. You're a great person and I am so fortunate to have you as my friend, hero, and father.

Love, Tom

This letter stands in marked contrast to the article written about his father by the young man awaiting trial in Atlanta. It expresses the positive rewards of the parenting relationship for both child and parent. It is obvious that Travis Simpkins, as he writes from prison, has been emotionally damaged by his perception of an absent parent who did not meet his expectations of what a father should provide. What will be the health implications of the stories of these two young men, both the same age, as they approach middle age?

Parental caring and health in midlife

From a study entitled, "Perceptions of Parental Caring Predict Health Status in Midlife: A 35-Year Follow-Up of the Harvard Mastery of Stress Study," we gain some powerful insights into this issue. The students were originally chosen at random from Harvard classes of 1952–1954. This study sought to determine how these young men reacted to stress and whether certain patterns were predictive of future health or disease. Two laboratory stressors were used in the original assessment of how the subjects coped with stress. One involved doing mental arithmetic while being harassed by the experimenters, and the other consisted of retelling a story from memory accurately and as quickly as possible under threat of electric shock. The subjects were given a detailed test after the stressors, and their style of coping was evaluated with emphasis on anxiety and anger directed at others or at one's self. One of the items in the psychological battery was perception of parental caring. Six positive reflections of parental caring (loving, just, fair, strong, clever, and hardworking) and eight possible negative qualities of parental caring (severe, stingy, brutal, mean, nervous, poor, punished frequently, and drunk) were evaluated. Of the 126 students in the original population, 116, or 92 percent of the sample, were included in the 35-year evaluation. Of those, researchers were able to locate 75 percent of the original scoring sheets which contained the ratings of parental caring. Subjects were divided into two groups: sick and well. Over half of the sick subjects had cardiovascular diseases, and the rest had ulcers, alcoholism, and miscellaneous disorders. Each of the positive items were rated higher in the well group and most of the negative items were scored lower.

Eighty-seven percent of those who rated both their mothers and fathers low in parental caring had diagnosed diseases in midlife, whereas only 25 percent of subjects who rated both parents as high in caring had diagnosed diseases in midlife. Those who had a caring mother but an uncaring father had a disease incidence of 70 percent, and those with a caring father and a non-caring mother had a 50 percent incidence of ill health conditions. When stress-coping styles were evaluated, 94 percent of those with low perceptions of parental caring and a severe anxiety coping style in dealing with laboratory stressors had diagnosed disease in middle age.

Drs. Russek and Schwartz, authors of this study, discuss several factors that could be influenced by parental caring and that would affect health outcomes including: nutrition and stress before and after birth; behaviors acquired during childhood such as amount of exercise, drug use, and sleep patterns; coping styles such as anxiety, anger, optimism, and self-esteem; and the support of parents in adult life. This Harvard study represented a sample of relatively privileged men from mostly intact families. The authors suggest that the association between parental caring and health may even be stronger today in populations suffering from more extreme family pathology.

This study provides excellent support for the PIERS concept, which states that disease and longevity are related to our physical, intellectual, emotional, relational, and spiritual nourishment. These Harvard students were all in good physical condition at their initial evaluation and were obviously intellectually gifted. So the first two features of PIERS were presumably similar among the subjects. Major differences, however, existed in the emotional and relational areas of their lives between those who developed diseases in midlife and those who were free of disease.

Points to Remember:

1 Traditionally, the family unit has been the bedrock of how we learn to relate. This institution has come under enormous stress in the past 30 years as the social development of our children has been turned over to schools, daycare centers, and the television set.

2 A third of all marriages end within the first four years, which leaves many homes without fathers.

3 Absent or abusive fathers are often at the core of these broken relationships.

4 The potential rewards to society of fathers being fathers is enormous.

5 Our relationship with our parents influences our health outcomes.

6 A thirty-five-year longitudinal study of the Harvard classes of 1952–54 examined the parental influences on health when the child reaches middle age. Eighty-seven percent of those who rated their mothers and fathers low in parental caring had diagnosed disease in midlife, whereas only twenty-five percent of subjects who rated both parents as high in caring had disease in midlife. Fifty to seventy percent of those with one caring parent had acquired disease.

7 When known biologic risk factors are controlled for, heart health is closely linked to significant relationships.

CHAPTER EIGHTEEN

Building Healthy Relationships

NOWING WHAT WE HAVE JUST LEARNED about the value of parental caring in the quality of life, how can we make our marriages stronger and thus preserve our children's health and happiness as well as our own? Perhaps one place to start is with those who have been happily married for most of their lives.

Rela, 91, and Gustave Burger, 97, were featured in *The Columbus Dispatch* on their 70th wedding anniversary. They emigrated from Hungary and raised their family in New York City; they were described as "husband and wife, friends and lovers." Mr. Burger is a joker and feels "That the best thing you can do is to make people laugh." The couple gave their children "love and time." Mr. Burger doesn't remember an argument, but his wife corrected him and says she can remember one! They go to sleep each night holding hands and with a prayer that God will keep their souls safe overnight. "We take care of each other," Mr. Burger said.

In the Burgers' marriage, we see many elements that go into making any successful relationship: friendship, kindness to one another, the rarity of explosive arguments, humor, common interests, shared experiences, a spiritual focus, and caring for one another.

Marriage

Dr. Judith Wallerstein has written a book, *The Good Marriage, How and Why Love Lasts.* Dr. Wallerstein is a psychologist and psychoanalyst who has been married 48 years and has studied divorce for more than 25 years. Her book details the relationships of 50 couples who have been happily married for many years. When interviewed, she stated, "There are a lot of people out there who love each other, respect each other, and think the other person they're with is worth loving. Marriage today is entirely different than it was in the past when it was pretty much held together by forces outside the marriage—the extended family, the church, the community, and even the job. That's no longer true. Marriage today is an institution that really is held up by each couple. The people I interviewed were keenly aware of this, and of the casualties all around them. They had a sense that they were doing something in their marriage that was different and wonderful." She feels that marriage partners must realize that their marriage is an entity in itself. "Divorced couples," she says, "were never able to think of their individual actions and ask 'Is this good for the marriage? Is it bad for it?' If you hold on to the self-centeredness of young adulthood and give up no part of it, you aren't going to have a marriage." Dr. Wallerstein advises nine actions for creating successful marriages:

- Create emotional distance from families and invest completely in your own marriage.
- Partners must develop their own areas of privacy and autonomy while building a sense of intimacy and togetherness with each other.
- Enjoy and raise children while protecting privacy as a couple.
- Confront and overcome difficult life events while maintaining the marriage bond.

- Create a safe haven for expressing disagreements and conflict.
- Establish a rich sexual relationship.
- Use laughter and humor to keep things in perspective.
- Nurture and comfort each other.
- Keep alive the idealized images of falling in love and sense of wonder about each other while facing the realities of changes wrought by time.

Gary Smalley, who has spent a career writing and speaking about marriage, would add to this list his five ingredients of a vital marriage. *The first vital sign of a healthy marriage is that all feel safe to think for themselves.* "We want our spouses to use their creativity and intelligence to complement our own. As someone has said of marriage, if both of us think exactly alike, one of us is unnecessary."

Secondly, each partner enjoys a sense of safety and value in sharing their feelings. "They avoid statements such as 'Oh grow up,' 'Lighten up,' 'You're making a mountain out of a molehill,' 'Give me a break.'"

The next vital sign of a healthy marriage is that each partner feels meaningfully connected. Smalley states, "You are connected when you regularly share your deepest feelings with one another. The opposite of this is a situation where a partner is either neglectful—perhaps a workaholic—or controlling. Neglect or control creates distance rather than connection."

The fourth vital sign of a healthy marriage is respecting the personal boundaries of your spouse. "It's asking for permission before entering another's space and being willing to accept the answer you have been given even if it's not the one you wanted. Asking permission is critical, but so is the ability to hear a no or not now with grace."

Finally, each marriage partner is encouraged to talk and know that their words will be valued. "When you talk, the other—your spouse, parent, boss, or whatever—listens with the attitude that what you are trying to express is greatly valued, even if the two of you disagree."

Listening

In my experience of dealing with strained relationships with family, friends, patients, and other professionals, usually at the center of the difficulty is the failure of one or both individuals to actively listen. This deficiency in our listening skills has enormous personal and societal costs. An essay by Cynthia Crossen entitled, "The Crucial Question For These Noisy Times May Just Be Huh?" provides a thoughtful look at the causes and consequences of poor listening skills. Here are some insightful quotes from this article for which she has interviewed experts who have dealt with this theme:

- We think listening is innate but it is not. It's a skill and we are not taught how to do it.
- We have become a nation of interrupters and we consider conversation as a competitive sport. The first one to take a breath loses.
- Why are Americans so bad at listening? We are always in a hurry. We are continually thinking—get to the point, we don't have time for the details—as we think about our perceived need to go to the store or church. Attentive listening takes time.
- Television encourages passive rather than active listening. It doesn't require that you remember anything and doesn't object if you leave the room. With people watching television five hours a day doing that kind of listening, it is not surprising that empathetic listening is an uncommon skill.
- Most people speak at a rate of 120 to 150 words per minute but our brains can process more than 500 words per minute. It takes an effort to stay focused and not fake it.
- Poor listening can cause disasters. Misunderstood instructions caused the death of 583 people in a runway collision in the Canary Islands. (Many malpractice cases in which I have been consulted, a fundamental flaw often found is that the health professional failed to listen attentively to either the patient or another health professional.)
- If every worker in America makes a $10 mistake a year because of poor listening, that would produce losses of more than a billion dollars a year.
- The opposite of talking isn't listening, it's waiting to talk. Often conversations become dueling monologues in the presence of a witness.

- The lack of listeners means full appointment books for counselors and support groups.
- Listening can be taught but it isn't as easy as it looks, for good listening means suspending your judgment and seeing the world through another person's eyes. When we do this we open ourselves up to the possibility that some of our ideas are wrong.
- People have an enormous need to be listened to, to be taken seriously, to be understood. If one listens to all the conversations of our world, between nations as well as between couples, they are for the most part dialogues of the deaf.

The lack of listeners is keeping the appointment books of mental health workers full. My son Kevin, who is a counselor, mentioned a client who he had recently seen for whom listening was a critical aspect of her problem. A young woman consulted him about problems involving traumatic family relationships. She was intelligent and articulate and said, "I know my problem, and I think I know how to solve it." When Kevin then asked why she was there, she said, "To have you listen to me." Those close to her had never valued her enough to actually "listen" to her. Numerous times during the visit she would ask Kevin a question concerning something she had said previously to see if he had been listening.

Steven Covey advises, "Seek first to understand, then to be understood," in his book *The 7 Habits of Highly Effective People.* He states, "Next to physical survival, the greatest need of a human being is psychological survival, to be affirmed, to be appreciated, to be understood. When you listen with empathy to another person, you give that person psychological air. Empathetic listening is a tremendous deposit in the emotional bank account of another."

A few minutes ago my wife came into my office. She had just had a stressful phone call about an employee who had been relating poorly with everyone in their work environment. Joan was upset. I listened, she talked, and soon calmness ensued, only to be pierced by the ringing of the phone. A colleague at work was incensed by the failure of a research collaborator to meet his obligations in a timely manner. He was very angry and stressed, and I could sense that his blood pressure or some other organ system was being adversely affected. In both instances, these people had spent time stating their expectations to others and believed they had been heard. When events proved otherwise, they responded physically to what they saw as a broken relationship and the violation of trust that had occurred. There is little we can do when we have not been listened to except to try again.

Similarly, if we don't listen to others, we don't relate as well; if we don't relate well, we receive less emotional support; and if we receive less emotional support, we are at more risk for illness. The development of good listening skills and the resulting positive influence on relationships may be an excellent strategy for those seeking good health. In her book *Kitchen Table Wisdom*, Dr. Naomi Remen, once a pediatrician at Stanford and now a counselor for people with cancer, eloquently states, "Listening is the oldest and perhaps most powerful tool of healing. It is often through the quality of our listening, not of our words, that we are able to effect the most profound changes in people around us. When we listen, we offer with our attention an opportunity for wholeness. Our listening creates sanctuary for the homeless parts within the other person, that which has been denied, unloved, and devalued by themselves and by others. Listening creates a holy silence. When you listen generously to people, they hear the truth in themselves, often for the first time."

The act of empathetic listening serves as a healing balm to others, but this quality is often absent from many marriages. Women are more often the ones who ask for a divorce, and frequently the man responds, "I didn't know there was a problem." Obviously these men have not been listening to their wives. Some consequences of divorce for men are that they either don't know or prefer not to discuss have been summarized in a research review by Rosanne Rosen.

- They do not readily seek professional help or the comfort of friends.
- They silently harbor emotional baggage and try to hide their embarrassment about being dumped, or they deny the guilt associated with breaking up their families.
- They manage better than women before a divorce is final, but the adjustment immediately afterward is more difficult.
- They need about 2 1/2 years to regain a sense of order in their lives.

- They tend to isolate themselves, date frenetically, work compulsively, or resort to alcohol and drugs.
- They are three times more likely than women to develop clinical depression.
- They express deep-seated anger toward their ex-spouse with its attendant health consequences a decade later.
- They are twice as likely as married men to be killed by stress-related illnesses—heart disease, stroke and hypertension.

Many are on second or third marriages, and often the problems experienced in the first marriage occur in the next relationship. Perhaps some credence should be given to the 1995 *Newsweek* essay by Maggie McKinney, who dealt with the question of why try to revive a dead marriage. She states, "When my husband of 20 years and I separated, people called, wrote letters, came visiting. Some promised, 'You'll marry again—and next time your marriage will last.' Others said, 'You're better off single.' Almost everyone encouraged me: Go for it! You can do it! Eighteen months later when my husband and I decided to try our marriage again, the support was subdued, often nonexistent. Except for friends among the religious right and not even all of them, people only asked questions or expressed shock and disbelief, 'I heard you two are back together. I hope to hell it isn't true.' 'When something is dead,' a minister told me, 'you need to bury it.' The media frequently deliver the same message: 'Why revive a failed relationship?'" She had been doing reasonably well when her husband asked if they could try again. She states that they recognized the problems and began coping with them. "Our separation taught us a little about what is and what isn't important. Forgiveness, we've learned, is essential. And we've avoided—at least so far—the anger and bitterness that can come from divorce. We won't have to go to our children's graduations, weddings, and other important occasions with an emotional cloud hanging over us." They learned to pay more attention to each other than they had in the past. She concludes, "The minister wasn't wrong. At the time I talked to him, the marriage was dead. But hasn't he heard of resurrection?"

It is not surprising that this article was written by a woman. Most women, as well as men, are aware that the marriage relationship often is treated with greater respect by women. Their actions and physiology speak to this point. In the study mentioned earlier in which I worked with Jan Kiecolt-Glaser and Ron Glaser, we evaluated the endocrine and immune effects of marital conflict and noted that both men and women had elevations in their stress hormones following the discussion of problem areas in their relationship. The endocrine levels of both men and women increased during the disagreement, but after the conflict the men's levels returned to normal whereas the women maintained higher values for many hours. The women ruminated throughout the day about the conflict, which probably kept their levels up while the men quickly turned to other pursuits and forgot about the episode.

Genes and strong relationships

There clearly are differences in how men and women relate, and now we have some genetic information that may explain some of the differences. In a 1997 article in the journal *Nature,* information was presented that the X chromosome may transmit information that influences our adeptness in social situations. The authors evaluated the social skills of women with Turner's syndrome, a condition caused by the deletion of an X chromosome in a woman. So instead of having an XX chromosome distribution, one from their father and one from their mother, they have a single X chromosome. The authors evaluated 80 girls and young women with Turner's who also had short stature and underdevelopment of secondary sexual characteristics at puberty. They found that the 25 girls who inherited the X chromosome from their mother had greater difficulty interacting socially with their peers than the 55 who inherited the X chromosome from their fathers. These single maternal X females had greater difficulty making or keeping friends, and they were not as sensitive to social cues as a tapping finger, a raised eyebrow, or a slightly higher tone of voice. Although genes contribute to how we relate in social situations, the authors realize that social behavior is complex and represents an interaction between environment and genetic factors. The good news was that they found that social sensitivity can be learned even if not inherited.

Our genes are not going to dictate the strength of our relationships, neither are our instincts, and there are also societal attitudes which do not promote relationship building. Leo Buscaglia has examined this challenge to human relationships as follows: "Most of us have been raised to believe that strength lies in independence. We see need as immature and dependence as weakness. We fear commitment in that it may destroy our individuality and our much-coveted freedom. In so feeling, we build self-imposed barriers to genuine encounters and the deep unions we desperately seek. This is indeed a curious paradox. Deeply committed to freedom, liberation, and independence on the one hand, and a deep need for togetherness on the other, we strive to unite in love. Such counterproductive belief and need systems only create more complex problems which, in the end, leave us frustrated, empty, and unexplained." He believes, "The only hope is a serious study of our relationships. We must try to better know who we are, who the other is, and what dynamics are required to keep us united. Our lives are intricate patterns of relationships in which our motivations, our desires, our beliefs, our needs, and our dreams are intricately attached." If we desire health-promoting relationships, he suggests that certain destructive characteristics have to be dealt with such as:

- The need to be always right.
- The need to be first in everything.
- The need to be constantly in control.
- The need to be perfect.
- The need to be loved by everyone.
- The need to possess.
- The need to be free of conflict and frustration.
- The need to change others for our needs.
- The need to manipulate.
- The need to blame.
- The need to dominate.

There is another group of Buscaglia relationship-builders that may prove helpful.

Always start a relationship by asking: Do I have ulterior motives for wanting to relate to this person? Is my caring conditional? Am I trying to escape something? Am I planning to change the person? Do I need this person to help me make up for a deficiency in myself? If your

*answer to any of these questions is "Yes," leave that person alone. He
or she is better off without you.*

If you take time to talk together each day you'll never become strangers.

*Value yourself. The only people who appreciate a doormat are people with
dirty shoes.*

*Don't be afraid of disagreements and arguments. The only people who
don't argue are people who don't care or are dead. In fact, don't have
short arguments. Make certain they are thoroughly over and done with.*

Don't take yourself so seriously, but never fail to take the other person seriously.

*Watch for little irritations, they grow into destructive monsters. Verbalize
them at once.*

Learn to listen. You don't learn anything from hearing yourself talk.

*If each partner in a relationship is willing to give 75 percent of him or her
self, then you will have 50 percent more than you need for a perfect
relationship.*

Remember that moral and spiritual values don't restrict, they protect.

Keep laughing. It exercises your heart and protects you from cardiac problems.

*Relationships are not sporting events. Stop wrestling for control. No one
ever wins this kind of match except divorce lawyers.*

*You are at the center of all your relationships, therefore you are responsi-
ble for your self-esteem, growth, happiness and fulfillment. Don't
expect the other person to bring you these things. You must live as if
you are alone and others are the gifts offered to help you enrich your life.*

When my son Gregg married Lanita, I suggested that they hold onto this
list and keep reviewing it in the future. Alternatively, they could periodically
place a copy on their mate's pillow, highlighting those items of concern.

Friendship

It seems that most of us have work to do in combating those influences
that are destructive to positive relationships. Not only are these characteristics deleterious to family relationships, but to our nonfamily friendships
and community relationships. The entire circle of friends that we support
and who likewise nourish us are critical for our happiness and well being.
Several days ago, I opened the mail and found four "important" items: first,

an update on a poorly performing mutual fund, and secondly, a season ticket application for Ohio State basketball, a sport which I really enjoy. The two remaining pieces were welcomed notes from family friends. Financial security and athletics are important to many of us, but expressions of gratitude and helpful insights from friends produce feelings of harmony and connectedness that can't be duplicated by these other pursuits. My wife was struggling with a family issue, as was our friend Judy at this point in time, and Judy sent this note:

Joan:

Your pain is all too clear to this household. I wish I could take it away. My pain was so deep I hurt throughout my body. I've learned I cannot protect them (our children) from the world or each other. But I have promised to continue to provide activity, the space and our home for them to heal their own wounds. We all learn at a different speed, a different pace, no two are alike—one year is five to one, ten to another. I will pray and wait for these gaps to close. We never know when their eyes will open…but I want to help them have that chance, no matter how long.

Love, Judy

Friendship implies helping others when it may have not been at the top of your wish list. It assumes we will place others' interests equal to our own and often above our self-interest. These statements are really just replays of the age-old "golden rule." But somehow it seems foreign to discuss such concepts in a 1990's society that fiercely worships individual freedom, independence, and self-interest while barely paying lip service to helping others. Self-centeredness is poor working material for the development of effective relationships that provide emotional support for all of us. It is even more difficult to muster any kind of attention to this area if we are struggling with all the other components of the PIERS plan. If we have neglected nourishment of the physical, emotional, and spiritual aspects of our being, it is unlikely that we can make much progress in relationship building.

In the research literature, social or emotional support has been defined as having available someone who will empathetically listen to your problems and help you with major decisions. It is this kind of support that seems to provide a buffer to all the emotional and biological forces that produce illness.

Points to Remember:

1 Many elements go into making any successful relationship: friendship, kindness to one another, humor, common interests, shared experiences, a spiritual focus, and caring for one another.

2 Gary Smalley's five ingredients of a vital marriage:
 • All feel safe to think for themselves.
 • Each partner enjoys a sense of safety and value in sharing their feelings.
 • Each partner feels meaningfully connected.
 • Respecting the personal boundaries of your spouse.
 • Each partner is encouraged to talk and know that their words will be valued.

3 People have an enormous need to be listened to, to be taken seriously, to be understood. Dr. Rachel Remen says, "Listening is the oldest and perhaps most powerful tool of healing. It is often through the quality of our listening, not of our words, that we are able to effect the most profound changes in people around us."

4 Self-centeredness is poor working material for the development of effective relationships that provide emotional support for all of us.

5 If we have neglected nourishment of the physical, emotional, and spiritual aspects of our being, it is unlikely that we can make much progress in relationship building.

SECTION SIX

Search for Harmony

Chapter Nineteen

Self-Care

ON December 22, 1992, James Scott, a 22-year-old fourth-year medical student from Australia, was hiking in the Himalayas when a blizzard hit. He was separated from his companion, and for two days he tried to get his bearings while falling into water, using up all of his food, and sleeping in freezing sub-zero temperatures. Three days later on Christmas Eve, his meal consisted of a caterpillar. During the night he could not keep from shivering, so he wrapped his head as well as his feet in towels and clothes to minimize heat loss. Each attempt to climb down the mountain was frustrated by the deep snow and his lack of energy. As the weeks passed he grew desperately lonely and anticipated dying. He had a copy of Dickens' *Great Expectations* and continually reread it from cover to cover. He received pleasure from snowflakes falling, birds flying over the rugged mountains, and avalanches tumbling over cliffs. He prayed for his loved ones and for his hiking companion. He imagined being back home with his fiancée,

family, and friends; to share his thoughts and express his love, he continued to write to them until his ink ran out. At that time he grew increasingly desperate. He became suicidal and stopped taking fluid. On the
third day of being semi-comatose, he had a dream that he was in
Australia with his family and fiancée. He woke up quite upset that he had
given up and once again began to drink snow water. On February 2, 1992,
42 days after being lost in the Himalayan blizzard, he was spotted by a
helicopter during the last of 26 rescue attempts. Today he is a practicing
physician, married, and the father of a daughter.

This story was reported in a 1997 *Annals of Internal Medicine* article,
accompanied by a critique of the factors that led to James Scott's survival.
He suffered from severe environmental and emotional stress, but he pos-
sessed personal qualities which helped him survive. He used his intelligence and imagination to remember pleasant times, practice karate
maneuvers, and repeatedly visualize rescue scenarios. Even while suffering from severely painful feet, fatigue, guilt, and doubt, he was able to
appreciate the wonders of nature. He was able to laugh at himself and the
remarkable resemblance between himself and Pip, a character in the
Dickens' novel. Finally, he prayed, mostly for others, for long periods of
time.

PIERS and self-care

We have discussed the importance of the various components of the
PIERS plan for combating stress and improving longevity. James Scott's
survival is an excellent example of these principles. Although deprived of
the basic elements of food and shelter, he was able to survive. Intuitively
he knew that his survival was dependent on his intelligence, being stable
emotionally, relating to the important loving relationships of his past, and
recognizing the importance of the spiritual dimensions for health and
survival. Deprived of the first element of PIERS, physical nourishment, he
relied heavily on the other elements. James Scott intelligently used the
knowledge available to him and exhibited those emotional attributes
which sustain health. He was able to reframe his situation by appreciating
nature's beauty while it was at the same time holding him captive. He rec-

ognized the power of relationships for survival, even though it was done through his imagination, and he frequently visited the spiritual dimension of his life by appreciating nature's beauty and by praying.

You and I are unlikely ever to find ourselves in such immediately life-threatening circumstances. However, as evident from the information we have reviewed on stress and toxic emotions, many of us are experiencing pressures in our health that are similar to being lost in the Himalayas. Loneliness, poor nutrition, fear of the unknown, regrets, doubts, and ideas that life is no longer worth living (which were frequent thoughts of James Scott) often reach us in our individual "Himalayan" experiences. Unlike James Scott, however, we may only give lip service to the importance of issues necessary for our health and survival. Meanwhile, cholesterol plaques may be forming in our coronary and carotid arteries, and our elevated blood pressure may be damaging our kidneys and heart.

The basic elements which were used by James for survival also form the basis for our own self-care. We have to recognize that our health and successful aging are not dependent on professional health care workers or the next breakthrough from medical research of the pharmaceutical industry, but rather on our day-to-day harmonizing of the physical, emotional, relational, and spiritual dimensions of our lives.

I believe that many have accepted the truth of these statements but seem unable to mobilize the energy to make the appropriate changes in their lives that are required to be seriously involved in self-care. There may be as many different reasons for this inability to make changes as there are people. However, the most common complaint I hear is that "I am on overload and don't have enough available time to incorporate all of these elements into my daily routine." As I discuss these issues with individuals in my medical practice, we often both become frustrated knowing the medication being prescribed may give short-term relief, but the major health risk behaviors are not going to be addressed.

In need of self-care

John, a middle-aged professional, consulted me for progressive impotence of several years duration. His testosterone was slightly decreased and he was seeing me for further evaluation and treatment. Some additional endocrine tests, pituitary imaging, and testosterone replacement therapy would probably take care of the problem, but was this the only or best approach to his problem? John also had high blood pressure and was on blood-pressure medicine that can influence potency. A major contributor to his high blood pressure was his excessive body weight which can also decrease testosterone levels. In addition, he was daily logging in a large number of stressful hours in his office and community work. By his own admission he was on overload. He wasn't sure how and why his work schedule had progressed to this point but it was influencing his increased intake of fast foods and lack of exercise. The following scenario was now clear; he was experiencing a stressful work situation leading to poor eating and exercise habits with a subsequent large weight gain; the weight gain preceded the development of high blood pressure and lowering of his testosterone levels; and the medication for his hypertension was also influencing his decreased potency. Therefore, the probable cause for his problem was unhealthy life choices which eventually progressed to impotence.

In John's story we see a breakdown in the self-directed care for healthy aging. First is the failure to utilize healthy aging strategies in order to help prevent or delay development of physical symptoms. Secondly, when physical symptoms and signs occurred without a diagnosable disease, John could have reviewed the various elements of the PIERS model to look for personal behaviors that may have been creating his signs and symptoms.

Dr. David Sobel has offered the following insights in regard to self-care. "What goes on in a person's head—the thoughts and emotions—can have a dramatic effect on the onset of some diseases, the course of many, and the management of nearly all. Nearly one-third of patients who visit a doctor have bodily symptoms as an expression of psychological distress. Another third have medical conditions resulting from behavioral choices such as smoking, alcohol and drug abuse, poor diets, and so forth. Among the remaining patients with medical diseases such as arthritis, heart failure, or pneumonia, the course of their illness can be strongly influenced by their mood, coping skills, and social support.

Points to Remember:

1 Our healthy aging is not dependent on health care workers or the next medical breakthrough but rather on the day-to-day harmonizing of the physical, intellectual, emotional, relational, and spiritual dimensions of our lives.

2 Many seem unable to mobilize the energy to make the appropriate changes in their lives that are required to be seriously involved in self-care.

3 A frequently voiced complaint for not being involved in self-care is that "I don't have time to incorporate all of these elements into my daily routine."

4 Self-directed care for healthy aging involves evaluating one's life in light of the PIERS model in order to prevent or delay the onset of physical symptoms or to deal with symptoms.

5 "What goes on in a person's head—the thoughts and emotions— can have a dramatic effect on some diseases, the course of many, and management of nearly all." (Dr. David Sobel)

Chapter Twenty

Medical Care Options

WHEN WE DEVELOP SYMPTOMS OF AN illness, how are we to decide on whom to ask for assistance? Fifteen years ago this would have been a ridiculous question, as an overwhelming number of people would simply consult a family physician. But in the last ten years, a variety of alternative approaches has evolved, such that one in three people is now using therapies other than those practiced by Western M.D.s. Sixty million Americans used alternative-medicine practices in 1990 at an estimated cost of 13 billion dollars. The estimated 425 million visits to alternative practitioners exceeded the 388 million visits to all U.S. primary-care physicians. In 1997, this gap widened with a 47 percent increase to 629 million visits to alternative-medicine practitioners.

Science and allopathic medicine

It is becoming increasingly popular to debunk much of what scientific medicine has to offer in favor of other approaches. Audiotapes arrive daily detailing the deficiencies of the medical profession in the areas of nutrition and preventive health. We are warned of the hazards of drug treatments and are urged that even the most difficult health problems can be solved outside of traditional medical approaches. Physicians are labeled as uncaring and seeking material gain via excessive charges to those least able to afford care. Although there is some truth in all these statements, it would be a tragic mistake if people were to disregard the services which Western medicine can uniquely provide: outstanding acute-care management, precision in diagnosis, a wide range of pharmacologic interventions, and an incredible research capability.

During a flight to Boston recently, I was reviewing my journals and came across an article in *Science* that tied together both the power and the humanistic aspects of Western science. In 1994, the Parseghian family found out that three of their four children suffered from Nieman-Pick disease, a rare illness in which cells become glutted with a fat-like molecule leading to progressive deterioration in organ function. Problems with vision, walking, hearing, and swallowing then follow, with death often occurring before adulthood. The family, along with their grandfather Ara Parseghian, a famous college football coach, formed a research foundation in the hope of finding a cure for this rare disease. Support from this foundation has led to two discoveries: the gene that causes the disease, and then the development of a mouse model that will permit further understanding of how the disease occurs and a system for testing possible treatments. This story illustrates how, with today's powerful research tools, important questions which would have been impossible to address a decade ago can be answered in a matter of several years.

A literal army of researchers over the past 50 years has made advances in health care that have saved millions of lives and improved the quality of life of millions more. I remember not being able to go to swimming pools in the summer because of the risk of contracting polio. When my young friend developed Hodgkin's disease in the '50s, he died; today his disease would have been cured. A torn cartilage no longer ends an athletic career or leads to crippling arthritis. Laser therapy prevents or retards blindness in diabetics, and angioplasties preclude the eight-inch scar which former-ly would have accompanied heart surgery to open up a blocked coronary artery. The CAT scan and MRI have replaced the pneumoencephalogram, which was once used to visualize brain lesions and led to excruciating headaches after the procedure. Laporoscopic surgery and microsurgery have markedly reduced postoperative pain and mortality. My wife's grandmother died as a young woman following the complications of a "routine cholestectomy" using older techniques which have now been replaced by laporoscopic surgery. An enormous battery of laboratory tests allows precision in our diagnoses. Transplantation of many organs is now available. New medicines for infections, high blood pressure, diabetes, ele-vated cholesterol, ulcers, and depression are introduced annually. Advances in the treatment of AIDS and aneurysms and a host of other conditions are in our papers daily. We have all been blessed by these con-tributions and hundreds more.

System failure?

Criticism of the medical profession, however, includes charges that physicians and other health care workers are not sufficiently caring, and are too oriented to crisis intervention and the use of pharmocologic solu-tions for every complaint. These complaints are voiced by nontraditional health practitioners, the general public, and even physicians involved in the practice of traditional medicine.

A review by researchers at the University of Toronto who examined 39 studies estimated that 75,000 to 137,000 deaths at U.S. hospitals in 1994 were due to drug reactions. The article places drug reactions as either the fourth or sixth leading cause of death behind heart disease (743,000), can-cer (530,000), and stroke (150,000), if one accepts the higher estimate.

An article in the *Annals of Internal Medicine* in 1997 reported on the pre-scribing practices of 112 physicians in Montreal, Canada, in order to deter-mine if non-steroidal anti-inflammatory drugs (NSAIDs) for chronic hip pain due to osteoarthritis were given according to accepted guidelines. They observed in this elderly population that unnecessary prescriptions for NSAIDs were written during 42 percent of office visits for this complaint.

Each year, 70 million prescriptions for NSAIDs are written in the United States. Their use accounts for 76,000 hospitalizations and 7,600 deaths annually, often from gastrointestinal side effects including bleeding. The authors of this article and the thoughtful editorial by Dr. Frank Davidoff suggest that the major reason for this serious problem is lack of time that physicians spend with patients. It is clear that both patients and physicians are not satisfied with the increasing pressure in the health care system to see more patients by decreasing the time spent with any individual patient. In these articles, the authors quote research which has shown that patients' feelings of confidence and ability to cope after an office visit is correlated to the length of the visit. The authors caution, however, that increased time is only useful if the practitioner has a high level of medical interviewing skill, an art which has taken a back seat in most educational programs due to the increased emphasis on technology.

Dr. Davidoff concludes his editorial by stating, "Imagine a future in which the time available for seeing a patient was determined primarily by the nature of the patient and the medical problem rather than by the dreams of system planners; in which there is time for taking an adequate medical history and doing the requisite physical examination; for actually discovering most of the patient's problems; for discussing management options and treatment effects to everyone's satisfaction; for providing screening efforts and health education on a regular basis; for patients to feel free to ask for, and get, medical information; for medical staff to give needed attention to psychosocial issues; and for patients and their physicians to sense that they have had time to see and hear, to be seen and heard. Bizarre! The very strangeness of the image says something about a medical-care system that is out of control and drifting farther all the time from its basic purpose of caring well for patients."

Health care options

We could debate the merits of this criticism of traditional medicine, but it is obvious that many people in our society are becoming more active in using preventive health strategies and looking for health options not usually considered under the purview of traditional general medical care. Hence the attraction of non-invasive and low-risk health initiatives for many patients. Acupuncture, aromatherapy, Ayurvedic medicine, biofeedback, cranial therapy, Chinese traditional medicine, guided imagery, herbal medicine, homeopathy, hypnotherapy, massage therapy, naturopathy, prayer, rolfing, touch therapy, and reflexology are constantly being discussed in the popular press as alternative approaches for prevention and management of physical symptoms.

These alternative forms have been referred to as complementary, holistic, and natural, and much heat but little light is usually produced by discussions concerning the appropriate terminology. As stated by Dr. Alan Berkenwald, alternative approaches to health are present, have always been present, and will always be present. They serve as challenges to the preeminent medical thinking of the day. He concludes that, "At the same time, the 'other' medicine will forever be rediscovering the alternatives, exploring their databases and paradigms, and publishing news of their 'resurgences.' Together, the systems are healer twins, a medical Gemini, like the two mythical brothers who were good companions and protectors of the brave. And, just like those mythologic twins who were set in the night sky by Jupiter, they may never appear together. They alternate forever before us, appearing in turn when we look to the heavens in our time of need, whatever we choose to call them."

There are thousands of individuals who can testify to how one or more of these alternative approaches have helped them after traditional treatments had failed. Objections by the supporters of traditional medicine to these observations and therapies include: 1) these are just anecdotes without clinical trials to support their validity; 2) they are obvious examples of the placebo effect which implies that we thought the treatment would work and so it set into motion healing properties; 3) many of the alternative practitioners are poorly trained and often engage in fraudulent practices; and 4) one puts one's self at risk when consulting these practitioners, as the side effects of their treatments are not well described, and they may miss a disorder that is easily diagnosed and treated by low-risk traditional methods.

I suspect that many M.D.s as well as alternative practitioners would agree with this list, but they would also add that some of these same criticisms could be leveled at traditional medical practices. The evidence that supports the utility of these approaches varies depending on the alternative practice. For example, acupuncture is gaining wider acceptance as evidenced by a 1997 National Institute of Health conference. The panel decided that acupuncture helped ease the nausea after chemotherapy or an operation, could alleviate morning sickness, and could numb pain after a dental procedure. They also felt that acupuncture might aid in the treatment of addiction, stroke rehabilitation, headache, menstrual cramps, tennis elbow, fibromyalgia (general muscle pain), low back pain, carpal tunnel syndrome, and asthma. Evidence supports the claim that opiate peptides, called endorphins, natural body chemicals that relieve pain, are released by acupuncture, and this at least partially explains its effect in pain management. Acupuncture may also stimulate the pituitary gland, which could produce a variety of systemic effects. Health maintenance organizations and insurance companies are now beginning to pay for these services.

The placebo effect

What about the criticism that the placebo effect is what makes alternative medicine effective? It has been known for a long time that people will respond to a treatment just because they believe it may help them. Therefore, when clinical trials are being performed to test a treatment, a control group of individuals who think they are receiving the active compound but are really ingesting inactive material is also included. What has always fascinated me from my earliest days in medical school is that a 30-percent or greater improvement can occur in the placebo group. The physiologic changes which occur in the brain and then in the rest of the body because the patient believes that he or she will improve is not understood. If the placebo effect is helping alternative treatment regimens produce symptomatic improvements in patients, it may still be a reasonable approach if the cost of treatment does not include harmful side effects. One way to partially resolve this dilemma on an individual basis is to have the patient keep a daily diary of treatment benefits while on traditional medications and then compare this response to those achieved while on alternative therapy.

Deceptive practices continue to be a problem with alternative treatments, but many states have licensing requirements, and references from other patients are also often helpful. Of course we need to be wary of anyone who promises cures for what we know is usually not curable. Another favorite technique of the charlatan is to claim that the government or others are holding back a particular alternative therapy to protect their own pocketbooks. They hope to make us paranoid about conspiracies that don't exist.

Complementary health services

It has been noted that more than 70 percent of patients who have used alternative services never mention it to their physicians. In a survey of 113 people visiting their family physicians in Portland, Oregon, half reported using an alternative treatment such as visiting a chiropractor, having massage treatment, or using herbal medicine, megavitamins, or meditation. About ten percent of patients reported using homeopathy, naturopathy, and acupuncture. The authors admit that their results are biased by the fact that Portland has several large centers for alternative medicine, but these numbers are still impressive. Some critics have assumed that poorly educated, neurotic, or ignorant people would be the most likely to use these services. Studies show that either educated, young to middle-aged, and financially well off patients are more likely to use alternative medicine, or that no associations with demographics can be found. It's unfortunate that patients sometimes don't feel comfortable sharing this information with their physician, as some of the preparations can interact with medications they are taking, and occasionally they contain potentially toxic substances such as the ephedrine contained in ma huang. Deaths from overdoses of this substance have been reported.

It has also been reported that over half of American parents turn to alternative therapies to help their children. These therapies have been used for children with life-threatening illness as well as in those with routine medical problems. In a study of 161 parents, 65 percent of the group seeking treatment for cancer used alternative treatments, and 55 percent of the parents whose children had other disorders used these services for their children. Prayer with their child was the alternative therapy of choice for 64 percent of parents of children with cancer, and 40 percent of parents with generally healthy children also turned to prayer as a method of healing. A quarter of seriously ill children experienced massage therapy, and 16 percent of young cancer patients received regular doses of medicinal herbs and/or megavitamins. It was stressed in the report that parents did not use alternative therapies because they disliked conventional medicine but because they believed in its efficacy and possibly because it helped them deal with their own feelings of hopelessness.

What I want in a health professional

How are we going to decide whether a particular condition would benefit from an alternative or complementary approach? This will continue to be a difficult question until there is a cadre of practitioners who have had experience with many of the reputable alternatives. Even more important, however, is to be associated with a health professional who has an appreciation of the various factors that influence our health and is willing to listen to our story.

Remember my friend, Maggie, who developed breast cancer? I was speaking to her six months following her surgery and asked her about her journey. She said dealing with the breast cancer was not that big a problem for her; her biggest concern was finding a physician who would help guide her through the maze of her various symptoms and concerns as well as the management of her high blood pressure. She related a particularly disturbing encounter with a neurologist who, after listening to her history for less than five minutes, told her she had tension headaches and needed two medications, including an antidepressant to which she had previously had a bad reaction. She said he was out of the examining room before she could provide this information. Feeling badly about this consultation, she elected not to take the antidepressant and when she returned for a follow-up visit and expressed her concern about the diagnosis and the prescription, she was scolded for not being a compliant patient. The exchange deteriorated when he then asked her what she thought her diagnosis should be, and she responded, "That is why I am in your office, to find out the nature of my problem." I wish this patient-physician encounter were an unusual event, but I have heard similar stories from other patients and friends. We all need a health professional who is willing to listen.

Does our personal health consultant emphasize the importance of proper nutrition and exercise, review important preventive health strategies, suggest relaxation therapy or other modalities in place of or along with medication for major stresses? When the condition is acute in onset or rapidly progressing, conventional treatments are usually most appropriate. However, when symptoms exist without a diagnosis or for chronic conditions, the addition of alternative treatments are probably going to have their greatest benefits.

The new medicine

James Gordon, M.D., is clinical professor of psychiatry and community and family medicine at Georgetown University School of Medicine, and his perspective on these issues is that we need a new way of approaching both alternative and traditional medical care. He writes in *Manifesto for a New Medicine*, "The new medicine that we are creating together appreciates the great value of surgery and drugs but sees them as last resorts, not first choices. It makes use of the most sophisticated modern diagnostic techniques and research studies, but also puts value on the learning and experience that humans have accumulated over millennia. It is a synthesis of modern technology and perennial wisdom, of powerful and definitive treatment and compassionate care, of Western and Eastern, high technology and indigenous and folk healing traditions. This new medicine insists that healing be a fully collaborative partnership in which teaching is as important as treatment, and it regards self-care—particularly through self-awareness, relaxation, meditation, nutrition, and exercise—as the true 'primary-care.' This new medicine is as concerned with enhancing wellness as it is with treating illness. It teaches us to mobilize our power to heal ourselves, and it makes full use of the extraordinary power of our minds to affect our bodies and of nondrug, physical approaches to enhance our mental and emotional functioning."

New approaches in managing illness may be as simple as a concerned phone call, as I recently heard at one of our medical conferences. Dr. Brandt, a professor of rheumatology at the University of Indiana, related his experience in managing patients with pain from osteoarthritis. He found that a weekly five-minute phone call asking how the patient was doing significantly improved the pain score when compared to the "drug only" patient group. This experience reminded me of a study related during a seminar by Dr. Ken Pelletier, of Stanford. Phone calls were placed frequently by nurses to individuals with significant risk factors for coronary artery disease. They explored issues with the patients, such as compliance with their diet. They found that this approach was more effective and less costly in improving cardiac risk factors than the traditional four visits a year to a cardiologist.

Simply holding a patient's hand can have health benefits. There is an ophthalmologist in California who has volunteers hold the hands of his patients during cataract surgery. They receive only local anesthesia, and having their hand held by volunteers, such as 83-year-old Mary Pickford, helps them to relax, which lowers their blood pressure and heart rate. Mary says that since volunteering in 1987, she has held the hands of about 1,400 patients. She can remember only three refusals, one being from a pompous tax collector who later apologized.

The value of human touch in the treatment and healing process became evident to me during a bout with a laryngeal disorder which temporarily shut off my breathing. This prompted a visit to the emergency room, where a diagnosis of reflux-induced spasm of the vocal cords was made. While waiting for the medication to work, I passed some anxious nights with disrupted sleep when a sense of choking frequently awakened me. During these anxious moments, my wife held my hand or massaged my back, and I then noticed an almost immediate decrease in my pulse rate and feeling of breathlessness. We can speculate about the different mechanisms responsible for this effect, but I feel comfortable calling it the healing touch.

Other nontraditional approaches in managing disease processes were documented in a study performed at UCLA, where patients with mild-to-moderate hypertension were taught assertiveness training, time management, and biofeedback, in addition to healthy ways of dealing with stress and anger. Seventy-three percent of those who entered the special program had reduced their blood pressure medication within 12 months. In addition, 55 percent of this group were normotensive and taken off all medication, compared to 30 percent in the control group.

Dr. David Eisenberg, in his article to doctors about "Advising Patients Who Seek Alternative Medical Therapies," proposes strategies for patient and physician in dealing with these issues, including developing a clear understanding of the patients' preferences and expectations, the recording of important symptoms while new alternative treatments are being used, and scheduling follow-up visits to monitor for potentially harmful situations. In the absence of professional, medical, and legal guidelines, the management plan encourages patient safety, documentation of outcomes, and the importance of shared decision-making. Dr. Eisenberg refers to a rabbi who, in her premarital counseling sessions, always asks the couple, "Tell me how you disagree. I'm not interested in what you disagree about, but rather how you work through your disagreement." The manner in which the patient and physician wrestle with disagreements about therapeutic choices helps define their relationship and its value to each party. No patient should be made to feel that their medical journey is to be taken alone.

Points to Remember:

1   Sixty million Americans used alternative medicine practices in 1990 at an estimated cost of 13 billion dollars, and the number of visits to alternative practitioners exceeded visits to all U.S. primary-care physicians. In 1997, the gap widened.

2   Western medicine can uniquely provide outstanding acute-care management, precision in diagnosis, a wide range of pharmacologic interventions, and an incredible research capability.

3   Drug reactions are a leading cause of death. Often prescriptions are written inappropriately which may be related to the lack of time that physicians spend with patients.

4   Our present medical-care system is out of control and moving further from its basic purpose of caring for patients.

5 "Alternative approaches to health care are present, have always been present, and will always be present." (Dr. Alan Berkenwald)

6 "Self-care—particularly through self-awareness, relaxation, meditation, nutrition, and exercise—is the true primary-care." (Dr. James Gordon)

7 "The manner in which the patient and physician wrestle with disagreements about therapeutic choices helps define their relationship and its value to each party. No patient should be made to feel that their medical journey is to be taken alone." (Dr. David Eisenberg)

CHAPTER TWENTY-ONE

How Can I Improve My Present Health-Related Behaviors?

T HE ONSET OF ILLNESS IS CERTAINLY A CALL TO action. Doctors who developed cancer and had successful outcomes have provided several recommendations. These physicians with cancer felt that being passive about cancer was the worst possible position and that one had to consider the diagnosis as a call to action. They suggested that discussing our fears and sharing them with someone helps our fears shrink. They also recommended that if one receives a diagnosis of cancer, he or she should get a second opinion, seek the best possible care, don't rush into treatment, ask disagreeing doctors to explain their opinions, be informed, tell family and friends about your disease, seek comfort from your relationships, and make lifestyle changes (such as nutrition and exercise). These principles, of course, can also be applied to other chronic illnesses.

Successful patients

Dr. Andrew Weil, who is closely identified with alternative health practices, has identified certain features that characterize patients who have recovered from difficult-to-cure illnesses. First, they did not accept discouraging words that there was nothing else that could be done for their condition. Instead they continued to hope that they would somehow find help. Secondly, they actively pursued information from health professionals, read books, wrote to authors, and asked for ideas from friends and neighbors. Information gathering is becoming easier with increased health data being available on the Internet.

Recently a patient came to my office with an unusual type of pituitary tumor that makes excessive amounts of growth hormone. When we began to discuss treatments, I was amazed at the amount of information she had acquired about her condition, more than most of our medical residents knew. She informed me that Internet searches had provided most of the information. During her time in my office, we were able to quickly focus on the issues about her disease that articles don't usually explore and were of major concern to her. I believe the Internet will become a powerful tool for individuals to enhance the quality of their self-care and improve the communication between health provider and patient. In a 1997 *Journal of the American Medical Association* article, nine of the most reliable and comprehensive cancer-related Web sites were provided. Presently even more information is available.

Dr. Weil also found that successful patients sought out others who had a similar illness and had been healed. In addition, they were also able to find a health professional who empowered them in their search for healing and made them feel they were not alone. These successful patients did not hesitate to make radical changes in their jobs, places of residence, diet, relationships, and habits. They saw these changes as necessary for personal growth, even though painful to enact.

Finally, these successful patients later came to regard their illness as a gift which provided the motivation to resolve some of the conflicts in their lives that had prevented their personal development. Although these qualities of successful patients have not been evaluated in a controlled study, I would personally subscribe to them if I were struggling with a difficult illness.

Good health habit formation

Although we all want to be successful patients, we would prefer to avoid becoming patients at all. One of the most difficult issues I face in my practice of medicine is helping individuals to change their destructive health behaviors. Often they see the logic of altering their life-style, but seem powerless to initiate or sustain any behavioral changes. We often talk about values clarification, journaling, and value-centered time commitments, but all is often discarded after leaving the office. If a minor change in a behavior or attitude is required, success is more common, but when major change is needed, success is infrequent.

The difficulty stems from the need for a paradigm shift (the way we see ourselves and the world around us). Earlier we explored the characteristics of men and women who were healthy 90- and 100-year-olds. They had many characteristics in common, including daily exercise, excellent nutrition, always learning, a spiritual dimension to their lives, lots of friends, and an excellent sense of humor. These habits were long-standing, and they organized each day around them. When it comes to understanding and communicating the development of effective habits, Stephen Covey does it as well as anyone. I have read his books, listened to his tapes, and attended his seminars, and I continue to be impressed by how clearly he has articulated the basic issues of habit formation and how to change or maintain them.

Often in the health arena, we search for the right book, diet, herb, guru, vitamin, or pill that will instantly transform behaviors that have been accelerating our aging for years. We want to polish over these behaviors and their subsequent health outcomes without devoting the time and energy to do the transforming work which produces long-lasting results. Stephen Covey states it this way: "There is no shortcut, no quick fix, to the development of a character or habits of effectiveness; we tend to reap what we sow." As the maxim goes: "Sow a thought, reap an action; sow an action, reap a habit; sow a habit, reap a character; sow a character, reap a destiny." The destiny we have been referring to is healthy aging, and this simple axiom describes the pathway we all must travel if we are to reap the rewards of good health. Remember, for example, that one-third of cancers in the U.S.A. are from cigarette smoking and one-third from poor nutritional choices, with coronary heart disease having a similar relationship to smoking and poor nutrition.

Recently I met Susan, a young woman who enjoyed telling me how much she loved her new job and how good she felt physically. This contrasted with her situation several years ago when she had a high-pressure selling job where satisfaction from a job well done could last no more than a day before she would hear the refrain, "What have you done for me today?" She acquired a big salary and equally abundant migraine headaches and gained weight from eating nothing but fast food. She was unable to find time to relax, and her relationships were evaporating due to neglect. She then met several people who counseled her by asking if she were headed in the direction she really wanted to be going, and if not, why not change? After some painful reflection, like how could she live on less money, she came to the conclusion that her present quality of life couldn't be called "living" by any stretch of the imagination. She then made a paradigm shift and began looking at herself and the world around her differently. Her new job, which paid less salary than her former position, was rewarding her with exciting challenges and personal satisfaction. In addition, she no longer had migraine headaches. It then became easier for her to make the other changes in her life, such as time each day for meditation, reflection on personal growth, improvements in her nutrition, and reestablishing lost relationships. She felt refreshed and looked younger.

I don't know if she ever heard of Covey's *Seven Habits,* but she had certainly employed them in making the necessary changes in her life. The first habit is to be "proactive" and to avoid the victim mindset that makes someone else responsible for our difficulty so that we cannot change our present condition. She quit blaming her boss for her problems and began to focus her time and energy on what she could control—her "circle of influence." One of her answers to being responsible and gaining control of her life was to find a new job.

She then exercised the second habit, which is to "begin with the end in mind." She decided what personal qualities meant the most to her and how she could make her job, other activities, and her relationships develop and sustain these qualities. She was more interested in being a human "being" than a human "doing." I'm not sure if she had ever heard of a personal mission statement, but she was certainly creating one.

The third habit of the seven habits is to "put first things first," and clearly Susan was engaged in this process. As Covey states, "Only by saying no to the unimportant can we say yes to the important." He argues that we need to spend more time in non-urgent but important activities as preparation, prevention, planning, values clarification, relationship building, needed relaxation, and empowerment. Of course without the second habit firmly in mind (begin with the end in mind), habit three is not very useful. Many time management programs and other aids may direct us in habit-three activities without emphasizing the importance of habit two. When I see destructive health behaviors before or after the onset of disease, they are often associated with a lack of a sense of mission or purpose in that individual's life which leads to such comments as, "We all have to die sometime," or "I can't give up all my vices."

We have emphasized the importance of close relationships in one's long-term health outlook. Covey emphasizes that effective relationships depend on having previously developed the first three habits which lead to personal effectiveness. Then one is prepared to listen empathetically to others and engage in using win-win strategies with them (habits four and five).

Habit seven is self-renewal, for which Covey suggests we commit an hour a day to building and sustaining our physical, emotional, and spiritual dimensions. He states, "Without this discipline the body becomes weak, the mind mechanical, the emotions raw, the spirit insensitive, and the person selfish." I would suggest that if we interviewed the successfully aging men and women that we know, many of them would have incorporated each of these habits into their lives.

Using our senses

If disordered thinking plays a role in health and disease, as suggested by increasing evidence, it occurred to me that using our senses appropriately could enhance our health by bringing us closer to our maximum physiologic potential. We have measurable physiologic reactions to negative sensory input, so why not establish a routine of providing positive sensory input into our minds as a contribution to daily self-renewal?

The dramatic colors of an autumn landscape, the pleasant aromas of food being prepared in the kitchen, the taste of our favorite foods and the calming effect that they produce, the touch of the soft skin of a baby, the hug of a close friend, the massaging of a sore muscle, and the notes of great music all are capable of evoking pleasant visual images and calming our anxieties. You might call this process and its subsequent results a poor man's antidepressant. Therefore, it isn't difficult to see why aromas, food, touch, music, and visual imagery have all been used to facilitate healing. Imagine during a stressful day or during an illness, that you are simultaneously provided with your favorite pastoral scene, food, aromas, and music, followed by a massage from your lover. Even the most strident critics of the concept that what we experience through our senses influences our health may have to soften their criticism as they contemplate this scenario.

There is more than anecdotal evidence that our senses provide important healing cues. An article in *Science* demonstrated that if a hospital room had a view of the outside landscape, patients could be discharged sooner than if their room did not provide such a view. The benefits of treatments which involve our sense of touch as provided by massage and acupuncture have been well demonstrated. Auditory stimulation with pleasant music is now being used to assist in the treatment of various disorders and has been shown to reduce the increased pulse rates of surgeons performing major operations. Also, the various tastes of food have served as a basic treatment modality in Ayurvedic and traditional Chinese medicine. Perhaps each day we should intentionally provide our senses with pleasant sensory input to enhance our health and hopefully to counteract some of the negative influences of the evening news reports.

A partnership

As we have previously noted, health is not something static but is an ever-evolving process intimately united with the aging process, much of which is under our control. When disease becomes established and we need the assistance of a health professional, it would be helpful to have on our side someone with the insight of Dr. Naomi Remen, who writes,

"Much in the concept of diagnosis and cure is about fixing, and a narrow focus on fixing people's problems can lead to denial of the power of the process. Years ago, I took full credit when people became well; their recovery was testimony to my skill and knowledge as a physician. I never recognized that without their biological, emotional, and spiritual processes which could respond to my interventions, nothing could have changed at all. All the time I thought I was repairing, I was collaborating. Seeing the life force in human beings brings medicine closer to gardening than carpentry. I don't fix a rosebush. A rosebush is a living process, and as a student of that process, I can learn to prune, to nurture, and cooperate with it in ways that allow it to best 'happen' to maximize the life force in it even in the presence of disease."

Points to Remember:

1 The onset of illness is a call to action.

2 Physicians who have had cancer suggest:
• Get a second opinion.
- • Seek the best possible care.
- • Don't rush into treatment.
- • Ask disagreeing doctors to explain their opinions.
- • Be informed.
- • Tell family and friends about your disease.
- • Seek comfort from your relationships.
- • Make lifestyle changes.

3 Dr. Andrew Weil's characteristics of successful patients:
• They do not accept discouraging words that there is nothing else that can be done for their condition.
- • They actively pursue information from health professionals, read books, write to authors, and ask for ideas from friends and neighbors.

- They seek out others who had a similar illness and have been healed.
- They find a health professional who empowers them in their search for healing and makes them feel they are not alone.
- They do not hesitate to make radical changes in their jobs, places of residence, diet, relationships, and habits.
- They later come to regard their illness as a gift which provides the motivation to resolve some of the conflicts in their lives that have prevented their personal development.

4 Better than being a successful patient is to avoid becoming a patient at all.

5 Often we gloss over health behaviors that have been accelerating our aging, and fail to devote the time and energy to do the transforming work which produces long-lasting results.

6 Often destructive health behaviors before or after the onset of a disease are associated with the lack of a sense of mission or purpose in a person's life.

7 "There is no shortcut, no quick fix, to the development of character or habits of effectiveness; we tend to reap what we sow." (Stephen Covey)

8 We have measurable physiologic reactions to negative sensory input, so why not establish a routine of providing positive sensory input into our minds as a contribution to daily self-renewal?

9 Health is not something static but is an ever-evolving process intimately united with the aging process, much of which is under our control.

CHAPTER TWENTY-TWO

Spirituality and Health

I N OUR SEARCH FOR PHYSIOLOGIC HARMONY, THE CONTRIBUTION of our spiritual life to the quality of our health is increasingly recognized. Of all the topics that have been addressed in this book, there is probably none more contentious than that which pertains to religion and/or spirituality and health. For some, this topic produces visions of witch doctors or small-town tent meetings where dramatic healings are witnessed by people throwing away their crutches and walking offstage. These issues have been frequently addressed in books, television, and theater. Criticism not only comes from the nonreligious but also from faithful followers of many religious traditions. In their perception, healing that occurs through meditation, prayer, or religious services not under their theological tradition is suspect.

The words religion and spirituality are often used interchangeably in both religious and scientific literatures, but when distinctions are made, spirituality is used in reference to the internal dialogue of an individual who is focused via meditation, prayer, or lifestyle on his relationship to

God and/or nature. Spirituality serves as a filter for interpreting life's events. In contrast, religiosity would refer to external functions such as church attendance, activities, and traditions.

Recently we have witnessed in America a resurgence in interest in religious and spiritual issues. This is reflected by the Promise Keepers march on Washington, D.C. in 1997 and the success of CBS's "Touched by an Angel" which attracts 25,000,000 viewers each week and has higher ratings than "60 Minutes." Several years ago, *Newsweek* ran a lead story on America's quest for spiritual meaning in which it found that 45 percent of people surveyed sense the sacred during meditation, 58 percent feel the need to experience spiritual growth, and 33 percent have had a religious or mystical experience. Evidence that spirituality is becoming "mainstream" is detailed in an article by Patricia Bellew Gray, entitled, "Want to Search Your Soul at a Monastery—Some Hot Spots for Hermits," which describes locations where one can experience a spiritual retreat.

The evidence

What is the evidence that religion and spirituality have an impact on health and aging? Drs. Oman and Reed of the Buck Center for Research in Aging in Novato, California followed a group of nearly 2,000 volunteers, aged 55 and older. Those who attended religious services were 24 percent less likely to have died during the intervening five years than those who did not attend services. This was the case even after other potential explanatory variables—such as age, sex, health and mental health status, and level of social support—were taken into account.

In a 1997 article in the *Journal of Gerontology*, Drs. Idler and Kasl at the Yale School of Medicine followed 2,812 elderly individuals in New Haven, Connecticut for 12 years and found that attendance at church services was positively related to improvement in their disabilities. The authors were not able to explain these findings by the subjects' health practices, social ties, or other indicators of well-being. They also noted that disability had minimal effects on church attendance and therefore argued that it was the beneficial aspects of being at church that were responsible for the observed decrease in disability. In their discussion of these findings, they mention that studies report that 76 percent of elderly people say that religion is very important in their lives. They feel that there is something unique about attendance at religious services that leads to better disability outcomes.

In the accompanying editorial, "Religion, Aging, and Health: Current Status and Future Prospects," Dr. Krause of the University of Michigan indicates that there is an impressive body of research that indicates that elderly religious people have improved physical health when compared to those who are less religious. He indicates that there is an increased interest in religion and health. This observation is supported by the increased number of scholarly papers and grants on this topic, the emergence of new journals devoted solely to religion and aging, and major funding agencies such as the Fetzer Foundation, the John Templeton Foundation, and the NIH that have sponsored committees and funded grants to examine these issues. He feels that this surge in interest reflects greater acceptance of religion among those who had traditionally avoided this subject, as well as interest by health care providers to explore any avenue that could reduce health care costs. He argues that one way to conceptualize the beneficial relationship of church attendance and health is that regular attenders get more religious support that leads to better coping strategies to deal more effectively with stressful life events.

In addition to helping people cope with disabilities, attendance at religious services or comfort from religious strength has been associated with improved survival after cardiac surgery and less depression in older adults. A study of heart transplant patients found that attendance at religious services decreased anxiety and improved physical functioning. They also found that private prayer aided patients in coping with difficult-to-follow drug regimens.

Also it has been found that those who attend services at least once weekly are 50 percent less likely to have elevated levels of an inflammatory protein (interleukin-6) that reflects inflammation in the body. It is usually produced by cells of the immune system and has previously been shown to be elevated in patients with diseases such as cancer, heart disease, and hypertension.

Even people who have had negative experiences with religions in the past are now beginning to see the importance of incorporating spirituality into their lives. Kathleen Norris, a Protestant who spent a year in a Benedictine monastery, writes in *The Cloister Walk,* "I hear many stories these days from people who are exiled from their religious traditions. They, also, speak from the margins. Many, like me, are members of the baby-boom generation who dropped religious observance after high school or college, and are now experiencing an enormous hunger for spiritual grounding."

Meditation

Meditation and prayer have now been incorporated into the daily practices of people who would not consider themselves religious. Some clarity on how meditative practices could influence our health was vividly described by reporter Ron Suskind during his visit to a meditation retreat. People from all walks of life, including corporate executives, gathered for days or weeks to practice daily silent meditation. They were reminded that most people spend each day thinking about the past, worrying about the future, participating in activities, or sitting in front of a TV. This leaves little time for focusing on the present and what we feel, see, or hear. The goal of their meditation was to live in the present, to become aware of things as they occur, and to avoid stress in their lives by accepting change rather than being frustrated by it. They were instructed on proper posture and on how to focus on their breathing. By the second day, the author began to notice a "lifting, expansive sensation. I feel weightless, aware and very much awake, but completely still."

Jon Kabat-Zinn comments about the misconception that meditation is a way to shut off the pressures of the world: "Meditation is neither shutting things out nor off. It is seeing things clearly, and deliberately positioning yourself differently in relationship to them." Stress is part of life, "So you can't artificially suppress the waves of your mind, and it is not smart to try. It will only create more tension and inner struggle, not calmness. That doesn't mean that calmness is unattainable. It's just that it cannot be attained by misguided attempts to suppress the mind's natural activity. It is possible through meditation to find shelter from much of the wind that agitates the mind. Over time, a good deal of the turbulence may die down from lack of continuous feeding. But ultimately the winds of life and of the mind will blow, do what we may. Meditation is about knowing something about this and how to work with it. You can't stop the waves but you can learn to surf."

Prayer

We have referred to prayer as a vehicle to help people in physical distress, as happened for James Scott lost in the Himalayas or children with malignancies. In our profiles of successfully aging seniors, we often found that prayer was a daily practice in their lives. The influence of prayer on health and disease has been a frequent topic in the media in recent years. *Newsweek's* feature on prayer sampled widely divergent points of view: Ninety-one percent of women and 81 percent of men pray; 82 percent say they ask for health or success for a child or family member when they pray; 79 percent say God answers prayers for healing someone with an incurable disease; 54 percent say that when God doesn't answer their prayers, it means that it wasn't God's will to answer; 82 percent don't turn away from God when their prayers go unanswered.

The issue of prayer and health had not been considered a topic for serious scientific discussion until ten years ago. At that time, Dr. Randolph Byrd published a paper stating that intercessory prayer had a positive health outcome for patients with heart disease who were admitted to the coronary care unit at San Francisco General Hospital. Three hundred ninety-three patients were entered into a traditionally-designed research protocol. Patients were randomly assigned to be prayed for or not to receive intercessory prayer. The author and medical staff did not know which patients were being prayed for. The praying was done outside the hospital by individuals whose lives were characterized by active daily devotional prayer. The patient's first name, diagnosis, general condition, and pertinent updates in their condition were provided to the intercessors. There were no differences between the two groups at entry to the study, but the hospital course for those individuals receiving prayer was of lesser severity and they required fewer diuretics, antibiotics, and ventilatory support.

There has been much criticism of this study, as one would expect from such explosive findings, but all clinical studies have weaknesses and therefore require replication before their conclusions are accepted. There are presently efforts to replicate this study, and additional studies have been funded to examine the role of prayer in influencing such conditions as AIDS, arthritis, alcoholism, and drug addiction.

Prayer was the center of a 1999 Duke University Medical Center news release of a study by Dr. Mitch Krucoff of 150 patients undergoing coronary angiography. Each subset received traditional medical therapies. One group received "noetic" therapies such as stress relaxation, guiding imagery, and touch therapy. One group had their names forwarded to religious groups including Buddhist monasteries in Nepal, a Carmelite nunnery in Baltimore, the Wailing Wall in Jerusalem, and to U.S. Christian congregations. Neither the staff nor the patient knew who was being prayed for. Patients who received prayers during their hospital stay did 50–100 percent better and those who received noetic therapies did 30–50 percent better than those patients who only received traditional treatments.

The efforts of Dr. Herbert Benson, a Harvard cardiologist, to critically examine the role of prayer in healing has gained enough visibility to make it the basis for discussion in the journal *Science,* which quotes Dr. Benson's 1996 book *Timeless Healing: The Power and Biology of Belief* that people are "wired for God," and that believing in God can improve health. Dr. Benson argues that, perhaps instinctively, humans have always known that worshipping a higher power was good for them, and that the calm instilled by faith itself can be a powerful force for healing. He has also promoted meditation and relaxation to treat numerous medical disorders, including hypertension and headaches. Several editorial comments in this same journal strongly criticize Dr. Benson's ideas: a New York University rheumatologist, Dr. Gerald Wiseman, for example, was quoted as saying that meditation is akin to "magic potions" and that these ideas are "of the worst sort preying on the sick." Even Christian scholars take shots at this type of inquiry by saying that this makes laboratory mice out of prayers.

Dr. Benson's ideas do go beyond the studies that we have previously discussed about the connections of better health and church attendance, in that he suggests that belief itself could affect health. He says, "I am coming closer to defining a biological role of belief in God, a line of inquiry I wasn't sure that either scientists or theologians would appreciate." He has reported that patients with various diseases who are being taught relaxation responses have "felt the presence of a power, a force, an energy close to them" during meditation, and that their conditions seemed to improve. His recent research interest is to replicate Dr. Byrd's finding that praying for someone else's health helps those being prayed for to get well.

In *The Gift of Peace,* completed just before he died of pancreatic cancer, Cardinal Bernadine commented, "My decision to go through my cancer in public had been to share a simple message: faith really matters. By talking about my inner peace, I hope people can see that there is a lot more to prayer and faith than words. God really does help us live fully even in the worst of times. And the capacity to do precisely this depends upon the deepening of our relationship to God through prayer."

Religious commitment and health

In an article entitled, "Making the Case for Bringing Religion to Patient Care," published in the *American College of Physicians Observer,* Dr. Dale Matthews, associate professor of medicine at Georgetown University, states, "I have come to the conclusion that religious commitment is usually good for your health." He reviewed 212 studies analyzing the link between religious commitment and health care outcomes. One hundred and sixty demonstrated a positive benefit of religious commitment, 7 percent found a negative effect, and 17 percent came to an indeterminate point of view. He mentions that Americans overwhelmingly believe in God, and that many believe that physicians should address spiritual issues and inquire into faith-healing experiences. Dr. Matthews quoted a *USA Today Weekend* poll that found that 79 percent of Americans believe that faith can help recovery from illness, and 63 percent think physicians should talk to patients about spiritual issues, yet only 10 percent recall any physician talking about faith and physical health. Dr. Matthews conducts "spiritual interviews" with certain patients during routine medical examinations to determine whether a patient's beliefs might someday help him or her cope with disease.

The importance of religious faith in recovery from depression was recently reported by a Duke University research team in *The American*

Journal of Psychiatry. They evaluated 94 individuals, all over 60 years of age, who had been diagnosed as being depressed when discharged from the hospital after an injury or illness. They used a questionnaire developed with the help of Christian ministers and Jewish rabbis to determine the individuals' own level of religiosity. They also evaluated the patients' religious practices such as prayer, Bible study, service attendance, and involvement in church activities. They found that patients with higher religiosity scores had more rapid remissions than patients with lower scores. Patients recovered 70 percent sooner for every ten-point increase in the religiosity test score. The researchers encouraged psychiatrists to initiate inquiries into a depressed patient's religious faith, as these beliefs may bring comfort and facilitate healing.

In a study reporting on the Spirituality and Healing in Medicine Symposium at Harvard medical school, Dr. David Larson commented on new medical school courses developed to train students on how to address the spiritual needs of their patients. A particular area of focus was that associated with the fear of dying for patients in the last year of life. Many of these medical school courses work with chaplains. Dr. Larson noted that 39 years ago, only three American medical schools taught courses on religion and spiritual issues, and now the number is almost 30.

The importance of a chaplain's role in affecting health outcomes was reported by Dr. Elisabeth McSherry, who evaluated 700 coronary artery disease patients in a V.A. hospital setting. These patients were being treated with complex and costly procedures such as coronary bypass and valve replacement surgery. One patient group received one hour of daily interaction with a chaplain, while the other group received three minutes a day. Individuals receiving the longer chaplain visits were discharged an average of two days sooner. Estimated increased costs of the chaplain visits were $100 per patient, but the earlier discharge date was estimated to save $4,000 per patient.

In a survey of 269 family doctors conducted at the American Academy of Family Physicians, 99 percent felt that religion could make people healthier. In discussing this topic in *Internal Medicine News*, Dr. Christina Puchalski mentions that critics worry that a trend toward spirituality in medicine may lead to an emphasis on specific dogmas. She disagrees, stating that spirituality usually revolves around an individual's relationship with God, but that it can also mean a connection with nature or music or whatever gives life meaning. She relates a story told to her by one of her patients suffering from terminal breast cancer. The woman revealed that when she first came to the hospital, she felt anonymous, similar to any other patient needing care. "What makes me different are my beliefs; my spirituality helps me cope with my dying. It's the most important part of my life."

Spirituality is the fifth element of the PIERS complex. In our search for harmony and healthy aging, spirituality is the element which ties the other aspects into an integrated unit. It provides what Frankl referred to in *Man's Search for Meaning* as the reason for our existence. Without this integrating spiritual influence in our lives, physical, intellectual, emotional, and relational aspects often suffer. Those who have lived long and productive lives often credit the spiritual and religious aspects for helping them to age successfully.

Reflection

While enjoying a Brahms symphony directed by Alesandro Siciliani and performed by the Columbus Symphony Orchestra last Saturday night, I reflected on these issues of health and healing, and the following metaphor came to mind. The Great Composer has placed a musical score in our DNA, and our bodies are the instruments chosen to produce the music as authentically as possible. Our minds serve as conductors of the symphony and strive to produce as error-free a rendition as possible. The goal is to have such balance and harmony in the performance of our lives, that an occasional missed note can't be heard because the overall presentation is so pleasant, so full of life and meaning.

Points to Remember:

1 Spirituality serves as a filter for interpreting life's events.

2 A twelve-year study of 2,812 elderly individuals found that attendance at church services was positively related to improvement in their disabilities.

3 Individuals who are more involved in religious pursuits recover more quickly from depression.

4 Attendance at religious services and comfort from religious strength or prayer have been associated with improved survival from cardiac surgery, and better coping with difficult-to-follow drug regimens.

5 76% of 212 studies analyzing the link between religious commitment and health care outcomes demonstrated a positive benefit of religious commitment, 17% demonstrated a neutral benefit, and 7% a negative effect.

6 In a survey of 269 family physicians, 99% felt that religion could make people healthier.

7 In our profiles of successfully aging seniors we often found that prayer was a daily practice in their lives.

8 Intercessory prayer has been reported to have a positive health outcome for patients with heart disease who were admitted to a coronary care unit.

9 "Humans have always known that worshipping a higher power was good for them, and that the calm instilled by faith can be a powerful force for healing. (Dr. Herbert Bensen)

10 Spirituality is the fifth element of the PIERS complex. In our search for harmony and healthy aging, spirituality is the element which ties the other aspects into an integrated unit.

11 Without an integrating spiritual influence in our lives, the physical, intellectual, emotional, and relational aspects often suffer.

SECTION SEVEN

Your Personal Profile on Your 100th Birthday

Chapter Twenty-Three

Predictors of Healthy Aging

SEVERAL YEARS AGO, I WAS ASKED TO GIVE A PRE-sentation on research we had done on aging and to make some general comments about the aging process. After discussing these issues, I summarized the presentation by describing the hypothetical personal characteristics of healthy peo-ple on their 100th birthday. They would have followed the PIERS plan con-scientiously: physically, intellectually, emotionally, relationally, and spiri-tually. First, in the physical area, they would probably be thin of body, hav-ing walked or engaged in yoga exercise daily and eaten low-calorie, high-fruit and vegetable diets. They would probably drink alcoholic beverages in moderation and have not smoked cigarettes for decades, if ever. They probably sleep well, and they rarely get sick. They probably have had little contact with the medical profession over the years, except for preventive services such as immunizations, mammograms, pap smears, and blood pressure checks. They have a positive outlook about their health, even though all of them have some physical disability.

They probably kept their minds very active both before and after retirement, which may not have occurred until late in their 70s. Their income was (and possibly still is) significantly above the poverty level. They devoted time each day to learning something new. Reading, although more difficult with failing eyesight, remained a passion. Although past experiences consume part of each day's thinking, they frequently reflect on the good things of their present life.

In the emotional arena, these centenarians are optimistic, hopeful, positive thinkers, dreaming of good days yet to come, and generally pleased with their lives. Their anger is short lived, they are rarely hostile to others, and they cope well with stress. They frequently tell funny stories and enjoy a good laugh when one is told to them. They still have many outlets for relaxation and recreation.

They are often involved in helping those less fortunate. They had successful marriages or had always been single. They have many younger friends in their 70s and 80s, which helps greatly as they are the last surviving members of their immediate family. They feel supported by a large social network and often attend social functions.

These centenarians have multiple spiritual commitments, which serve to provide a sense of purpose and meaning in their lives. They appreciate the beauty of nature, pray and/or meditate daily, and are frequent attenders of religious services.

Although the person who embodies all of these characteristics may not exist, you and I have all met elderly individuals who embody many of these qualities and are aging healthfully. If we begin to discard these qualities, we probably change our aging pattern, and with extensive erosion of these principles we develop accelerated aging. We all have seen individuals who possess few of these qualities and have seen them age very quickly.

Stanford researchers have recent data to support these observations in a study of 1,741 male and female University of Pennsylvania alumni first evaluated in 1939–40 and then at various times from 1962–94. The low-risk group postponed significant functional impairment by more than five years compared to the high-risk group. Exercise, weight, and smoking history were predictors of future disability. They also found that low-risk participants had half the disability acquired throughout the life span as it was postponed and compressed into fewer years at the end of life.

The PIERS plan empowers us to effectively cope with risk areas. Remember the PIERS review? Why not retake it? Have you made any changes since first taking the review?

The good news is that if we have an undesirable score, it is not fixed in stone but can be increased as our behavior improves. Simply being aware of these issues may be all that is needed for an individual with a score of 60 to take a personal inventory and then target certain areas for renewed effort for improvement. For example, if work is consuming an abundance of your time and emotional energy, then strategies to redefine how you look at your career may lead to a job change so that more time can be spent developing the important relationships in your life. We frequently read in the popular press about people who have "downsized" in order to enjoy and develop other areas of their lives. We can also reevaluate our core values and make the continual adjustments needed for us to achieve our health objectives.

PIERS Review

Physical:

_____ I eat properly.
_____ I exercise.
_____ I am free of illness.
_____ I abstain from smoking and drinking excessively.
_____ I get refreshing sleep.

Rarely (if ever)   scores 1 point
Occasionally   scores 2 points
Above average   scores 3 points
Very frequently   scores 4 points

This will produce a maximal score of 100 if you obtained four points for every question.

Intellectual:

_____ I am analytical.
_____ I read.
_____ I am learning.
_____ I use my mental ability at work.
_____ I reflect on my life.

Emotional:

_____ I am peaceful.
_____ I like myself.
_____ I am optimistic.
_____ I laugh.
_____ I relax.

Relational:

_____ I am a good listener.
_____ I feel supported by friends.
_____ I attend social functions.
_____ I talk with my parents/family members.
_____ I feel close to my co-workers.

Spiritual:

_____ I pray or meditate.
_____ I appreciate nature.
_____ I give to or serve others.
_____ I attend religious services.
_____ I feel my life has meaning.

Points to Remember:

Personal characteristics of healthy people on their 100ᵗʰ birthday:

Physical:
Thin, exercise daily, low-calorie high-fruit and vegetable diet, non-smoker, moderate alcohol intake, sleep well, infrequently ill, use preventive health services, have a positive outlook about their health.

Intellectual:
Kept their minds active before and after retirement which occurred in their 70s, learned something new each day, reading and discussing current events remained a passion, often reflect on the good things of life.

Emotional:
Optimistic, pleased with their lives, their anger is short-lived, are rarely hostile to others, cope well with stress, have a good sense of humor, many outlets for relaxation and recreation.

Relational:
Are frequently helping others, have successful marriages or have always been single, have many young friends in their 70s and 80s, feel supported by a large social network and often attend social functions.

Spiritual:
Have multiple spiritual commitments which serve to provide a sense of purpose and meaning. They appreciate the beauty of nature, pray and/or meditate daily, and are frequent attenders of religious services.

The more closely one can identify with these characteristics, the more likely you are aging healthfully. Conversely, those who possess few of these attributes often are seen to have accelerated aging.

Chapter Twenty-Four

A Recipe for Change

ISHING FOR IMPROVEMENT MAY HELP set into motion positive change. Often, however, wishing is not enough as the stress in our lives and our response to it has severely limited our ability to change our behavior, and associated physical complaints may already be producing repeated physician visits. Just as piers placed in the ocean prevent erosion of the beach, so can the PIERS components of our lives help prevent the erosion of our health. These PIERS areas of our lives serve as a buffer to the agents of aging and disease which are ever-present as they move us from harmonious health to the development of symptoms and eventual disease. Following an evaluation by a physician which provides or fails to provide a specific disease diagnosis, other professional consultation may be desirable.

Strategies

Dr. Nicholas Cummings coined the term "somatization" to refer to the situation in which a person's physical complaints are really manifestations of unconscious emotional conflicts. Remember that over 60 percent of patients in a generalist's office do not receive a disease diagnosis, but are having symptoms that are reflections of somatized stress. The goal of psychotherapy is to help the person discover alternatives to translating stress into physical symptoms and hopefully to resolve the emotional issue that is the cause of the problem. Brief psychotherapy, which may take one to five sessions, is effective for 85 percent of individuals who are experiencing somatized stress. Of course, we need an experienced clinician to assure us initially that established disease is not present, which in most cases can be done with one or two office visits. Unwillingness to accept a nonorganic diagnosis by the patient, or fear of malpractice by the physician if a diagnosis is missed, may set into motion repeated behaviors that will eventually be harmful to the individual's health and somebody's wallet.

Another therapeutic approach to improving tension, stress, and physical problems related to it without resorting to drug therapy is utilizing the relaxation response as described by Dr. Herbert Benson: sitting in a comfortable position, closing your eyes, relaxing your muscles, breathing slowly and naturally, and focusing on a word, phrase, or prayer that is rooted in your personal belief system. This is practiced for 10 to 20 minutes once or twice a day. It has been shown to positively influence hypertension, pain, infertility, insomnia, anxiety, anger, hostility, and depression.

Eight weeks of mindful meditation has been found by Dr. Jon Kabat-Zinn to reduce pain, depression, and anxiety, enhance feelings of trust, and help patients to improve their health behaviors. He feels that there is nothing magical or mystical about meditation; rather it is about paying attention, purposely, in the only time you live, namely this present moment. It is the practice of observing your thoughts, feelings, and sensations, in order to achieve a broader and calmer perspective on them. It can be performed while sitting, lying, or in the midst of any daily activity. Through this process, you deepen self-understanding and reduce the tendency to react automatically to stressful life events or circumstances.

Creating positive visual images is pleasant and helps people get into a relaxed state. Its proponents feel it brings positive physiologic changes, provides psychological insight, and enhances emotional awareness. My patient for many years, Gail is a woman with breast cancer and endocrine problems. Yesterday she asked me if I had included her story of using meditation and visualization to cure her breast cancer. I said not yet, but I told her that her story should be told. Gail has a Ph.D. and teaches at a local college. She had the misfortune of developing breast cancer in her 30s. At the same time, two of her close friends who were the same age, were also diagnosed with stage-two breast cancer, and all three had the same treatment regimens. One woman became depressed and was convinced she would be dead in a few years, and her prophecy was accurate, with death occurring within several years of her diagnosis. The other friend became consumed with turning her life into evaluating everything that was written about breast cancer. One day she came to a breast cancer support meeting and stated that she had just spent six hours on the Internet researching one small aspect of breast cancer. Gail said breast cancer had become a "cult" to her friend. She also died several years after her diagnosis. In contrast to her friends, Gail's response to her diagnosis was to reevaluate those areas in her life that required change and to begin meditation with visualization each morning and evening. She would imagine that her immune cells were NATO forces capable of killing enemy tumor cells. If she felt aggressive in the morning, her tumor cells might be German forces or, if she was in a romantic mood, French forces. She would see these immune killer cells going through her various organs and engulfing each tumor cell that was visible that day. It has been ten years since her diagnosis, and she does not use this technique very often now. But she is convinced that it was vital to her cure or at least her excellent course to this point in time. Stories like Gail's do not fall into the category of scientific proof. Given the research we have discussed in these pages, however, her interpretation of her present good health being secondary to her visualization practice is competitive with other explanations we might offer.

Biofeedback is another behavioral technique used for some symptoms and disorders such as headaches. It is a treatment that uses the body's own signals, such as pulse rate, and puts them in visual displays like a computer screen. You may be given a stressful scenario to visualize and the reactivity of your pulse or other physiologic marker is recorded. You would then attempt to relax and bring your pulse back to baseline.

Exercise is very useful to enhance relaxation. There is also a place for medication in certain situations. For example, if you are so clinically depressed that you find it difficult to initiate even basic activities of living, you may need medication before you embark on a program of self-improvement. Whatever approach we take to deal with stress when health professionals are involved, we want a skilled provider. Personal recommendations and professional accreditation are all we have to guide us in this important selection process. When evaluating the benefits of any of the above approaches, keeping a daily journal of your symptoms or emotional state will be useful. Our memories often need assistance in assessing benefits or lack thereof.

Your belief system and religious tradition may already have tools in place for you to greatly improve your emotional state and physical symptoms. In the Old Testament of the Bible, anxiety is frequently mentioned in the book of Psalms, and prayer and meditation are referred to as being helpful in combating anxiety's ill effects. The New Testament book of Philippians advises, "Do not be anxious about anything, but in everything by prayer and petition with thanksgiving present your requests to God. Finally, whatever is true, whatever is noble, whatever is right, whatever is pure, whatever is lovely, whatever is admirable—if anything is excellent or praiseworthy—think about such things and the God of peace will be with you." (4:6–8) This is a very old antidote for anxiety, but it has the elements of what we would today call developing a sense of gratitude, positive thinking, optimism, visual imagery, and brief psychotherapy: all very helpful health practices. Meditation and prayer are found in every religious tradition and perhaps for some individuals could serve as an acceptable alternative for medication. However, we should not forget the usefulness of professional consultation and medication in the treatment of anxiety and depression.

The benefit of service

Another opportunity for upgrading oneself on the PIERS scale is through serving others. I have been impressed by many people whom I have met over the years who frequently volunteer to help others, and they seem to possess many of the positive qualities that are outlined in the PIERS review. One could argue that it is because they have these qualities that they volunteer rather than obtaining them after volunteering. Often, however, I hear people say how helping others has taken their minds off their own troubles and has even diminished problems as they serve other people with much greater needs and problems. Serving others has often helped them grow in each of the five areas of the PIERS plan. Personal growth seems to occur when we reject the scarcity mindset and accept an abundance mentality view of life. The scarcity view of living sees giving of time, talent, money, possessions, or emotional energy as leaving little for the giver. The opposing abundance mindset argues that when I give in any of these areas to others in my community, I get back much more than was given.

Dr. Parker Palmer discusses in an essay the scarcity assumption which seems to govern so much of human behavior: "Nature is in sharp contrast to human nature, which seems to regard perpetual scarcity as the law of life. Daily I am astonished at how readily I believe that something I need is in short supply. If I hoard possessions, it is because I believe that there are not enough to go around. If I struggle with others' power, it is because I believe that power is limited. If I become jealous in relationships, it is because I believe that when you get too much love I will be short-changed. Even in writing this essay I have had to struggle with the scarcity assumption. It is easy to stare at the blank page and despair of ever having another idea, another image, another illustration. It is easy to look back at what one has written and say, that is not very good but I had better keep it, because nothing better will come along. It is difficult to trust that the pool of possibilities is bottomless, that one can keep diving in and finding more. The irony, often tragic, is that embracing the scarcity assumption, we create the very scarcities we fear. If I hoard material goods, others will have too little and I will never have enough. If I fight my way up the ladder of power, others will be defeated and I will never feel secure. If I get jealous of someone I love, I am likely to drive that person away. If I cling to the words I have written as if they were the last of their kind, the pool of new possibilities will surely go dry. We create scarcity by fearfully accepting it as law, and by competing with others for resources as if we were stranded on the Sahara at the last oasis. Authentic abundance does not lie in secured stockpiles of food or cash or influence or affection but in belonging to a community where we can give those goods to others who need them—and receive them from others when we are in need." We don't need to go to the extreme of Mother Teresa who worked until her death, asset-poor and quality-of-life rich. But there is a growing group of seniors who are grateful for having incorporated these principles into their lifestyles.

Wealth and health

I have said very little in regard to wealth as it relates to health. Research suggests that people who live below the poverty line have increased risk for illness and a shortened life span. Many of these studies use $50,000 per year as the top income level. But often the creation of "excessive" wealth requires such an enormous commitment of time and energy to the work-place that other areas of one's life become neglected. This is compounded by what I call the burden of ownership: the new time commitment we have in protecting our wealth from the IRS and others, managing the staffs of two or three homes, getting all the cars serviced, and keeping the power boat running.

Seventy-hour workweeks drain time and energy from all the five elements of PIERS and lead to poor health. Richard is a 45-year-old executive with a Silicon Valley high-tech firm who has been a friend of mine for many years. One day, while riding his bicycle in the San Jose hills, he noted chest pain which was fleeting but returned during the same ride and again the following week. A visit to a cardiologist was followed by a catherization revealing a tight stenosis of a coronary artery. During the next year, three angioplasties and coronary bypass surgery were required to treat his problem. Without a family history of heart disease, he began to inventory the events that created premature coronary artery disease. A 60-plus-hour work week on high-tech projects for years; decreased exercise; weight gain;

disrupted sleep; extensive travel; frequent and stressful presentations; less time for recreation, friends, and church activities; the death of his wife; and the subsequent responsibility for raising two teenage sons seemed to provide fertile soil for the development of heart disease. I asked Richard to take the PIERS review as he remembers his situation several years ago and he scored in the low 60s.

This heart disease made him a believer in the importance of the emotional, relational, and spiritual aspects of his life, and these were changed along with his diet and renewed exercise program. On the basis of published research, Richard, with his new health behaviors and some medications, can expect to see regression of the plaques that had formerly been blocking coronary blood flow.

An intense drive to create wealth and possess a financially-secure retirement package between age 40 and 60 may have unexpected and often undesirable consequences. This issue was brought home to me yesterday in a conversation with my friend, Jay. For an alumni function, he was in the process of calling classmates who had graduated from Princeton approximately 40 years ago. During the conversations, he asked over 40 alumni how they viewed their upcoming retirement. He noted that he was able to predict those who were going to retire completely from those who planned to work part-time for many years by the amount of energy transmitted in their voices. The high-energy responses were from those who planned to keep doing what was a very important part of their lives even though with reduced effort. The low-energy responses were from individuals such as CEOs who often were being forced into retirement and were not sure what was going to fill that void. They were aware that they would soon grow weary from a full menu of travel, gardening, and golf. These items which brought great pleasure as a diversion from work seemed much less attractive when seen as, "That's all that's left!"

Perhaps some of us need to spend less time with our financial planners and more time with "life" planning so that every day will be more intensely experienced and each tomorrow more warmly anticipated. For some, this may mean downsizing now so as to improve the balance and, hence, quality of life in the present. Imagine the scenario of a 40- to 45-hour workweek, evenings and weekends with family and friends, a modest lifestyle, and an enjoyable workplace experience while working until age

75. Remember we have had presidents in their 70s and leaders in their 90s. Your retirement package would need to be much less, as the gap between when you would retire from making money and your death would be significantly narrowed. In addition, your probability of having acquired an illness based on violation of the PIERS principles would be diminished.

Presidential stress

As I contemplate bringing this book to a close, I am looking at an editorial written in *Psychosomatic Medicine* by Dr. Joel Dimsdale entitled "President Lincoln: An Instance of Stress and Aging." In this article are included photographs of face masks of Abraham Lincoln that were made in 1860, just before he was nominated by the Republican National Convention, and the other in 1865, two months before his assassination. In those five years he was elected president, the Civil War had started, and its merits were contested by congress and his own cabinet. From the beginning, the war went badly at Bull Run, Shiloh, Fredericksburg, and Antietam, with casualties exceeding all the American deaths from the War of 1812, the Mexican-American War, and the Spanish-American War together. He had enemies on the battlefield, in Congress, and in his cabinet. His son died, and his wife was bringing in charlatans who were holding seances so she could speak to her dead son. These face masks reveal the lines and expressions that unremitting stress can produce. This accelerated aging produced by chronic stress is revealed not only in an individual's face but also in the internal organs that supply us with life.

The stressful events in our lives and our response to them will have a major impact on our aging. I was contemplating this fact this past summer as I was sitting in a car during a storm that was blowing over Ocean Shore Drive in Newport, Rhode Island. This was the first time Joan and I had been back to our home of 30 years ago, where I had served as a general medicine officer with the U.S. Navy. It was a bad northeaster with 20-foot-plus waves crashing over the rocks which guarded the cove where we were watching the storm. The clouds were thick as we were pelted with rain and gale-force winds. As we observed this scene in the comfort of our car I noticed a sea gull right above us, and I wondered why it was flying in this mess. It was then that I noticed that the gull was not flying but rather stationary with only an occasional flap of its wings to keep hovering above the cove. The gull appeared to be heading into the wind with an almost effortless motion. The gull didn't seem to be worried about being blown into outer space or dashed on the rocks below. When a new major gust of wind would hit the cove, there was a slight adjustment of wing position, and the gull continued effortlessly in the same spot. What appeared to take so little energy and was being done so gracefully depended on a fine-ly-tuned navigational system that produced almost automatic responses to the rigors of the storm. There was no evidence of worry, fear, or panic.

Most of us don't respond like this to the storms or even the breezes of life. It appears as if many of us are in need of fine-tuning or perhaps an overhaul of our navigational systems. Through reflection, exploration of our core values, and a renewed interest in the physical, intellectual, emotional, relational, and spiritual aspects of our lives, we can develop better balance. Hopefully we will then glide more gracefully though the hassles and storms to live the good, long life.

Bibliography

Introduction

Berkman L.F., Leo-Summers L., Horwitz R.I., Emotional support and survival after myocardial infarction. *Annals of Internal Medicine.* 1992; 117:1003–1009.

Cohen S., Tyrrell D.A., Smith A.P., Psychological stress and susceptibility to the common cold. *The New England Journal of Medicine.* 1991; 325:606–612.

Remen RN., *Kitchen Table Wisdom, Stories That Heal.* New York: Berkeley Publishing Group, 1996.

Tournier P., *Learn to Grow Old.* London: SCM Press Ltd., 1972.

Section One: Am I Aging Healthfully?

Chapter 1
Stress, Relationships, and Disease

Glaser R., Kiecolt-Glaser J.K., Bonneau R., Malarkey W.B., Hughes J., Stress-induced modulation of the immune response to recombinant hepatitis-B vaccine. *Psychosomatic Medicine.* 1992; 54:22–29.

Kiecolt-Glaser J.K., Glaser R., Cacioppo J.T., Malarkey W.B., Marital stress: Immunologic, neuroendocrine, and autonomic correlates. *Annals of the New York Academy of Sciences.* 1998; 840:656–663.

Kiecolt-Glaser J.K., Glaser R., Gravenstein S., Malarkey W.B., Sheridan J., Chronic stress alters the immune response to influenza virus vaccine in older adults. *Proceedings of the National Academy of Science, USA.* 1996; 93:3043–3047.

Kiecolt-Glaser J.K., Malarkey W.B., Chee M.A., Newton T., Cacioppo J.T., Mao H.Y., Glaser R., Negative behavior during marital conflict is associated with immunological down-regulation. *Psychosomatic Medicine.* 1993; 55:395–409.

Kiecolt-Glaser J.K., Malarkey W.B., MacCallum R.C., Cacioppo J.T., Glaser R., Longitudinal changes in marital satisfaction, cellular immunity, and health in newly-weds. *Psychosomatic Medicine.* 1999.

Kiecolt-Glaser J.K., Marucha P.T., Malarkey W.B., Mercado A.M., Glaser R., Slowing of wound healing by psychological stress. *The Lancet.* 1995; 346:1194–1196.

Malarkey W.B., Kiecolt-Glaser J.K., Pearl D., Glaser R., Hostile behavior during marital conflict alters pituitary and adrenal hormones. *Psychosomatic Medicine.* 1994; 56:41–51.

McTiernan A., Exercise and breast cancer—time to get moving? *The New England Journal of Medicine.* 1997; 336:1311–1312.

Spiegel D., Bloom J.R., Kraemer H.C., Gottheil E., Effect of psycho-social treatment on survival of patients with metastatic breast cancer. *The Lancet.* 1989; 2:888–891.

Chapter 2
Aging: Accelerated or Healthy?

Bueno J., Bodybuilding gets new contestants: Old guys muscle in. *The Wall Street Journal.* 1996; August 23:B1.

Campion E.W., The oldest old. *The New England Journal of Medicine.* 1994; 330:1819–1820.

Chopra D. *Ageless Body, Timeless Mind.* New York: Harmony Books, 1993.

Cooper B., *Tale of Tiny.* Runner's World. 1995; December: 80.

Delany A.L., Delany S.L., *Having Our Say: The Delany Sisters' First 100 Years.* New York: G.K. Hall & Company, 1994.

Delany, S.L., *On My Own at 107: Reflections On Life Without Bessie.* New York: HarperCollins, 1997.

Finch C.E., Tanzi R.E., *Genetics of Aging.* Science. 1997; 278:407–416.

Knight-Ridder Newspapers. Thurmond gears up again at 93. *The Columbus Dispatch.* 1996; February 25.

Newsweek. Tallying 21st-century America: Bigger, older, and more diverse. *Newsweek.* 1997; January 27:59.

People. The old man and the ski. *People.* 1997; February 24:71.

Rowe J.W., Kahn R.L., Human aging: Usual and successful. *Science.* 1987; 237:143–149.

Rubinstein E.A., The not so golden years. *Newsweek.* 1991; October 7:13.

Seaver A.M.H., My world now. *Newsweek.* 1994; June 27:11.

Weimers L. Still learning at 77, she gives new meaning to "late bloomer." *The Columbus Dispatch.* 1996; December 22.

Section Two: Nutrition and Health

CHAPTER 4

WHAT SHOULD I EAT?

Ames B.N., Shigenaga M.K., Hagen T.M., Oxidants, antioxidants, and the degenerative diseases of aging. *Proceedings of the National Academy of Science.* 1993; 90:7915–7922.

Bairati I., Meyer F., Fradet Y., Moore L., Dietary fat and advanced prostate cancer. *The Journal of Urology.* 1998; 159:1271–1275.

Flier J.S., Underhill L.H., Caloric intake and aging. *The New England Journal of Medicine.* 1997; 337:986–994.

Henderson D.K., Hardened fats, hardened arteries? *The New England Journal of Medicine* 1997; 337:1544–1545.

Hu F.B., Stampfer M.J., Manson J.E., Rimm E., Colditz G.A., Rosner B.A., Hennekens C.H., Willet W.C., Dietary fat intake and the risk of coronary heart disease in women. *The New England Journal of Medicine.* 1997; 337:1491–1499.

Kalmijn S., Feskens E.J., Launer L.J., Kromhout D., Polyunsaturated fatty acids, antioxidants, and cognitive function in very old men. *The American Journal of Epidemiology.* 1997; 145:33–41.

Osei, K., Metabolic consequences of the West African diaspora: Lessons from the thrifty gene. *Journal of Laboratory and Clinical Medicine.* 1999; 133:98–111.

CHAPTER 5

I'M OVERWEIGHT. SO WHAT?

Bouchard C., Tramblay A., Després J-P., Nadeau A., Lupien P.J., Thériault G., Dussault J., Moorjani S., Pinault S., Fournier G., The response to long-term overfeeding in identical twins. *The New England Journal of Medicine.* 1990; 322:1477–1482.

Bougnères P., Stunff C.L., Pecqueur C., Pinglier E., Adnot P., Ricquier D., In-vivo resistance of lipolysis to epinephrine. *Journal of Clinical Investigation.* 1997; 99:2568–2573.

Danforth, Jr. E., Sims E.A.H., Obesity and efforts to lose weight. *The New England Journal of Medicine.*1992; 327:1947–1948.

Eckel R.H., Obesity and heart disease: A statement for healthcare professionals from the Nutrition Committee, American Heart Association. *Circulation.* 1997; 96:3248–3250.

Enerback S., Jacobsson A., Simpson E.M., Guerra C., Yamashita H., Harper M.E., Kozak L.P., Mice lacking mitochondrial uncoupling protein are cold-sensitive but not obese. *Nature.* 1997; 387:90–97.

Fleury C., Neverova M., Collins S., Raimbault S., Champigny O., Levi-Meyrueis C., Bouillaud F., Seldin M.F., Surwit R.S., Ricquier D., Warden C.H., Gene turns the heat on fat. *Nature Genetics.* 1997; 15:269–272.

Huang Z., Hankinson S.E., Colditz G.A., Stampfer M.J., Hunter D.J., Manson J.E., Hennekens C.H., Rosner B., Speizer F.E., Willett W.C., Dual effects of weight and weight gain on breast cancer risk. *The Journal of the American Medical Association.* 1997; 278:1407–1411.

Huang Z., Willett W.C., Manson J.E., Rosner B., Stampfer M.J., Zpeizer F.E., Colditz G.A., Body weight, weight change, and risk for hypertension in women. *Annals of Internal Medicine.* 1998; 128:81–88.

Kassirer J.P., Angell M., Losing weight-an ill-fated New Year's resolution. *The New England Journal of Medicine.* 1998; 338:52–54.

Levine J.A., Eberhardt N.L., Jensen M.D., Role of nonexercise-activity-thermogenesis in resistance to fat gain in humans. *Science.* 1999; 283:184–185.

Lichtman S.W., Pisarska K., Berman E.R., Pestone M., Dowling H., Offenbacher E., Weisel H., Heshka S., Matthews D.E., Heymsfield S.B., Discrepancy between self-reported and actual caloric intake and exercise in obese subjects. *The New England Journal of Medicine.* 1992; 327:1893–1898.

Montague C.T., Farooqi I.S., Whitehead J.P., Soos M.A., Rau H., Wareham N.J., Sewter C.P., Digby J.E., Mohammed S.N., Hurst J.A., Cheetham C.H., Earley A.R., Barnett A.H., Prins J.B., O'Rahilly S., Congenital leptin deficiency is associated with severe early-onset obesity in humans. *Nature.* 1997; 387:903–908.

Ravussin E., Danforth Jr. E., Beyond sloth—physical activity and weight gain. *Science.* 1999; 283:184–185.

Ravussin E., Lillioja S., Knowler W.C., Christin L., Freymond D., Abbott W.G.H., Royce V., Howard B.V., Bogardus C., Reduced rate of energy expenditure as a risk factor for body-weight gain. *The New England Journal of Medicine.* 1988; 318:467–472.

Ravussin E., Pratley R.E., Maffei M., Wang H., Friedman J.M., Bennett P.H., Bogardus C., Relatively low plasma leptin concentrations precede weight gain in Pima Indians. *Nature Medicine.* 1997; 3:238–240.

Ristow M., Müller-Weiland D., Pfeiffer A., Krone W., Kahn C.R., Obesity associated with a mutation in a genetic regulator of adipocyte differentiation. *The New England Journal of Medicine.* 1998; 339:953–959.

Stevens J., Cai J., Pamuk E.R., Williamson D.F., Thun M.J., Wood J.L., The effect of age on the association between body-mass index and mortality. *The New England Journal of Medicine.* 1998; 338:1–7.

Stunkard A.J., Sørenson T.I.A., Hanis C., Teasdale T.W., Chakraborty R., Schull W.J., Schulsinger F., An adoption study of human obesity. *The New England Journal of Medicine.* 1986; 314:193–198.

CHAPTER 6

I'M READY TO LOSE SOME WEIGHT

Chase M., Getting a bit thick in the middle? It's not hopeless after all. *The Wall Street Journal.* 1997; June 16:B1.

Connolly H.M., Crary J.L., McGoon M.D., Hensrud D.D., Edwards B.S., Edwards W.D., Schaff H.V., Valvular heart disease associated with fenfluramine-phentermine. *The New England Journal of Medicine*. 1997; 337:581–588.

Hecht K., Oh, come on fatties! *Newsweek*. 1990; September 3:8.

Khan M.A., Herzog C.A., St. Peter J.N., Hartley G.G., Madlon-Kay R., Dick C.D., Asinger R.W., Vessey J.T., The prevalence of cardiac valvular insufficiency assessed by transthoracic echocardiography in obese patients treated with appetite-suppressant drugs. *The New England Journal of Medicine*. 1998; 339:713–718.

National Task Force on the Prevention and Treatment of Obesity. Long-term pharmacotherapy in the management of obesity. *The Journal of the American Medical Association*. 1996; 276:1907–1915.

Nonas C.A., Aronoff N.J., Pi-Sunyer F.X., Dietary strategies for weight loss. *Endocrine Practice*. 1995; 1:280–286.

Parsi A.F., Diet-Drug Debacle. *Annals of Internal Medicine*. 1998; 129:903–905.

Tanofsky M.B., Wilfley D.E., Spurrell E.B., Welch R., Brownell K.D., Comparison of men and women with binge eating disorder. *International Journal of Eating Disorders*. 1997; 21:49–54.

CHAPTER 7

SHOULD I USE NUTRITIONAL SUPPLEMENTS?

Alpha-Tocopherol, Beta-Carotene Cancer Prevention Study Group. The effect of Vitamin E and beta-carotene on the incidence of lung cancer and other cancers in male smokers. *The New England Journal of Medicine*. 1994; 330:1029–1035.

AuGraham I.M., Daly L.E., Refsum H.M., et al., Plasma homocysteine as a risk factor for vascular disease. *The Journal of the American Medical Association*. 1997; 277:1775–1781.

Benton D., Haller J., Fordy J., Vitamin supplementation for one year improves mood. *Neuropsychology*. 1995; 32:98–105.

Blusztajn J.K., Choline: A vital amine. *Science*. 1998; 182:794–795.

Brown J.E., Jacobs Jr. D.R., Hartman T.J., Barosso G.M., Stang J.S., Gross M.D., Zeuske M.A., Predictors of red cell folate level in women attempting pregnancy. *The Journal of the American Medical Association*. 1997; 277:548–552.

Chandra R.K., Effect of vitamin and trace-element supplementation on immune responses and infection in elderly subjects. *The Lancet*. 1992; 340:1124–1127.

Christen S., Woodall A.A., Shigenaga M.K., Southwell-Keely P.T., Duncan M.W., Ames B.N., Gamma-tocopherol traps mutagenic electrophiles such as NO(X) and complements alpha-tocopherol: Physiological implications. Proceedings of the National Academy of Sciences. 1997; 94:3217–3222.

Colditz G.A., Selenium and cancer prevention. *The Journal of the American Medical Association*. 1996; 276:1984–1985.

Colston K.W., Perks C.M., Xie S.P., Holly J.M., Growth inhibition of both MCF-7 and Hs578T human breast cancer cell lines by Vitamin D analogues is associated with increased expression of insulin-like growth factor binding protein-3. *Journal of Molecular Endocrinology*. 1998. 20:157–162.

Dawson-Hughes B., Harris S.S., Krall E.A., Dallal G.E., Effect of calcium and Vitamin D supplementation on bone density in men and women sixty-five years of age or older. *The New England Journal of Medicine*. 1997; 337:670–676.

Diaz M.N., Frei B., Vita J.A., Keany J.F., Antioxidants and atherosclerotic heart disease. *The New England Journal of Medicine*. 1997; 337:408–416.

Epstin F.H., Homocysteine and atherothrombosis. *The New England Journal of Medicine.* 1998; 338:1042–1050.

Fata F.T., Herzlich B.C., Schiffman G., Ast A.L., Impaired antibody responses to pneumococcal polysaccharide in elderly patients with low serum Vitamin B12 levels. *Annals of Internal Medicine.* 1996; 124:299–304.

Ford E.S., Will J.C., Bowman B.A., Narayan K.M., Diabetes mellitus and serum carotenoids: Findings from the Third National Health and Nutrition Examination Survey. *The American Journal of Epidemiology.* 1999; 149:168–176.

Gale C.R., Martyn C.N., Winter P.D., Cooper C., Vitamin C and risk of death from stroke and coronary heart disease in cohort of elderly people. *British Medical Journal.* 1995; 310:1563–1566.

Giovannucci E., Stampfer M.J., Colditz G.A., Hunter D.J., Ruchs C., Rosner B.A., Speizer F.E., Willett W.C., Multivitamin use, folate, and colon cancer in women in the nurses' health study. *Annals of Internal Medicine.* 1998; 129:517–524.

Heinonen O.P., Albanes D., Virtamo J., et al., Prostate cancer and supplementation with alpha-tocopherol and beta-carotene: Incidence and mortality in a controlled trial. *Journal of the National Cancer Institute.* 1998, 90:440–446.

Hu G., Zhang X., Chen J., Peto R., Campbell T.C., Cassano P.A., Dietary Vitamin C intake and lung function in rural China. *The American Journal of Epidemiology.* 1998; 148:594–599.

Johnston C.S., Thompson L.L., Vitamin C status of an outpatient population. *Journal of the American College of Nutrition.* 1998; 17:366–370.

Kawano Y., Matsuoka H., Takishita S., Omae T., Effects of magnesium supplementation in hypertensive patients: Assessment by office, home, and ambulatory blood pressures. *Hypertension.* 1998; 32:260–265.

Keski-Oja J., Vitamin D3 derivatives (deltanoids) in the treatment of tumor cell invasion. *Journal of Laboratory and Clinical Medicine.* 1999; 133:95–97.

Lehr H-A, Weyrich A.S., Saetzler R.K., Jurek A., Arfors K.E., Zimmerman G.A., Prescott S.M., McIntyre T.M., Vitamin C blocks inflammatory platelet-activating factor mimetics created by cigarette smoking. *Journal of Clinical Investigation.* 1997; 99:2358–2364.

Looker A.C., Dallman P.R., Carroll M.D., Gunter E.W., Johnson C.L., Prevalence of iron deficiency in the United States. *The Journal of the American Medical Association.* 1997; 277:973–976.

Malinow M.R., Duell P.B., Hess D.L., Anderson P.H., Kruger W.D., Phillipson B.E., Gluckman R.A., Block P.C., Upson B.M., Reduction of plasma homocysteine levels by breakfast cereal fortified with folic acid in patients with coronary heart disease. *The New England Journal of Medicine.* 1998; 338:1009–1015.

Mark S.D., Wang W., Fraumeni Jr. J.F., Li J.Y., Taylor P.R., Wang G.Q., Dawsey S.M., Li B., Blot W.J., Do nutritional supplements lower the risk of stroke or hypertension? *Epidemiology.* 1998; 9:9–15.

McAlindon T., Felson D.T., Nutrition: Risk factors for osteoarthritis. *Annals of the Rheumatic Diseases.* 1997; 56:397–402.

Meydani S.N., Meydani M., Blumberg J.B., Leka L.S., Siber G., Loszewski R., Thompson C., Pedrosa M.C., Diamond R.D., Stollar B.D., Vitamin E supplementation and in-vivo immune response in healthy elderly subjects. A randomized controlled trial. *The Journal of the American Medical Association.* 1997; 277:1380–1386.

Mills J.L., Simpson J.L., Cunningham G.C., Conley M.R., Rhoads G.G., Vitamin A and birth defects. *American Journal of Obstetrics and Gynecology.* 1997; 176:31–36.

Nygård O., Nordrehaug J.E., Refsum H., Ueland P.M., Farstad M., Vollset S.E., Plasma homocysteine levels and mortality in patients with coronary artery disease. *The New England Journal of Medicine.* 1997; 337:230–236.

Orr W.C., Sohal R.S., Extension of lifespan by overexpression of superoxide dismutase and catalase in *drosophila melanogaster. Science.* 1994. 263:1128–1130.

Perrig W.J., Perrig P., Stahelin H.B., The relation between antioxidants and memory performance in the old and very old. *Journal of the American Geriatrics Society.* 1997; 45:718–724.

Prince R.L., Diet and the prevention of osteoporotic fractures. *The New England Journal of Medicine.* 1997; 337:701–702.

Pyapali G.K., Turner D.A., Williams C.L., Meck W.H., Swartzwelder H.S., Prenatal dietary choline supplementation decreases the threshold for induction of long-term potentiation in young adult rats. *Neurophysiology.* 1998, 79: 1790–1796.

Rimm E.B., Stampfer M.J., Ascherio A., Giovannucci E., Golditz G.A., Willett W.C., Vitamin E consumption and the risk of coronary heart disease in men. *The New England Journal of Medicine.* 1993; 328:1450–1456.

Rothman K.J., Moore L.L., Singer M.R., Nguyen U-S.D.T., Mannino S., Milunsky A., Teratogenicity of high Vitamin A intake. *The New England Journal of Medicine.* 1995; 333:1369–1373.

Salonen J.T., Nyyssönen K., Tuomainen T-P., Mäenpää P.H., Korpela H., Kaplan G.A., Lynch J., Helmrich S.P., Salonen R., Increased risk of non-insulin dependent diabetes mellitus at low plasma Vitamin E concentrations: A four year follow up study in men. *British Medical Journal.* 1995; 311:1124–1127.

Sano M., Ernesto C., Thomas R.G., Klauber M.R., Schafer K., Grundman M., Woodbury P., Growdon J., Cotman C.W., Pfeiffer E., Schnedier L.S., Thal L.J., A controlled trial of selegiline, alpha-tocopherol, or both, as treatment for Alzheimer's disease. *The New England Journal of Medicine.* 1997; 336:1216–1222.

Sempos C.T., Looker A.C., Gillum R.F., Makuc D.M., Body iron stores and the risk of coronary heart disease. *The New England Journal of Medicine.* 1994; 330:1119–1124.

Simon J.A., Hudes E.S., Serum ascorbic acid and other correlates of gallbladder disease among U.S. adults. *American Journal of Public Health.* 1998; 88:1208–1212.

Slifman N.R., Obermeyer W.R., Aloi B.K., Musser S.M., Correll W.A., Cichowicz S.M., Betz J.M., Love L.A,. Contamination of botanical dietary supplements by digitalis lanata. *The New England Journal of Medicine.* 1998; 339:806–811.

Stampfer M.J., Hennekens C.H., Manson J.E., Colditz G.A., Rosner B., Willett W.C., Vitamin E consumption and the risk of coronary disease in women. *The New England Journal of Medicine.* 1993; 328:1444–1449.

Tang A.M., Graham N.M., Semba R.D., Saah A.J., Association between serum Vitamin A and E levels and HIV-1 disease progression. *AIDS.* 1997; 11:613–620.

Westerveld G.J., Dekker I., Voss H.P., Bast A., Scheeren R.A., Antioxidant levels in the nasal mucosa of patients with chronic sinusitis and healthy controls. *Archives of Otolaryngology.* 1997; 123:201–204.

Wood R.J., Zheng J.J., High dietary calcium intakes reduce zinc absorption and balance in humans. *American Journal of Clinical Nutrition.* 1997; 65:1803–1809.

Zhang H.M., Wakisaka N., Maeda O., Yamamoto T., Vitamin C inhibits the growth of a bacterial risk factor for gastric carcinoma: *Helicobacter pylori. Cancer.* 1997; 80:1897–1903.

Section Three: Your Health and Exercise

CHAPTER 9
I DON'T HAVE TIME

Barinaga M., How much pain for cardiac gain? *Science.* 1997; 276:1324–1327.

Buchner D.M., Physical activity and quality of life in older adults. *The Journal of the American Medical Association.* 1997; 277:64–66.

Cerhan J.R., Chiu B.C-H., Wallace R.B., Lemke J.H., Lynch C.F., Torner J.C., Rubenstein L.M., Physical activity, physical function, and the risk of breast cancer in a prospective study among elderly women. *Journal of Gerontology: Medical Sciences.* 1998; 53A:M251–M256.

Cohen H.A., Newman I., Nahum H., Blocking effect of Vitamin C in exercise-induced asthma. *Archives of Pediatrics and Adolescent Medicine.* 1997; 151:367–370.

Ettinger W.H., Burns R., Messier S.T., Applegate W., Rejeski W.J., Morgan T., Shumaker S., Berry M.J., O'Toole M., Monu J., Craven T., A randomized trial comparing aerobic exercise and resistance exercise with a health education program in older adults with knee osteoarthritis. *The Journal of the American Medical Association.* 1997; 277:25–31.

Fiatarone M.A., O'Neill E.F., Ryan N.D., Clements K.M., Solares G.R., Nelson M.E., Roberts S.B., Kehayias J.J., Lipsitz L.A., Evans W.J., Exercise training and nutritional supplementation for physical frailty in very elderly people. *The New England Journal of Medicine.* 1994; 330:1769–1775.

Fulcher K.Y., White P.D., Randomised controlled trial of graded exercise in patients with the chronic fatigue syndrome. *British Medical Journal.* 1997; 314:1647–1652.

Hakim A.A., Petrovitch H., Burchfiel C.M., Ross W., Rodriguez B.L., White L.R., Yano K., Curb J.D., Abbott R.D., Effects of walking on mortality among nonsmoking retired men. *The New England Journal of Medicine.* 1998; 338:94–99.

Kujala U.M., Kaprio J., Sarna S., Koskenvuo M., Relationship of leisure-time physical activity and mortality: The Finnish twin cohort. *The Journal of the American Medical Association.* 1998; 279:440–444.

Leitamann M.F., Giovannucci E.L., Rimm E.B., Stampfer M.J., Spiegelman D., Wing A.L., Willett W.C., The relation of physical activity to risk for symptomatic gallstone disease in men. *Annals of Internal Medicine.* 1998; 128:417–425.

Pereira J., This is a huge relief for those who opt to just up and run. *The Wall Street Journal.* 1997; April 28:A1.

Sherrill D.L., Kotchou K., Quan S.F., Association of physical activity and human sleep disorders. *Archives of Internal Medicine.* 1998; 158:1894–1898.

Slemenda C., Brandt K.D., Heilman D.K., Mazzuca S., Braunstein E.M., Katz B.P., Wolinsky F.D., Quadriceps weakness and osteoarthritis of the knee. *Annals of Internal Medicine.* 1997; 127:97–104.

Strauss R.H., Lanese R.R., Malarkey W.B., Weight loss in amateur wrestlers and its effect on serum testosterone levels. *The Journal of the American Medical Association.* 1985; 254:3337–3338.

Thune I., Brenn T., Lund E., Gaard M., Physical activity and the risk of breast cancer. *The New England Journal of Medicine.* 1997; 336:1269–1275.

Women's Sports Foundation. Work & Play: The Balancing Act II (*A Working Woman's Guide to Health & Fitness*). 1997.

CHAPTER 10
YOUR PERSONAL EXERCISE PRESCRIPTION

Kushi L.H., Fee R.M., Folsom A.R., Mink P.J., Anderson K.E., Sellers T.A., Physical activity and mortality in postmenopausal women. *The Journal of the American Medical Association.* 1997; 277:1287–1292.

CHAPTER 11
MOTIVATION AND EXERCISE

Doheny K., The inspiration for perspiration. *The Columbus Dispatch.* November 4, 1996.
McGinnis J.M., The public health burden of a sedentary lifestyle. *Medicine and Science in Sports and Exercise.* 1992; 24:S196–S200.

Section Four: Stress, Emotions, and Health

CHAPTER 13
EVERYDAY HASSLES AND HEALTH

Bishop J.E., Secrets of the heart: Can it be broken? *The Wall Street Journal.* 1994; February 14:B1.
Brett K.M., Strogatz D.S., Savitz D.A., Employment, job strain, and preterm delivery among women in North Carolina. *American Journal of Public Health.* 1997; 87:199–204.
Cook P.J., Lip G.Y.H., Davies P., Beevers D.G., Wise R., Honeybourne D., *Chlamydia pneumoniae* antibodies in severe essential hypertension. *Hypertension.* 1998; 31:589–594.
Epstein S.E., Speir E., Zhou Y.F., Guetta E., Leon M., Finkel T., The role of infection in restenosis and atherosclerosis: Focus on cytomegalovirus. *The Lancet.* 1996; 348:s13–s17.
Everson S.A., Lynch J.W., Chesney M.A., Kaplan G.A., Goldberg D.E., Shade S.B., Cohen D., Salonen R., Salonen J.T., Interaction of workplace demands and cardiovascular reactivity in progression of carotid atherosclerosis: Population-based study. *British Medical Journal.* 1997; 314:553–557.
Gelman D., Friday C., Overstressed by success. *Newsweek.* 1991; June 3:56.
Grau A.J., Buggle F., Becher H., Zimmermann E., Spiel M., Fent T., Maiwald M., Werle E., Zorn M., Hengel H., Hacke W., Recent bacterial and viral infection is a risk factor for cerebrovascular ischemia: Clinical and biochemical studies. *Neurology.* 1998; 50:196–203.
Grau A.J., Buggle F., Ziegler C., Schwarz W., Meuser J., Tasman A.J., Buhler A., Benesch C., Becher H., Hacke W., Association between acute cerebrovascular ischemia and chronic and recurrent infection. *Stroke.* 1997; 28:1724–1729.
Gullette E.C., Blumenthal J.A., Babyak M., Jiang W., Waugh R.A., Frid D.J., O'Connor C.M., Morris J.J., Krantz D.S., Effects of mental stress on myocardial ischemia during daily life. *The Journal of the American Medical Association.* 1997; 277:1521–1526.
Gupta S., Leatham E.W., Carrington D., Mendall M.A., Kaski J.C., Camm A.J., Elevated *chlamydia pneumoniae* antibodies, cardiovascular events, and azithromycin in male survivors of myocardial infarction. *Circulation.* 1997; 96:404–407.
Johnson J.V., Stewart W., Hall E.M., Fredlund P., Theorell T., Long-term psychosocial work environment and cardiovascular mortality among Swedish men. *American Journal of Public Health.* 1996; 86:324–331.

Juvonen J., Juvonen T., Laurila A., Kuusisto J., Alarakkola E., Särkioja T., Bodian C.A., Kairaluoma M.I., Saikku P., Can degenerative aortic valve stenosis be related to persistent chlamydia pneumoniae infection? *Annals of Internal Medicine.* 1998; 128:741–744.

Kario K., Matsuo T., Kobayashi H., Yamamoto K., Shimada K., Population-based analysis of the effect of the Northridge Earthquake on cardiac death in Los Angeles County, California. *Journal of the American College of Cardiology.* 1997; 29:926–933.

Liese B., Mundt K.A., Dell L.D., Nagy L., Demure B., Medical insurance claims associated with international business travel. *Occupational and Environmental Medicine.* 1997; 54:499–503.

Luecken L.J., Suarez E.C., Kuhn C.M., Barefoot J.C., Blumenthal J.A., Siegler I.C., Williams R.B., Stress in employed women: Impact of marital status and children at home on neurohormone output and home strain. *Psychosomatic Medicine.* 1997; 59:352–359.

Lupien S.J., de Leon M., de Santi S., Convit A., Tarshish C., Nair N.P.V., Thakur M., McEwen B.S., Haugr R.L., Meaney M.J., Cortisol levels during human aging predict hippocampal atrophy and memory deficits. *Nature Neuroscience.* 1998; 1:69–73.

Lupien S.J., Gaudreau S., Tchiteya B.M., Maheu F., Sharma S., Nair N.P.V., Hauger F.L., McEwen B.S., Meaney M.J., Stress-induced declarative memory impairment in healthy elderly subjects: Relationship to cortisol reactivity. *Journal of Clinical Endocrinology and Metabolism.* 1997; 82:2070–2075.

Lynch J., Krause N., Kaplan G.A., Salonen R., Salonen J.T., Workplace demands, economic reward, and progression of carotid atherosclerosis. *Circulation.* 1997; 96:302–307.

Manuck S.B., Marsland A.L., Kaplan J.R., Williams J.K., The pathogenicity of behavior and its neuroendocrine mediation: An example from coronary artery disease. *Psychosomatic Medicine.* 1995; 57:275–283.

Meier C.R., Derby L.E., Jick S.S., Vasilakis C., Jick H., Antibiotics and risk of subsequent first-time acute myocardial infarction. *The Journal of the American Medical Association.* 1999; 281:461–462.

Pedersen D., A lonely death in Texas. *Newsweek.* 1997; March 31:53–54.

Rettig M.B., Ma H.J., Vescio R.A., Põld M., Schiller G., Belson D., Savage A., Nishikubo C., Wu C., Fraser J., Sad J.W., Berenson J.R., Kaposi's sarcoma-associated herpesvirus infection of bone marrow dendritic cells from multiple myeloma patients. *Science.* 1997; 276:1851–1854.

Sapolsky R.M., Why stress is bad for your brain. *Science.* 1996; 273:749–750.

Seeman T.E., McEwen B.S., Singer B.H., Albert M.S., Rowe J.W., Increase in urinary cortisol excretion and memory declines: MacArthur studies of successful aging. *Journal of Clinical Endocrinology and Metabolism.* 1997; 82:2458–2465.

Shellenbarger S., Work & family: Some readers saw the burnout coming, and many empathized. *The Wall Street Journal.* 1997; July 9:B1.

Syme S.L., Balfour J.L., Explaining inequalities in coronary heart disease. *The Lancet.* 1997; 350:231–232.

Thomas E., Barry J., Vistica G.L., A matter of honor. *Newsweek.* 1996; May 27:24–29.

Vahtera J., Kivimaki M., Pentti J., Effect of organisational downsizing on health of employees. *The Lancet.* 1997; 350:1124–1128.

Williams R.B., Barefoot J.C., Blumenthal J.A., Helms M.J., Luecken L., Pieper C.F., Siegler I.C., Suarez E.C., Psychosocial correlates of job strain in a sample of working women. *Archives of General Psychiatry.* 1997; 54:543–548.

Yeung A.C., Vekshtein V.I., Krantz D.S., Vita J.A., Ryan T.J., Ganz P., Selwyn A.P., The effect of atherosclerosis on the vasomotor response of coronary arteries to mental stress. *The New England Journal of Medicine.* 1991; 325:1551–1556.

CHAPTER 14
ANGER

Adler J., "Road rage": We're driven to destruction. *Newsweek.* 1997; June 2:70.

Anderson G., *The 22 Non-Negotiable Laws of Wellness: Feel, Think, and Live Better Than You Ever Thought Possible.* New York: HarperCollins Publishers, 1995.

Associated Press. "Road rage" blamed for carnage. *The Columbus Dispatch.* 1997; July 19.

Bear Heart, Larkin M., *The Wind Is My Mother.* New York: Clarkson N. Potter, 1996.

Blumenthal J.A., Burg M.M., Barefoot J., Williams R.B., Haney T., Zimet G., Social support, Type-A behavior, and coronary artery disease. *Psychosomatic Medicine.* 1987; 49:331–40.

Covey S., *The 7 Habits of Highly Effective People : Powerful Lessons In Personal Change.* New York: Fireside, 1990.

DeBeauport E., *The Three Faces of Mind.* Wheaton, IL: Quest Books, 1996.

Everson S.A., Kauhanen J., Kaplan G.A., Goldberg D.E., Julkunen J., Tuomilehto J., Salonen J.T., Hostility and increased risk of mortality and acute myocardial infarction: The mediating role of behavioral risk factors. *The American Journal of Epidemiology.* 1997; 146:142–152.

Frankl V., *Man's Search for Meaning.* New York: Touchstone, 1984.

Goleman D., *Emotional Intelligence.* New York: Bantam, 1997.

Ironson G., Taylor C.B., Boltwood M., Bartzokis T., Dennis C., Chesney M., Spitzer S., Segall G.M., Effects of anger on left ventricular ejection fraction in coronary artery disease. *American Journal of Cardiology.* 1992; 70:281–285.

Kiecolt-Glaser J.K., Glaser R., Cacioppo J.T., MacCallum R.C., Snydersmith M., Kim C., Malarkey W.B., Marital conflict in older adults: Endocrinological and immunological correlates. *Psychosomatic Medicine.* 1997; 59:339–349.

Kiecolt-Glaser J.K., Malarkey W.B., Chee M.A., Newton T., Cacioppo J.T., Mao H.Y., Glaser R., Negative behavior during marital conflict is associated with immunological down-regulation. *Psychosomatic Medicine.* 1993; 55:395–409.

Kiecolt-Glaser J.K., Newton T., Cacioppo J.T., MacCallum R.C., Glaser R., Malarkey W.B., Marital conflict and endocrine function: Are men really more physiologically affected than women? *Journal of Consulting Clinical Psychology.* 1996. 64:324–332.

Malarkey W.B., Kiecolt-Glaser J.K., Pearl D., Glaser R., Hostile behavior during marital conflict alters pituitary and adrenal hormones. *Psychosomatic Medicine.* 1994; 56:41–51.

Stoney C.M., Matthews K.A., McDonald R.H., Johnson C.A., Sex differences in lipid, lipoprotein, cardiovascular, and neuroendocrine responses to acute stress. *Psychophysiology.* 1988; 25:645–655.

Temoshok L., Personality, coping style, emotion, and cancer: Towards an integrative model. *Cancer Surveys.* 1987; 6:545–567.

Testa K., Father in landmark right-to-die case commits suicide. *The Columbus Dispatch.* 1996; August 20:A1.

Thomas S., Jefferson C,. *Use Your Anger.* New York: Pocket Books, 1996.

Williams R.B., Hostility and the Heart. *In Mind Body Medicine* (Goleman D., Gurin J., editors) Yonkers, NY: Consumer Reports Books, 1993.

CHAPTER 15
OPTIMISM AND HEALTH

Associated Press. Study: Good outlook keeps patients' hearts ticking. *The Columbus Dispatch.* 1994; April16:7A.

DeBeauport E., *The Three Faces of Mind.* Quest Books: Wheaton, IL, 1996.

Everson S.A., Kaplan G.A., Goldberg D.E., Salonen R., Salonen J.T., Hopelessness and four year progression of carotid atherosclerosis. The Kuopio Ischemic Heart Disease Risk Factor Study. *Arteriosclerosis Thrombosis and Vascular Biology.* 1997; 17:1490–1495.

Kubzansky L.D., Kawachi I., Spiro A., Weiss S.T., Vokonas P.S., Sparrow D., Is worrying bad for your heart? A prospective study of worry and coronary heart disease in the normative aging study. *Circulation.* 1997; 95:818–824.

Milbank D., Here's good news! And if we're right you won't read it. *The Wall Street Journal.* 1997; March 31:1A.

Mother Theresa, *A Simple Path.* New York: Random House, 1995.

Peale N.V., *The Power of Positive Thinking.* New York: Ballantine, 1996.

Peterson C., Seligman M.E.P., Yurko K.H., Martin L.R., Friedman H.S., Catastrophizing and untimely death. *Psychological Science.* 1998; 9:127–130.

Swan W., *How To Be a Better Me.* Bisbee, AZ: Swan Enterprises, 1991.

Temoshok L.R., We need to study the psychosocial impact of medical interventions. *Advances: The Journal of Mind-Body Health.* 1997; 13:51–53.

Section Five: Relationships and Health

CHAPTER 16
CAN MY RELATIONSHIPS INFLUENCE MY LONGEVITY?

Albers L.H., Johnson D.E., Hostetter M.K., Iverson S., Miller L.C., Health of children adopted from the former Soviet Union and Eastern Europe. Comparison with preadoptive medical records. *The Journal of the American Medical Association.* 1997; 278:922–924.

Bartrop R.W., Luckhurst E., Lazarus L., Kiloh L.G., Penny R., Depressed lymphocyte function after bereavement. *The Lancet.* 1977; 1:834–836.

Belsky J., Hsieh K.H., Crnic K., Mothering, fathering, and infant negativity as antecedents of boys' externalizing problems and inhibition at age three years: Differential susceptibility to rearing experience? *Development and Psychopathology.* 1998; 10:301–319.

Berkman L., The role of social relations in health promotion. *Psychosomatic Medicine.* 1995; 57:245–254.

Berkman L.F., Leo-Summers L., Horwitz R.I., Emotional support and survival after myocardial infarction. *Annals of Internal Medicine.* 1992; 117:1003–1009.

Cerhan J.R., Wallace R.B., Change in social ties and subsequent mortality in rural elders. *Epidemiology.* 1997; 8:475–481.

Dimsdale J.E., Social support—A lifeline in stormy times. *Psychosomatic Medicine.* 1995; 57:1–2.

Fawzy F.I., Fawzy N.W., Hyun C.S., Elashoff R., Guthrie D., Fahey J.L., Morton D.L., Malignant melanoma: Effects of an early structured psychiatric intervention, coping, and affective state on recurrence and survival six years later. *Archives of General Psychiatry.* 1993; 50:681–689.

Francis D., Diorio J., LaPlante P., Weaver S.H., Seckl J.R., Meaney M.J., The role of early environmental events in regulating neuroendocrine development. *Annals of the New York Academy of Science.* 1996; 794:136–152.

Gatchel R.J., Schaeffer M.A., Baum A., A psychophysiological field study of stress at Three Mile Island. *Psychophysiology.* 1985; 22:175–181.

Hebert E., Schwebel S., Pain led to death wish. *The Columbus Dispatch.* 1996; June 22:1A

Hymowitz C., Narisetti R., A promising career comes to a tragic end, and a city asks why. *The Wall Street Journal.* 1997; May 9:A1.

Krumholz H.M., Butler J., Miller J., Vaccarino V., Williams C.S., de Leon C.F., Seeman T.E., Kasl S.V., Berkman L.F., Prognostic importance of emotional support for elderly patients hospitalized with heart failure. *Circulation.* 1998; 97:958–964.

Liu D., Diorio J., Tannenbaum B., Caldji C., Francis D., Freedman A., Sharma S., Pearson D., Plotsky P.M., Meaney M.J., Maternal care, hippocampal glucocorticoid receptors, and hypothalamic-pituitary-adrenal responses to stress. *Science.* 1997; 277:1659–1662.

Nouwen H.J.M., *The Wounded Healer.* Image Books: New York, 1979.

Oxman T.E., Freeman D.H., Manheimer E.D., Lack of social participation or religious strength and comfort as risk factors for death after cardiac surgery in the elderly. *Psychosomatic Medicine.* 1995; 57:5–15.

Penninx B.W., van Tilburg T., Kriegsman D.M., Deeg D.J., Boeke A.J., van Eijk J.T., Effects of social support and personal coping resources on mortality in older age: The Longitudinal Aging Study. Amsterdam. *The American Journal of Epidemiology.* 1997; 146:510–519.

Schaeffer M.A., Baum A., Adrenal cortical response to stress at Three Mile Island. *Psychosomatic Medicine.* 1984; 46:227–237.

Seligmann J., For longer life, take a wife. *Newsweek.* 1990; November 5:73.

Spiegel D., Bloom J.R., Kraemer H.C., Gottheil E., Effect of psychosocial treatment on survival of patients with metastatic breast cancer. *The Lancet.* 1989; 8668:888–891.

Van Boven S., Giving infants a helping hand. *Newsweek Special Issue.* 1997, Spring-Summer:45.

Yasuda N., Zimmerman S.I., Hawkes W., Fredman L., Hebel J.R., Magaziner J., Relation of social network characteristics to five year mortality among young-old versus old-old white women in an urban community. *The American Journal of Epidemiology.* 1997; 145:516–523.

CHAPTER 17

Our Key Relationships Are in Trouble: Health Implications

Bacorn C.N., Dear dads: Save your sons. *Newsweek.* 1992; December 7:13.

Bauer G.L., Forbes S., Hudson D.W., DeWine M., Horn W.F., Rush A., Buckley C., Arkes H., McCartney B., Mohammed I.W.D., Why we celebrate Father's Day. *The Wall Street Journal.* 1997; June 13:A18.

Blankenhorn D., The American family is in big trouble. *Bottom Line/Personal.* 1991; July 15:7.

Russek L.G., Schwartz G.E., Perceptions of parental caring predict health status in midlife: A thirty-five year follow-up of the Harvard mastery of stress study. *Psychosomatic Medicine.* 1997; 59:144–149.

Simpkins T., Growing up is hard to do. *Newsweek.* 1993; June 21:12.

CHAPTER 18
BUILDING HEALTHY RELATIONSHIPS

Buscaglia L., *Loving Each Other.* SLACK Incorporated: Thorofare, NJ, 1984.

Covey S., *The 7 Habits of Highly Effective People: Powerful Lessons In Personal Change.* New York: Fireside, 1990.

Crossen C., The crucial question for these noisy times may just be: "Huh?" *The Wall Street Journal.* 1997; July 10: A1.

Kiecolt-Glaser J.K., Newton T., Cacioppo J.T., MacCallum R.C., Glaser R., Malarkey W.B., Marital conflict and endocrine function: Are men really more physiologically affected than women? *Journal of Consulting Clinical Psychology.* 1996; 64:324–332.

Larson D.B., Swyers J.P., McCullough M.E., Scientific research on spirituality and health: A consensus report. *National Institute for Healthcare Research.* 1998.

McKinney M., Return to the future. *Newsweek.* 1995; March 6:21.

Remen, R.N., *Kitchen Table Wisdom; Stories That Heal.* New York: Riverhead Books, 1996.

Rosen R., Divorce, masculine style. *The Columbus Dispatch.* 1997; October 24:1H.

Skuse D.H., James R.S., Bishop D.V., Coppin B., Dalton P., Aamodt-Leeper G., Bacarese-Hamilton M., Creswell C., McGurk R., Jacobs P.A., Evidence from Turner's syndrome of an imprinted x-linked locus affecting cognitive function. *Nature.* 1997; 387:705–708.

Smalley G., *Making Love Last Forever.* Dallas: Word, 1996.

Smeltzer N.J., Couple celebrates seven decades of love. *The Columbus Dispatch.* 1997; March 7.

Wallerstein J.S., Blakeslee S., *The Good Marriage.* New York: Warner Books, 1996.

Section Six: Search for Harmony

CHAPTER 19
SELF-CARE

Zimmerman M.D., Appadurai K., Scott J.G., Jellett L.B., Garlick F.H., Survival. *Annals of Internal Medicine.* 1997; 127:405–408.

CHAPTER 20
MEDICAL-CARE OPTIONS

Davidoff F. Time. *Annals of Internal Medicine.* 1998; 127:483-485

DeShazo R.D., Kemp S.F., Allergic reactions to drugs and biologic agents. *The Journal of the American Medical Association.* 1997; 278:1895–1906.

Eisenberg D.M., Davis R.B., Ettner S.L., Appel S., Wilkey S., Van Rompay M., Kessler R.C., Trends in alternative medicine use in the United States, 1990–1997: Results of a follow-up national survey. *Journal of the American Medical Association.* 1998; 280:1569–1575.

Eisenberg D.M., Advising patients who seek alternative medical therapies. *Annals of Internal Medicine.* 1997; 127:61–74.

Elder N.C., Gillcrist A., Minz R., Use of alternative health care by family practice patients. *Archives of Family Medicine.* 1997; 6:181–184.

Gordon J.S., *Manifesto for a New Medicine.* New York: Addison-Wesley, 1996.

Pennisi E., Newfound gene holds key to cell's cholesterol traffic. *Science.* 1997; 277:180–181.

Shapiro D., Hui K.K., Oakley M.E., Pasic J., Jamner L.D., Reduction in drug requirements for hypertension by means of a cognitive-behavioral intervention. *American Journal of Hypertension.* 1997; 10:9–17.

Tamblyn R., Berkson L., Dauphinee W.D., Gayton D., Grad R., Huang A., Isaac L., McLeod P., Snell L., Unnecessary prescribing of NSAIDs and the management of NSAID-related gastropathy in medical practice. *Annals of Internal Medicine.* 1997; 127:429-438.

CHAPTER 21

How Can I Improve My Present Health-Related Behaviors?

Covey S., *The 7 Habits of Highly Effective People: Powerful Lessons In Personal Change.* New York: Fireside, 1990.

Meyer M., Rao L., How top cancer docs beat (their own) cancer: What they learned could save your life. *Prevention.* 1997; May:85–93.

Remen R.N., *Kitchen Table Wisdom; Stories That Heal.* New York: Riverhead Books, 1996.

Sikorski R., Peters R., Oncology A.S.A.P., Where to find reliable cancer information on the Internet. *The Journal of the American Medical Association.* 1997; 277:1431–1433.

Sobel D.S., Health in cyberspace. *Mind/Body Health.* 1997; V(4):1–2.

Ulrich R.S., View through a window may influence recovery from surgery. *Science.* 1984; 224:420–421.

Weil A., *Spontaneous Healing.* New York: Knopf, 1995.

CHAPTER 22

Spirituality and Health

Bernardin J.L., *The Gift of Peace: Personal Reflections.* Loyola Press: Chicago, 1997.

Byrd R.C., Positive therapeutic effects of intercessory prayer in a coronary care unit population. *Southern Medical Journal.* 1988; 81:826–829.

Gesensway D., Making the case for bringing religion to patient care. *ACP Observer.* 1997; July/August:5.

Gray P.B., Want to search your soul at a monastery? Get in line. *The Wall Street Journal.* 1997; December 19:B1.

Idler E.L., Kasl S.V., Religion among disabled and nondisabled persons II: Attendance at religious services as a predictor of the course of disability. *Journal of Gerontology: Social Sciences.* 1997; 52B:S306–S316.

Kabat-Zinn J., *Wherever You Go, There You Are: Mindfulness Meditation.* Hyperion: New York, 1994.

Kantrowitz B., King P., Rosenberg D., Springen K., Wingert P., Namuth T., Gegax T.T., In search of the sacred. *Newsweek.* 1994; November 28:52–62.

Kennedy G.J., Kelman H.R., Thomas C., Chen J., The relation of religious preference and practice to depressive symptoms among 1,855 older adults. Journal of Gerontology: *Psychological Sciences.* 1996; 51B:P301–P308.

Kilgore C., Some medical schools push for spirituality training. *Internal Medicine News.* 1997; June 15:5.

Koenig H.G., Cohen H.J., George L.K., Hays J.C., Larson D.B., Blazer D.G., Attendance at religious services, interleukin-6, and other biological parameters of immune function in older adults. *The International Journal of Psychiatry in Medicine.* 1997; 27:233–250.

Koenig H.G., George L.K., Peterson B.L., Religiosity and remission of depression in medically ill older patients. *American Journal of Psychiatry.* 1998; 155:536–542.

Krause N., Religion, aging, and health: Current status and future prospects. *Journal of Gerontology: Social Sciences.* 1997; 52B:S291–S293.

Larson D.B., Swyers J.P., McCullough M.E. (editors), Scientific research on spirituality and health: A consensus report. *National Institute for Healthcare Research.* 1998.

Lyon J.L., Klauber M.R., Gardner J.W., Smart C.R., Cancer incidence in Mormons and non-Mormons in Utah, 1966–1970. *The New England Journal of Medicine.* 1976; 294:129–133.

Norris K., *The Cloister Walk.* New York: Riverhead Books, 1996.

Oman D., Reed D., Religion and mortality among the community-dwelling elderly. *American Journal of Public Health.* 1998; 88:1469–1475.

Oxman T.E., Freeman D.H., Manheimer E.D., Lack of social participation or religious strength and comfort as risk factors for death after cardiac surgery in the elderly. *Psychosomatic Medicine.* 1995; 57:5–15.

Pitt Medicine. The healing power of faith. *Pitt Medicine.* 1997; Spring:2–4.

Roush W., Herbert Benson: Mind-body maverick pushes the envelope. *Science.* 1997; 276:357.

Strawbridge W.J., Cohen R.D., Shema S.J., Kaplan G.A., Frequent attendance at religious services and mortality over twenty-eight years. *American Journal of Public Health.* 1997; 87:957–961.

Suskind R., Silent treatment: Our reporter tries the meditative life. *The Wall Street Journal.* 1994; November 16:A1.

Thomas G., Doctors who pray: How the medical community is discovering the healing power of prayer. *Christianity Today.* 1997; 41:20–28.

Underwood A., Foote D., Kalb C., Stone B., Talking to God. *Newsweek.* 1992, January 6:39–64.

Yahoo! News Reuters Health. Prayers may have helped heart patients. *Yahoo! News Reuters Health.* 12/24/1998.
http://dailynews.yahoo.com/tx/19981224/hl/prayer1_1.html.

Section Seven: Your Personal Profile on Your 100th Birthday

CHAPTER 23
PREDICTORS OF HEALTHY AGING

Vita A.J., Terry R.B., Hubert H.B., Fries J.F., Aging, health risks, and cumulative disability. *The New England Journal of Medicine.* 1998; 338:1035–1041.

CHAPTER 24
A RECIPE FOR CHANGE

Benson H., The relaxation response. *In Mind Body Medicine* (Goleman D, Gurin J, editors). Yonkers, NY: Consumer Reports Books, 1993:233–257.

Cummings N., Somatization: When physical symptoms have no medical cause. *In Mind Body Medicine* (Goleman D, Gurin J, editors). Yonkers, NY: Consumer Reports Books, 1993:221–230.

Dimsdale J.E., President Lincoln: An instance of stress and aging. *Psychosomatic Medicine.* 1998; 60:2–6.

Dossey L., *Healing Words.* New York: HarperCollins, 1993.

Hixson K.A., Gruchow H.W., Morgan D.W., The relation between religiosity, selected health behaviors, and blood pressure among adult females. *Preventive Medicine.* 1998; 27:545-552.

Kabat-Zinn J., Mindfulness meditation: Health benefits of an ancient Buddhist practice. *In Mind Body Medicine* (Goleman D, Gurin J, editors). Yonkers, NY: Consumer Reports Books, 1993:259–275.

Kabat-Zinn J., *Wherever You Go, There You Are: Mindfulness Meditation.* New York: Hyperion, 1994.

Lynch J.W., Kaplan G.A., Shema S.J., Cumulative impact of sustained economic hardship on physical, cognitive, psychological, and social functioning. *The New England Journal of Medicine.* 1997; 337:1889–1895.

Pappas G., Queen S., Hadden W., Fisher G., The increasing disparity in mortality between socioeconomic groups in the United States, 1960 and 1986. *The New England Journal of Medicine.* 1993; 329:103–109.

Parker P., Fetzer Institute. *Seasons: A center for renewal.* Brochure, undated.

Rossman M.L., Imagery: Learning to use the mind's eye. *In Mind Body Medicine* (Goleman D, Gurin J, editors). Yonkers, NY: Consumer Reports Books, 1993:291–300.

Schwartz M.S., Schwartz N.M., Biofeedback: Using the body's signals. *In Mind Body Medicine* (Goleman D, Gurin J, editors). Yonkers, NY: Consumer Reports Books, 1993:301–313.

INDEX

Dr. William Malarkey has been a practicing physician for over 30 years. He received his medical training at the University of Pittsburgh, The Ohio State University, Washington University in St. Louis, and the University of Colorado. He is board certified in Internal Medicine and in Endocrinology. He has received recognition for his clinical expertise and is referred patients from throughout Ohio and surrounding states. He has been on numerous "best doctors" lists in various publications.

Dr. Malarkey's internationally recognized work in endocrinology has emphasized breast cancer, pituitary tumors, and stress research. He is Director of The Ohio State University Clinical Research Center. His work has led to over 150 research publications and book chapters as well as over 100 published research abstracts, many of which he has presented at national meetings. He has served on numerous national committees and editorial boards.

His wife Joan is CEO and President of Community Connection, a non-profit organization that deals with offenders and ex-offenders. They have been married for 37 years and have three children, Kevin, Gregg, and Ashley, and two grandchildren, Alex and Chase. They share an interest in travel, bicycling, kayaking, reading, movies and spending time with family and friends.